What Are People Saying About Broken in the Stronger Places: From Resilience to Resourcefulness?

"In this poignant and powerful narrative, Elizabeth courageously shares a personal journey that begins and ends with trauma, offering a beacon of hope to survivors of domestic violence and sexual assault. This book is not just a recounting of personal experiences; it is a testament to resilience and the strength of the human spirit." – *Stephanie Gattas, CEO/Founder, The Pink Berets*

"Elizabeth words are moving and powerful. A true testament to her and what she has given to the women veteran community. She tells a story that truly needs to be told. – *Lucy Del Gaudio, Advocate, U.S. Army Veteran*

"Broken in the Stronger Places by Elizabeth A. Estabrooks is a memoir that is a potent experiential brew of personal and professional insights on the wounds that women in military and civilian life incur over time at work and in families in their relationships with toxic men. Of equal importance, the book excavates the many forms of healing and transformation that such women are capable of achieving." – *Barbara Levy Simon, Professor Emerita , Columbia University School of Social Work*

Elizabeth Estabrooks' Broken in the Stronger Places is a deeply moving and powerful memoir that sheds light on the complexities of trauma, healing, and resilience. Drawing from her personal experiences in the military and her decades of work in the fields of domestic violence and sexual assault advocacy, Estabrooks weaves a narrative that is both intensely personal and widely relevant. She eloquently challenges the conventional notion that trauma makes us stronger in the broken places, instead offering a more nuanced and compassionate perspective on the cyclical nature of healing and retraumatization.

What sets this book apart is its seamless blend of memoir, social commentary, and professional insight. Estabrooks does not merely recount her own experiences but situates them within a broader historical and systemic context, illustrating the evolving role of women in the military and the persistent barriers they face. She also provides valuable guidance for mental health professionals and advocates, ensuring that the book serves as both a personal testament and a resource for those working to support survivors. Her honest and unfiltered storytelling invites readers into the complexities of trauma, making it an essential read for anyone seeking to understand the long-term effects of trauma and violence.

At its core, Broken in the Stronger Places is a testament to the resilience of survivors while also acknowledging the ongoing challenges they face. Estabrooks' writing is both raw and insightful, creating a space for reflection, validation, and action. Whether you are a survivor, an advocate, or someone looking to deepen your understanding of trauma and healing, this book is a profoundly important and enlightening read. –*Emily Miles, Executive Director, New York Alliance Against Sexual Assault*

"Broken in the Stronger Places will not only move but bring awareness to those who have a passion for helping survivors and victims in crimes against women. A much-needed approach where Ms. Estabrooks examines and shares not only her personal encounter but with life experiences working in the field of social work. She understands firsthand the various challenges faced by the next generation of those who have the desire to work with victims and survivors of domestic violence and sexual assault.

When it comes to women veterans, Liz brings the knowledge we all can learn from along with solutions for those of us who have past trauma experience. In the end, "Like burning embers that melt the plastic marshmallow package at a campfire," will stay with me." – Regina Vasquez / USMC Veteran and Founder of Fatigues Clothesline

BROKEN IN THE STRONGER PLACES:

From Resilience to Resourcefulness

Elizabeth A. Estabrooks, MSW

Broken in the Stronger Places: From Resilience to Resourcefulness

Copyright © 2024 by Elizabeth A. Estabrooks, MSW

Manufactured in the Unites States of America. All rights reserved. No other part of this book may be reproduced in any form or by any electronic or mechanical means including information storage and retrieval systems without permission in writing from the publisher, except by a reviewer, who may quote brief passes in a review. Published by A Woman's Voice Press, 2230 Campbell St., Baker City, OR 97814

Permissions

Although the author has exhaustively researched all sources to ensure the accuracy and completeness of the information contained in this book, we assume no responsibility for errors, inaccuracies, omissions, or any other inconsistency based herein. Any slights against people or organizations are unintentional.

Attention Colleges and universities, corporations, and writing and publishing organizations: Quantity discounts are available on bulk purchases of this book for educational training purposes, fund-raising, or gift giving. Special books, booklets, or book excerpts can also be created to fit your specific needs. For information, contact A Woman's Voice Press, 2230 Campbell Street. Baker City, OR 97814, (541)350-6525, elizabeth@awomansvoicepress.com

ISBN 979-8-9920055-0-9
Library of Congress Control Number: 2025902554
Book cover designed by Carly Newberg, Sincerely Carly, Baker City, OR

To those who came after me and wanted to know. You know who you are.

To my sisters Theresa and Kelley for their unwavering support, even when it was hard.

To my loved ones, my sister Ritha and my mom, Irene. Although they are no longer with us, the story could not have happened without them. I believe they would be proud.

To my personal book consultant, cover designer, question answerer, and photographer, Carly Newberg, whose support and counsel were invaluable.

Mostly to the women who trusted me for so many years. Thank you for the life you breathed into my soul.

Contents

Author's Notes 3
Introduction 5
Chapter 1—Tell Me What I Need to Know to Help You 11
    Listening in Silence 14
Chapter 2—Life as Imitation of Art 19
    Confusing Gold with Perfection 19
    Crossing Streams 21
Chapter 3—Trauma—Broken and Healed 27
    Unpacking the Definitions 28
    Through the Lens Darkly 41
Chapter 4—Broken in the Stronger Places 49
    Retraumatization 49
    Real People = Valid Experiences 50
    Trauma Informed: The Missing Link 53
    The 5-4-3-2-1 Exercise 54
Chapter 5—I Do Solemnly Swear 59
    This Man's Army 61
    Early Decisions, Late Mistakes 63
    The Indoctrination Is Strong 67
    Eyes Wide Open 70
    No Girls Allowed 74
    Onward, with Hope 81
    The Wheels of Harassment Grind Slowly 82
    Saying the Quiet Stuff Out Loud 88

Chapter 6—The Order of Things **93**
    Home Again, Home Again 93
    Trauma Is as Trauma Does 95
    In the Words of Dory: Just Keep Swimming 101
    Small Town, Small Ideas 102

Chapter 7—A Sea Change **107**
    When Yes Turns into a Career 108
    Passion, Anger, and a New View 110
    Lacquer Up and Keep Going 112

Chapter 8—Into the Deep End **117**
    A Woman's Voice 117
    The Measure of Misogyny 119
    If Not Me, Who? If Not Now, When? 121
    Political Winds and Breaking News 125
    The Places We Belong 127
    Activate Life: Phase 2 129

Chapter 9—A New Path **135**
    A New Old Decision 135
    There's Nothing to See Here 138
    No Safe Place, Still 138
    Life Happens Upstream 143
    The Things We Live With 146

Chapter 10—Work Now, Heal Later **153**
    Breaks, Deep, and Wide 160
    Lessons Learned—Sort of 162
    It All Matters 169

Chapter 11—Dreams and Nightmares **175**
    The End Game 175
    One Step Forward, Two Slides Back 181
    The Emperor's New Clothesxxxvi 183
    When Hope Is Gone 189

Chapter 12—And Just Like That **193**
    A Ragged Break 199

Chapter 13—Out of the Fire 207
    Finding Hope 209
    Sunshine and Gifts 214
    The Grief of Life 215
Epilogue **221**
    Moving Toward Next Steps..222
    Crisis Resources 228
Building a safe workplace **229**
    Workplace Safety 230
    Employee Assistance Program (EAP) 232
    Environment..232
Building a trauma and survivor informed organization **235**
    Hiring practices 238
    Veterans 239
Resourcefulness: Tools that get us through **241**
    There's an app for that!... 247
Acknowledgments **251**
About the Author **255**
Glossary **257**
References **263**

Women should be tough, tender, laugh as much as possible, and live long lives. The struggle for equality continues unabated, and the woman warrior who is armed with wit and courage will be among the first to celebrate victory.

—**Maya Angelou**

Author's Notes

For Victims and Survivors: Know that as you read this story, you will read references to other women's stories. Although these references are not detailed accountings of assaults, they may cause a distressing emotional or trauma reaction in you. My story cannot be told without at least these mentions made at a high level. I tell my story and lessons learned in hopes that you will know you are not alone and in the hope that you may find some connection and recognition in these pages. Skip ahead where you need to or take the time to sit with what you are reading and how you are feeling. More important than all of that is that you take good care of yourself as you journey with me through this book

For Readers: One of my goals with this book is to expand awareness of trauma and post-traumatic stress (PTS) from a real-life perspective, as opposed to through a researcher or clinical lens. Therefore, I have included definitions, recommendations, and suggestions that any reader can benefit from. These areas are identified with a key symbol. 🗝

For Veterans: While this book is not solely about veterans, it is important for veterans to understand that if they have post-traumatic stress and are survivors of intimate partner violence (IPV) / domestic violence as well as sexual harassment, assault, and rape while surviving in the military, they may be eligible to obtain service-connected disability benefits for any PTS or physical conditions related to their trauma from these experiences. More importantly, even if a veteran does not have a service-connected disability for IPV or sexual trauma, they are eligible to receive free care from the Veterans Administration (VA) for related health and mental health conditions.

The following page includes a list of crisis resources that can be utilized by those in crisis and those who live and/or work with people who live with the aftermath of traumatic experiences.

Introduction

In December 1977, I joined the United States Army, the oldest and largest military branch in the United States, uniquely connecting me to the three million women who have served since the American Revolution. My service was not a new event, but at that time, still uncommon for women. Unbeknownst to me then, there had been numerous laws over the decades that broadened military opportunities for women and led to our expanding enlistment in 1977. The most impactful change was the passage of the Women's Armed Services Integration Act in 1948, which gave women permanent, regular military status but also limited the number of women who could serve. The '70s saw great change for women from 1975–1979, with regulations eliminating involuntary discharge for pregnancy; allowance of mandatory defensive weapons training; and authorization for women to serve the same length of tours of duty overseas as men. In 1977, coed basic training was authorized at Ft. McClellan, Alabama, and Ft. Jackson, South Carolina.

Plenty of people, including US Army leaders, were adamantly opposed. The first five minutes of my basic training made it clear they had no use for women in "This Man's Army." That attitude from men toward women defined my three-year Army experience, but it was not what started me on my path to social justice. My feet were set there when I was young, the first time I watched my mom reel from the punch landed by my stepfather.

Broken in the Stronger Places: From Resilience to Resourcefulness

Spending most of thirty years in the field of domestic violence and sexual assault meant engaging with the stories of thousands of women. Although I entered the arena carrying my own trauma, it was from these women that I gained my expertise on interpersonal violence and trauma. My transition to working with women veterans has helped me more thoroughly understand retraumatization: a phase of trauma that is insufficiently discussed and too often overlooked.

The full spectrum of life as a survivor can mean resilience and strength, but it can also include the opposite end of the spectrum. There is a brokenness within that not even therapy or treatment can heal. Or seen differently, a brokenness that heals but then is subject to rebreaks, even in those areas we have worked to strengthen. This kind of brokenness counters psychology's theory of being stronger in the broken places, a theory developed from the ancient Japanese art of kintsugi. With this art form, the cracks in treasured and valuable porcelain are repaired with lacquer and precious metals to add to their beauty and history. As the art form goes, breaking and repairing is believed to show value and honor to the broken item, making it stronger in its once-broken places.

However, decades of experience with survivors and recognizing and managing my own post-traumatic stress, including vicarious trauma, have taught me that these stronger places can and do break.[1] Even with all of the right tools, such as therapy and treatment, the lacquer and precious metal of our being can fall apart from one or multiple incidents that trigger retraumatization; the loss of a loved one; an event similar to the original trauma; an errant comment. The issue is not only that we sometimes find ourselves broken in these stronger places, but that those within the field may tend to ignore the breaking, expecting survivors—specifically women—to continue life as normal. There is little space in our culture for the breaking of women. We have instead employed phrases like "You are the strongest person I know. You got this! Pull through it—the kids need you" to silence women in their pain and need.

The book goes beyond being a simple memoir. My education, experience, and knowledge are guides that add value to this story. Nevertheless, it is a story that needs definitions, data, resources, and references to help clarify what I mean when talking about being "broken in the stronger places." It is

Introduction

also about women only, as women are the sum of my whole career. While initially intended for survivors of interpersonal violence, it will also be suitable for anyone in the mental health, community safety, or social justice field to help expand awareness that the path of trauma can and often does include this level of retraumatization. Retraumatization can occur and can be especially confusing even after "being healed," when it is believed that healing is done. It serves as a reminder that post-traumatic stress does not go away.

For organizations and individuals interested in understanding how to do better for the victims and survivors they knowingly or unknowingly serve, you will find a guide section at the end of the book and on my website that will be helpful for those interested in examining their practice and workplace to help build a safe, trauma-informed space for anyone who is a trauma survivor.[2]

The story held in these pages starts and ends with trauma. I hope other survivors can recognize themselves and their journeys, that they are not alone, and hope that professionals and family members can gain some additional practical understanding about the impact and reality of retraumatization. Over the decades, I helped so many women who were harmed almost exclusively by men in ways that ranged from sexual harassment to being brutalized in some exceedingly nightmarish ways, but this book will not be about their stories. It is about my story and how it intertwines with all these women.

For the readers who have trauma experiences, know that I will not be sharing stories except on a very high level (for example, referring to a woman who was sexually assaulted or raped but giving no further detail). I will also somewhat share my own experiences of sexual harassment and assault in the Army. These references will be told from a high-level viewpoint without getting into the weeds of details and facts.

Nearly half of my life has been dedicated to hearing the stories of women, which is why this book is only about women and through a women's lens. Yes, sexual assault and violence happen to men too, but because this is my story, it is exclusively about women. Throughout these pages, I will also refer to men as the perpetrators of violence, sexual harassment, assault, and rape. Why? Of all the women I have worked with or spoken to over the decades, all but a handful were harmed by men. Nevertheless, this book is inclusive of women who were harmed by women because their pain and trauma are as real.

Broken in the Stronger Places: From Resilience to Resourcefulness

Except for what is in the introduction, you will rarely see anything that relates to men as victims or survivors in this book. This is not meant to negate the experiences of the male population who have suffered from violence or harm or those experiences of people who were abused by women, but to keep it as my accounting of my experiences in working with women throughout my career.

I am fully aware that folks in the mental health field may dispute what I am saying, and there may be "but-the-men" arguments, and that is OK. What I own is that this is my story and my way of sharing the experiences and lessons learned while trying desperately to hold together my stronger places.

It is my commitment to write this through my lens as a woman who intentionally chose the path of helping women for the better part of thirty years and not turn this into a clinical or academic missive. My path has followed the blood-, trauma-, and anguish-stained road of women who experienced or witnessed behavior ranging from bad to dangerous and, in some cases, lethal. For nearly thirty years, I listened to and studied the stories told by women, some worse than anything most people can imagine is even possible, all stowed away inside my soul. My work always had one purpose, which was to bring positive change and justice for women and make this a world that is a little bit safer for them in every way.

However, much of what I discuss does need the context that comes from including research and data, so although this is not a textbook, white paper, or journal submission, sections that contain clinical theory, definitions, and data or research are included. Also included at the end is a guide for how organizations and individuals can improve their direction and outcomes and avoid contributing to the cycle or trauma. Insight comes to us from many directions, and I am hopeful this book will provide that to the reader, whether you are a survivor or victim of violence, a family member or friend, a clinical or other mental health professional, or all of the above.

A strong mom's resilience and determination serve as an inspiration for her children to overcome obstacles and achieve their dreams.

—**Serena Williams**, *Interview with Vogue (2020)*

CHAPTER 1

Tell Me What I Need to Know to Help You

In 1993, a friend asked me to serve on the board of directors for the local domestic violence/sexual assault crisis intervention center in rural Eastern Oregon, which turned out to be life-altering in so many ways. This simple request started a journey that, for me, became a dedication to hearing the stories of women who had been harmed through violence. Like a storm out of the clear blue sky, it began with no warning.

Although I almost said no when she asked, what came out of my mouth was, "I'll think about it." Through that process of thoughtfulness, I began scrolling back through the memories of women I had known throughout my life, including myself, who had been physically, emotionally, sexually assaulted, or raped by their husband or partner. The numbers rose steadily as I repeated their names to myself, recalling their stories, as well as the events I had witnessed unfolding with some of them.[i] There were so many, both friends and family members, that I soon became overwhelmed with the reality of their experiences.

As the numbers grew and the list of names expanded, I could not see how there was any possible answer except yes, so I called her back and said, "I'll do

Broken in the Stronger Places: From Resilience to Resourcefulness

it." It was a call that set me on a thirty-year path of listening to other women tell their stories of interpersonal violence.

The phrase "tell me what I need to know to help you" became the way I learned to open my conversations with women because it was the most natural way to tell women that I was there to hear and help them. It was not because I was a trained clinician or social worker at the time. When I first started, it was without even the forty hours of training then required by the Oregon Coalition Against Domestic Violence and Sexual Assault of an advocate in the field of domestic violence and sexual assault. What I discovered—much to my surprise—was that sometimes asking was not even necessary; women just started sharing with me.

That is how it happened with my mom; she just started talking while we were on a long road trip from Colorado to Oregon. Road trips are wonderful occasions for just chatting it up, sharing secrets, laughing, learning things you did not know about your fellow traveler—and honest conversations. I had some of the best, most honest conversations ever while driving with my kids, friends, and family.

Mom and I were traveling from Southeastern Colorado to Eastern Oregon in the early '90s and decided to take I-70 through Grand Junction from Denver. I do not remember why it is the thing my brain held on to, but the Green River sign is permanently etched into my memory banks. That sign is where Mom just started talking about her stepdad and how he began molesting her when she was only nine years old. She went on to tell me about the different men who sexually assaulted and raped her until she was fifteen. She spoke of her anger and shame, her sadness, and her grief over her lost childhood.

When talking about her anger, there was a fierceness to that emotion. She knew the anger was inside of her, and as kids, we witnessed it. With tears in her eyes, she admitted how she knew it changed the way she loved as a wife and a mother. I do not remember how long she talked or I listened; it was just that while she spoke, acknowledging I heard what she was saying and felt her pain was important. This is the type of story or memory we never want to hear about a parent—in adulthood or otherwise—but it is a story that survivors need to tell when the time is right and they feel safe. Her time was right with me.

Tell Me What I Need to Know to Help You

Her tears fell, but mine did not. I knew instinctively that my tears would make my mother stop talking, and she needed to tell her story and for me to listen quietly and not judge or question. She told me she had never had anyone just sit in silence and listen before, not even the therapist she once tried to visit but gave up on when it ended with her spiraling into more shame and self-blame.

When she was done, she dried her tears, looked at me, apologized, and said, "I don't know where that came from. You didn't need to hear that from your mother. I shouldn't have shared that with you. I'm sorry."

I assured her that it was OK, I was so very sorry it happened to her, no one deserved that, and no victim was ever to blame for what someone else chose to do to them. I tried to assure her it was not her fault. I also told her that if she ever wanted to talk or if she wanted my help with anything, all she needed to do was ask.

Over the next few years, she did ask, and we did talk about it. She asked me for tools that might help her, since going to a therapist again was not something she was willing to try. I gave her a few books and a workbook developed for survivors. She made her way through the workbook, but she never shared if she thought it helped. Eventually, she stopped talking about it. Over the years, I speculated as to whether opening that wound again through discussions was somehow just too much for her or whether she had found some peace and healing, but since she was a private person and prone to occasional angry outbursts relating to herself or life, I feared treading on that sensitive topic, lest it cause more pain.

While my mother and I were never close, I came to understand in adulthood that her pain and my life were inextricably bound. Her childhood and adult traumas impacted the way she mothered, the way she viewed life, and defined for her everything about herself. Her sharing with me permanently altered how I viewed not only everything I did for the rest of my career but also how I viewed the world of men, women, violence, and their aftermath—especially for the survivors.

Listening in Silence

My mother's story was one of the first stories of sexual assault I ever heard told as a story. By that, I mean although I was aware of it happening to others in my life, few had ever really shared their story. Rather, they had just dropped the information during a conversation. Because of my mother, I learned in those moments the importance of sitting in silence and listening when a survivor is speaking. As part of my journey into advocacy for women and girls who had experienced these terrible things, one thing that arose from somewhere inside of me and that I held on to throughout my career was the understanding that this was her time to cry, not mine. Although it was never a conscious effort, somehow, I knew instinctively not to shed a single tear when women were sharing the stories of their pain and abuse.

I learned to sit, listen, acknowledge, and absorb. In doing this work, there grew an inner awareness, which I failed to notice until the end of my career, that in choosing this path, I would need to either stuff away or patch together my own broken places (some of which were, unknowingly, a result of my mother's trauma) making my own wounds and breaks strong enough to withstand what was to come. For the next thirty years, I used those carefully managed stronger places to fight the fight, absorb the pain of others, and help heal their broken places.

It worked—until it didn't.

I spent the better part of my career taking in these stories, investing in the field of domestic violence and sexual assault as an advocate, community planner, researcher, and activist, asking women to tell me what I needed to know to help them. Eventually came the realization that, as in my mother's case, it was often not even necessary to ask. There was something about my demeanor that women just knew they could open up, so they kept talking, and I kept listening.

My yes, when asked to join the board of the domestic violence organization in 1993, led to me later serving as the co-executive director alongside my older sister, Ritha. Eventually, she resigned and left the work to me. Over the next four years, I worked with women who had been abused physically, emotionally, and sexually by their partners, mostly men, sometimes women.

Tell Me What I Need to Know to Help You

Being a fierce advocate meant gaining knowledge about the sexual assault and domestic violence field and all its nuances. In 1993, it was still common for cops not to make arrests in these cases, judges not to convict, and society to judge and blame the victims. I could not be an advocate without also engaging in activism to drive change that benefited victims and survivors. So, even after leaving that job in 1997, my work in community safety and training continued to evolve, which meant continuing to expand my knowledge base for a deeper understanding of what I needed to know to help women.

I stayed the course after earning both my bachelor's and master's degrees, continuing my advocacy and social work as the Oregon Women Veterans Coordinator, working with women veterans, community partners, and policymakers. My graduate school research had focused on the experiences of women both as veterans and service members, specifically related to interpersonal violence, so I went into that job with awareness and knowledge. My research, along with my conversations with women veterans that had prevailed since 1993, deepened my awareness and understanding of women veterans and their unique experiences, challenges, issues, and needs. But still, once I was boots on the ground as the Coordinator, I realized how great the need was among this population of women—a vast number that, at that time, almost no research covered.

Years later, I was invited to join the Department of Veterans Affairs (VA) Center for Women Veterans (CWV) in Washington, DC, as the deputy director. We had a system where the staff managed complaints and concerns that came in from women veterans, and I became the person who—because of my expertise—consulted on, and in some cases managed, the worst cases (on staff request). In each case, I reached out personally to the woman veteran, and they shared all they had experienced and how those experiences were impacting them now: insomnia, fear, ongoing sense of betrayal, anger, depression, eating disorders, mistrust, relationship problems, and more. In many of those cases, I also worked directly with VA reps who could provide the best direction and outcomes.

As happened in Oregon, I heard stories of events so brutal I would sometimes hang up and wonder why the victim had not died as a result—then or since. I would sit in amazement at the sheer resilience of these women who had

Broken in the Stronger Places: From Resilience to Resourcefulness

so often lived in silence and fought the internal battle necessary to stay alive, sometimes for decades, recognizing the resourcefulness that kept them alive. Frequently, what I heard in the end was some version of "Thank you for listening. I've never told that to anyone before. I feel like I said too much, but thank you for being here, caring, and believing me."

This was my professional journey in the field from 1993–2022. My personal journey began in my youth while bearing witness to the abuse women experience, as well as my own experiences of harassment as a young woman in the workplace, sexual harassment and assault in the Army, and abusive relationships thereafter. To walk this path, I needed to cover up my own trauma—trauma I did not realize I carried. Consciously or subconsciously, I managed everything by covering my wounds to make my broken places stronger, just as is done through the art of kintsugi, I thought covering my pain with lacquer and gold would ensure that I was functional and beautiful.

For most people, understanding sexual harassment, assault, and rape is difficult. This may sound ridiculous, but it is true. What is the difference, and why is it important? Words matter, definitions change, and specifics are part of the conversations. For instance, sexual harassment. Unlike others, VA says that the person must feel threatened, which I frequently challenged, both before and after going to work for VA. What I learned over the years is that institutions change language so that it is easier for them. Almost never, though, does that mean it is easier for the population they serve.

---

i. Sexual harassment, assault, and rape are classified differently, depending on the state, workplace guidelines, and sometimes even the law. As an example, in some guidelines and laws, groping and grabbing in a sexual way falls under the term "harassment," which is wholly insufficient in addressing the reality of this action. Mostly, these actions are identified as assault. For this book, when I am using the word harassment, it verbal and emotional assault; sexual assault, includes groping, grabbing, or any other physical contact short of rape. Rape is just that: rape. Each of these actions and behaviors, from harassment to assault, are perpetrated without consent.

A work of art does not answer questions, it provokes them; and its essential meaning is in the tension between the contradictory answers.

—**Leonard Bernstein**

CHAPTER 2

Life as Imitation of Art

Confusing Gold with Perfection

As previously mentioned, the art of kintsugi, literally translated to mean "golden joinery or golden repair" is an ancient Japanese technique of repairing broken items with lacquer and then applying gold or other precious metal powder to strengthen the repair, making the piece more beautiful. Although the origin of kintsugi is unknown, it is believed to have been developed under the command of Japanese shogun Ashikaga Yoshimasa when his favorite tea bowl was broken.

The story is that the shogun sent the bowl out to his own artisans for repair but was unhappy with the results when they returned an ugly, leaking piece. Following multiple attempts, he eventually employed a local craftsman to come up with a better solution. The craftsman, with a view to the symbiotic nature of art and life, chose a unique and custom approach. Instead of trying to cover the scars of the repaired bowl, he chose to allow the broken places to shine with renewed beauty because of the repair.

Kintsugi can take weeks or months, depending on the size and type of the piece, with multiple layers of lacquer being applied, each layer cured,

Broken in the Stronger Places: From Resilience to Resourcefulness

and a new one applied. In the end, as the precious metal powder is applied, it appears that the repair or scar is flowing. The broken item is repaired in a way that still shows the broken place, maintains the function, and adds to the beauty of the item.

It is said that the broken object, once repaired, is not only more beautiful but stronger in those broken places. The scars are seen as acknowledging an object's past while honoring its living history. It is believed that the value becomes even greater because of what the break and piece embody and where it has come in its journey.

Kintsugi has also become a metaphor used in mental and behavioral health teachings today to help guide people through navigating perceived failure, understanding that, even in trauma, we can heal, and recognizing through a powerful visual how we can be stronger in the broken places. The scars we bear symbolize our life experiences, even those that were painful. Rather than hiding them away, they make us who we are. They can serve as a reminder that healing is a process and each person's path and life is unique and continues to have value.

The technique of adding lacquer, which metaphorically comes from therapy, self-care, forgiveness, resilience, and moving through grief, leaves space for the application of the precious metals that are made up of honoring and valuing ourselves and understanding that our past, present, and future lives can be celebrated and do hold value. The scar itself represents healing and resilience. The act of overcoming is a sign of the resourcefulness we employ during or after the breaking happens.

It is the healing process allowed by various forms of therapy that helps us put gold and other precious metals over our scars, whereby we recognize they exist. Through whatever the chosen modality, those past traumas and pain are acknowledged as part of our past, but they make us no less beautiful. We do not hide from the trauma or its effects; we honor it and become stronger in spite of it.

When analyzing trauma treatment and recovery through the lens of this ancient Japanese art form of kintsugi, we look at these objects that have been so carefully and beautifully mended with great attention and love over time, and we use that as a metaphor for how those of us with trauma can be put back together or mended. The idea is that by using appropriate therapeutic modalities (like Cognitive Behavioral Therapy) we gain tools that help us function and deal better with life that comes after trauma. Treatment serves as the lacquer that helps heal our broken places. Our improved self-esteem and life function are the gold that covers the scar. Theoretically, if we use enough lacquer and shine it up with gold, we get better and stronger, and our trauma is minimized enough for us to get through the daily grind.

This sounds lovely, doesn't it? It is a wonderful theory and one that I used to acknowledge and even embrace. But then life happened, and I spent the better part of thirty years listening to thousands of women tell me about despicable acts committed by other humans against them, as well as living with my PTS, a condition which unknowingly grew worse with each year.

My experience over the decades brought with it the understanding that the kintsugi metaphor was not complete—that it fell short of acknowledging retraumatization. As I fully realized this, I began to also understand the importance of appreciating the reality of how retraumatization can mean turning the metaphor on its head: breaking us in our stronger places.

Crossing Streams

For years, I did not recognize my trauma because I compared my experiences to those who had been sexually assaulted and raped. My trauma came from a nonstop onslaught of sexual harassment (and assault) wherein the men constantly derided and sexualized me verbally, groped and grabbed me, followed me during my three years in the Army. So many of the women I spoke to and the stories I read were horrific and brutal experiences; how could I have trauma when my experience was not like that? What I found in my work with women veterans was that many who endured sexual harassment and groping believed similarly: it could not be trauma if I was not raped.

But trauma does not know what it is and is not supposed to do. There are no rules with trauma.

As I frequently say, there was no place safe and no safe place. It was not until I was in graduate school that someone I knew identified a direct line from my military and other experiences, to my vicarious trauma as an advocate,

Broken in the Stronger Places: From Resilience to Resourcefulness

to my own trauma. I eventually came to understand the impact this trauma I carried for myself and others had on me in my lifetime; but for decades I ignored the feelings and memories and pushed through and forward, doing what I needed to do to take care of myself so I could do my work, care for my kids, and take care of others.

Vicarious trauma is an occupational hazard for people who work with victims and survivors of violence and other trauma experiences. Law enforcement, advocates, social workers, medical personnel, and first responders are all susceptible. Listening to stories, watching videos, responding to scenes—these are all exposures that can and do lead to vicarious trauma. For those who are survivors of their own trauma, it is a volatile mixture.

As with other traumas, people who are exposed to vicarious trauma respond in different ways. According to the Office of Victims of Crime, vicarious trauma changes your world view. More specifically, they state the change is "inevitable."[ii] A person may become negative, cynical, and fearful, or the opposite could occur, and they could come to appreciate their lives in a fuller way. Alternatively, a person's responses may change from positive to negative or vice versa with prolonged exposure. While that may sound counterintuitive, some examples of positive outcomes might be increased empathy and compassion for victims and survivors or experiencing inspiration after witnessing victim/survivor resilience and fortitude in overcoming trauma.

I designed the patches on my broken parts with layers of lacquer and beautiful gold that shone like the sun so the world could see what they wanted to see and what I needed to show and give them. It was never because anyone asked this of me, but because I wanted to be strong for my mother, my family, my friends, my children, and what turned out to be thousands of women who needed strength to be both shown and given so they could heal. Still, even though I had taught about vicarious trauma, it was something I failed to acknowledge or recognize in myself.

There were children to raise, bad relationships to get through, money to earn, and social justice battles to win. My chosen field included being thee for women who had been raped, abused, and assaulted. I needed to be strong so they could get through their trauma and live their lives. Every day I needed to get up and keep moving for them.

Life as Imitation of Art

Half a lifetime of being the strong one meant more lacquer and more gold, a process that has for centuries held together and strengthened even the rarest porcelains made and broken. But I am not a vase or dishware. I am human. Eventually, what was broken was weakened over the decades of constant use, and I began seeing small, chipped breaks and noticing light leaking from the cracks like liquid seeps through a cracked cup. More lacquer was applied, but the strong space needed for it to adhere was losing its integrity.

The pieces breaking off were too small and required constant, daily attention. Eventually, as much as I had perfected my ability to repair what was broken, I could feel it weakening. Not even the newest lacquer and strongest metals could hold it together, and it began to come apart. For instance, I began to realize more and more often that my emotions, while not flat lined, were dulling or, alternatively, turning into anger. I was no longer an emotionally healthy person.

When my son was little, he used to bring me all his toys to fix, even from his father's home. One day, I asked him why he did not just have his Dad fix it, and he said, without hesitation, "Because you can fix anything, Mom." I always found a way to get it fixed, even if it meant taking it to someone, which led him to believe I could fix anything. My years of success at being a fixer had led me to the same conclusion that I could fix anything. Unfortunately, I underestimated the sheer tenacity of trauma, the impact of vicarious trauma, and my own history.

In listening to an endless expanse of pain, sorrow, anger, and hell over nearly thirty years, on top of my own trauma experiences, I ultimately came to recognize how my field of vision began to expand when it came to the psychological theory of kintsugi.

In listening to thousands of women, reading their stories, as well as a never-ending stream of research, I learned that kintsugi is a good theory, but we are not inanimate objects and fixing the vase is not the end of the story. As much as we all try to make those scars pretty in gold and strong as the lacquer, that broken place remains, and over time, if enough pressure is applied or the repair is weakened through an unexpected event, that stronger place risks breakage. For anyone living with trauma or working with humans who have trauma, that needs to be the story in itself.

As I journey with myself over the past decades, I contemplate all of this and more.

---

ii   Office of Victims of Crime. What is Vicarious Trauma? https://ovc.ojp.gov/program/vtt/what-is-vicarious-trauma Viewed 11/01/2024.

Don't dare presume there's shame in the lot of a woman who carries on.

—**Barbara Kingsolver,** *The Poisonwood Bible*

CHAPTER 3

Trauma—Broken and Healed

As a writer, it falls on me to make sure that the reader understands what I am talking about, so let's jump into talking about trauma—what it means, the various forms, what it looks like. Over the years, I learned that because a person experienced a traumatic event, it does not follow that they understand trauma or PTS. So, this chapter delves into trauma and PTS, what they look like, and what we can do with and about them. It also gets into what I mean when I talk about "broken in the stronger places."

Simply put, post-traumatic stress is a mental health condition that is a mental, physical, and/or emotional response stemming from a stressful, traumatic event that puts someone in danger of serious injury, harm, or death. The event can be an act of interpersonal violence, combat, a plane crash, a mass shooting, and more. While my focus is on women who have experienced interpersonal violence, it *is not meant to exclude* those who have PTS due to some other trauma-inducing experience. What I write here may relate to you as well.

Broken in the Stronger Places: From Resilience to Resourcefulness

Unpacking the Definitions

My experience has been that there is often confusion around the terminology used in discussions of sexual assault, domestic violence, and more. You will find definitions, chosen from the most common sources, in the glossary at the end of the book.

IPV, simply put, is "a worldwide systemic, cultural problem that activists and advocates began to address in the nineteenth century." In 1871, Alabama and Massachusetts were the first states to pass laws criminalizing assaults by husbands against wives, while marital rape was first recognized legally in 1874 by New York. It took another seventy-one years—until 1945—for marital rape to be outlawed nationally, but it was not until 1972 that the first women's shelter was opened (in Washington, DC). This timing coincided with the formation of the Battered Women's Movement by feminist activists and survivors. Over the ensuing decades, women began building shelters and crisis centers while recognizing that existing policy and law were either insufficient or being ignored by law enforcement and the courts, leading to decades of fighting not for improved laws and policies but for mandatory action by the law and judicial systems.

Until 1996, the military mostly failed to acknowledge domestic violence or sexual assault. On September 30, 1996, the US Congress passed the Lautenberg Amendment, which makes it illegal for anyone convicted of a domestic violence misdemeanor to own or possess. firearms.[iii] Because this law could potentially impact military and law enforcement members who have these convictions, it was fraught with disputes and problems. Unfortunately, the military found a way around this law by offering waivers to individuals who are enlisting if it is deemed that their talent or skill serves "the greater good" enough so that the law does not apply to them. For military leaders, the solution applied to those serving has been to simply overlook their personal crimes of violence. For victims, even those serving in the military, this translates to a lack of protection from military police or judicial systems.

By many, especially veterans and veteran families, the VA is widely seen as an extension of the military, because VA care and services are frequently tied to military service. For more than a hundred years, their focus was on veteran men, with women seen as a sidenote. What this meant to women veterans was that the VA had no system in place to provide appropriate victim or survivor services and care. However, in 2012 a tragedy prompted then Department of Veteran Affairs (VA) Secretary Eric Shinseki to take action to improve services to victims and survivors of intimate partner violence. To jumpstart the process, he ordered the formation of the Domestic Violence Task Force. The duties of the task force were to develop a protocol that would guide the VA in recognizing and providing care to veterans who are survivors of IPV. As an outsider, I was honored to be invited to participate. From this task force was born the VA's Intimate Partner Violence Assistance Program, which included the addition of IPV coordinators at hospitals around the United States.

One of my biggest concerns has been and remains that the people they hire as IPV coordinators too often have little to no knowledge or experience with the topic, which reduces their effectiveness and can cause harm. Additionally, it is common for them to fail to collaborate with the local domestic violence organizations—people who have deep knowledge of the topic and can provide excellent resources as partners. These two system weaknesses can and do have negative impacts on survivors.

On numerous occasions over the years, I encountered VA IPV Coordinators who had never worked in the field and literally had no idea what they were doing. I recall meeting an IPV coordinator who freely admitted he was underwater because his specialty was HIV care, and he knew nothing about IPV. He was not alone among these coordinators. They are simply tasked with doing the work but with inadequate training, knowledge, or background. Placing an unskilled, unqualified worker in such a position can be very harmful to both survivors and victims when this unskilled person fails to give them proper advice or counsel.

Understanding the various forms of violence against women and how they intersect is vital for anyone interacting with victims and survivors. While IPV is acknowledged as dangerous and harmful, it does not exist in a vacuum, but frequently alongside other forms of violence, especially sexual violence. Another seemingly innocuous type of violence against women is sexual harassment. We experience it in the home, on the street, in the workplace, in public spaces, and in the military. In fact, unchecked, it is seen as a foundation for more severe forms of sexual violence.

Sexual harassment is a broad term that includes many types of unwelcome verbal and physical sexual attention. Allow me to state the obvious here: "unwelcome" is about what the person who is the target of the comments feels—not what the person doing the harassing thinks. For those who minimize sexual harassment as anything serious enough to lend itself to PTS or military sexual trauma (MST), I encourage you to rethink that position. Studies have found a strong link between sexual harassment, sexual assault, and post-traumatic stress, especially when sexual harassment and assault are combined. Moreover, it is recognized as an ongoing stressor for women (as in my case) in the military. One VA study found that sexual harassment during military service was significantly associated with PTSD symptom severity. In fact, it was similar to that of combat exposure for men and sexual assault for women.[iv]

Sexual harassment generally violates civil laws and is not a criminal offense —you have a right to work or learn without being harassed. Sadly, current reports show that workplace harassment continues to exist in large numbers. Equal Employment Opportunity Commission (EEOC) reports show that between FY 2018 and FY 2021, "sexual harassment charges constituted 35.4 percent of the total charges (277,872) received by the EEOC." Of these charges, 78 percent were filed by women, whereas 62 percent of all harassment charges were filed by women during that same time period. Seventy-one percent of the sexual harassment charges were concurrently filed with race charges by Black/African American women.[v] This latter part is just one of many important realities for women of color and LGBTQIA+, who contend with increased rates of discrimination, harassment, and assault compared to their white, straight, cisgendered women counterparts.

Problematic as it is, the VA has its own definition of sexual harassment, which narrows the context because of it use of the phrase, "which is threatening in character," as part of the definition. A Google search of the definition of sexual harassment found no other uses of "threatening" in this context. The problem with including the word "threatening" as part of the definition is that it is limiting and inaccurate when it comes to real-life harassment. While sexual harassment *can* be threatening, and other definitions do allow for that, the addition of this phrase in the Department of Veterans Affairs definition can and sometimes is used as a means to refuse MST benefits.

When I was being harassed by all those men over the three years I served, they were not using language that was threatening in character. However, the fact is that it was a relentless onslaught all day every day for three years. This frequency and duration, combined with my inability to escape and a lack of support from leaders, caused trauma that had a lifelong impact. Harassment does not have to include threatening language to cause long-term harm.

Let me reiterate clearly: any woman who has been subjected to sexual harassment can tell you that it does not need to be "threatening in character" to cause fear, embarrassment, intimidation, anxiety, or more. The more you are exposed to this behavior, with no ability to get away from it, being forced to work daily—side by side—with the perpetrators, the more trauma exposure you have.

Sexual assault is a criminal offense, although it is sometimes reduced to harassment by those who are in the law enforcement and criminal justice arenas. In both military and civilian domains, it refers to physical sexual contact that occurs without the consent of the victim.

The phrase "military sexual trauma" (MST) was not coined until 1992, when it was defined in the newly passed US Code 1720D that paved the way for treatment at the Department of Veterans Affairs (VA) (see glossary for expanded definition). Unfortunately, this code also uses the above-written VA definition of sexual harassment.

Fortunately, over the years, both law and policy have changed in a way beneficial to veteran survivors with MST-related PTS. Today, any veteran who experienced any type of unwilling or inappropriate sexual encounter in the military can obtain treatment from the VA, even if they do not have an MST-related service-connected benefit for this as a disability. Despite the military's efforts at addressing sexual violence incidents within their ranks, they do not acknowledge the phrase "military sexual trauma."

It is also important to recognize the importance of confusing language concerning the VA and MST. With the VA, there is no such thing as an MST disability. One can have a diagnosed physical or mental health condition related to MST, but one does not have an MST diagnosis. The condition one has and files a claim for is MST-related PTS, depression, anxiety, substance abuse disorder, physical disability, or more.

One of my pet peeves is that the VA and others, while acknowledging in some places that it is the experience or event, refer to MST as the event, not the result. For instance, they ask, "Did you experience military sexual trauma?" There is an important distinction in how this phrase is used. An experience of harassment, assault, or rape can be defined as a traumatic experience. The VA, however, in an attempt to abbreviate the conversations around sexual harassment, assault, and rape in the military, began referring to *the event* as "military sexual trauma," which led to a *reframing of the experience* as the psychological trauma now held. This is grammatically and experientially incorrect.

MST-related PTSD is what you have, not what happened to you. The life experience that took place was physical assault, sexual harassment, assault, and/or rape. Military-sexual-trauma-related PTS (or other) **is an identifier** that labels the trauma you have **because of** that experience(s).

The greatest problem of this incorrect verbiage is that veterans are asked if MST happened to them; and too often, they answer no, even when they did experience one of these interpersonal violence events. Why? Because although it happened to them, they may lack a full understanding of what MST meant/means, perhaps because they were not diagnosed, perhaps because, like me, they did not think their experience fell under the definition. Simply put: it is confusing to people, and that confusion may mean that too many people who have MST because of harassment, assault, and rape go without their service-connected disabilities or treatment. *Ask instead if they experienced sexual harassment, assault, rape, or intimate partner violence and see how many more positive responses you receive.*

Consider this in the context of other traumas and PTS. We do not ask people if IPV trauma, disaster trauma, or accident trauma happened *to* them. We do not ask civilian survivors of sexual assault or domestic violence if sexual or IPV trauma happened *to* them. We instead speak of the experience as just that and seek to help with the post-traumatic stress *related to* that event. We ask questions that help us understand the nature of the trauma as it relates to their current condition. For instance, did they experience violence or any type of abuse in the home or by a partner?

Trauma—Broken and Healed

Using MST as the defining event instead of the identifier of the condition that results from an event (e.g., PTS, insomnia, depression, and so on) causes confusion and fails to acknowledge the reality and severity of the event that occurred. We use MST as a substitute for using the words sexual harassment, assault, or rape. Until we can have these honest conversations about what causes their MST, we fail to properly acknowledge the existence of these grave problems, and people who have these experiences may fail to self-identify.

Finally, it is important to understand the aftermath of sexual harassment, assault, and rape. For those survivors who live with trauma, they may experience one or more of the many associated symptoms, including insomnia, disturbing nightmares, feeling unsafe, depression, anxiety, numbness, difficulty with anger and irritability, and substance use. These are serious symptoms that many people live with, not even knowing they are symptoms of their MST-related PTS.

Moreover, it is vital that we all begin to see MST and other sexual-assault-related trauma as a leading risk factor in substance abuse, suicide, and homelessness among all women. A few little-known facts:

- Women generally have higher rates of suicide ideation than men but lower rates of suicide completion.

Among the woman veteran population, they experience a higher rate of suicide than civilian women, primarily due to their use of weapons when attempting suicide.

- While the suicide rate among veteran men is declining, it continues to rise among the women veteran population.
- The rate of homelessness among women veterans continues to rise while homelessness among their male and nonveteran counterparts is on the decline.

According to the World Health Organization, 26 percent of women have been subjected to some form of physical and/or sexual violence from a current or former partner or spouse at least once in their lifetime.[vi] Sexual assault is frequently perpetrated in intimate relationships. When looking at sexual assault data, it generally does not include sexual assault experienced as part of a relationship. Those are two different measures. So, when we see 26 percent here and a different number altogether for sexual assault, know that although we are talking about the same acts, we are referring to two separate populations.

When it comes to all trauma, the numbers, no matter how or where, are nearly the same. A 2016 study that looked at over sixty-four thousand people across twenty-four countries found that over 70 percent of respondents had at least one traumatic experience, with 30.5 percent having been exposed to four or more.[vii] A 2022 Department of Veterans Affairs fact sheet tells us that about six of every ten men (or 60 percent) and five of every ten women (or 50 percent) experience at least one trauma in their lives, and the National Council for Behavioral Health checks in with data that is similar to the 2016 study, citing that 70 percent of US adults have experienced trauma at some point in their life.[vii,ix]

This is not to say we are all hot messes. Not all people who experienced something traumatic have PTS, *but all people who have PTS experienced something traumatic.* Also, some traumas are more likely to cause PTS than others. One study found that women with both MST and high combat exposure have significantly higher PTS compared to those without MST.[x] It is also important to acknowledge that two people can have the same experience, but one may come through it with no negative residual effects, while the other may present with PTS.

Resilience, coping skills, and resources/resourcefulness play a part in making sure that we can function, mostly or partly, through that trauma and live our daily lives. The type and frequency of trauma make a difference in the onset, presence, and duration of PTS. When we think of frequency, it could mean a singular incident (for instance, a rape) or an experience where the trauma experience is ongoing. Relationships or situations where there is emotional, physical, sexual, spiritual, financial, or other types of violence or abuse are an example of ongoing trauma.

In 1996, psychologist Jennifer Freyd developed the phrase "institutional betrayal" and recognized it as a contributing factor to PTS, depression, anxiety, and more.[xi] In short, she found that being in an unsafe environment where there is no protection or support—when the people who are supposed to be your allies turn into an enemy from which there is no escape—can contribute to the onset of the mental health conditions listed above. An example of institutional betrayal is my three years in the military that were a constant barrage of sexual harassment and assault I could not escape. No one cared. I had no support from peers or military leaders when attempting to address the problem. I and other women were on our own to maneuver through this sick, twisted environment every day. It was an example of ongoing trauma that ultimately led to me developing post-traumatic stress.

The type of trauma we experience can also matter. As previously mentioned, among women veterans, it has been found that combat alone is less of a predictor of PTS than sexual assault, and when sexual harassment is added, the combination becomes a stronger predictor.

PTS, known for decades as PTSD (*D* stands for disorder), is the body and mind's response to trauma. Although the name was not in use until 1980, when it made its debut in the mental health bible that is the *Diagnostic and Statistical Manual of Mental Health Disorders* (DSM), it has always been around, with professionals recognizing its existence among veterans back to the Civil War. Due to the stigma associated with mental health conditions, there has been a move to leave behind the word "disorder" in hopes to remove the stigma. In 2012, with the impending publication of the DSM-V, one of the challenges in front of the American Psychological Association (APA) was whether to remove the word "disorder"—a movement led by leadership at the US Army. Although the decision was made to retain "disorder," the field has seen an informal move to change it to simply post-traumatic stress, or PTS. Both the US military and the Pentagon have dropped the *D*.

In fact, a 2023 survey of clinical patients, about half of whom had a PTS diagnosis, showed a preference for removal of the D to reduce stigma and increase or improve treatment seeking. More specifically, they supported replacing the D with an I (injury). As a social worker and one experienced in the field, I find agreement with this movement to remove the D. Therefore, this book will refer to post-traumatic stress, or PTS.

With or without a letter after the PTS, it is recognized as a mental health condition that results from a traumatic experience that is considered a catastrophic stressor resulting from exposure to war, assault, a vehicle accident or plane crash, and more.

PTS comes with a long list of symptoms that fall under four categories:[xii]

- Intrusion
- Avoidance
- Alterations in cognition and mood
- Alterations in arousal and reactivity

A list of symptoms is found under each category, and in order to be diagnosed, a person must present with one or more symptoms in each. These can include flashbacks, nightmares, insomnia, avoiding places or people, hyperarousal, risky behaviors, negative thoughts, inability to maintain relationships, and more.

Importantly, PTS is unique for everyone, and so it may look different for each of us. The intention and duration may be more or less for some, depending on the type and duration of their trauma-inducing experience, whether they had multiple experiences and the amount of positive support they obtained following the traumatic experience. Some new studies even show that where a woman is in her menstrual cycle can affect the strength and duration of her PTS.[xiii]

Complex PTS (C-PTS) is PTS on steroids. In other words, it is PTS, but different. It most often occurs as a result of repeated or prolonged exposure (e.g., frequent community violence), trauma in childhood, and, to the point of this book, sexual abuse (including trafficking) and domestic violence. Studies have found that among teen girls who experienced sexual assault[xiv] and victims who experienced institutional betrayal, the rate of C-PTS is higher than among other groups.

The nature of C-PTS and its causes can lead to a more negative impact on the nervous system, which can lead to more difficulties connected to attachment or interpersonal relationships. Some additional markers of C-PTS that separate it from PTS are emotional dysregulation, negative self-cognitions, and interpersonal hardship.[xv]

Trauma—Broken and Healed

Trauma is not over and done. It does not just go away because a therapist said so and told you that you have the tools to manage and are well enough to move on. Mental health professionals acknowledge that trauma still exists as part of the life that made you and will always be there, and both theory and practice say that through therapy and work we learn to manage our trauma and its consequences.

"The symptoms of PTSD really never go away," Dr. Sanjay Gupta told CNN. "Here is why: There is a profound psychological and physiological reaction to something traumatic. That traumatic event can't be completely undone, though it can be diminished in the mind."

It is true that folks with PTS learn to face life with that trauma inside of us but, hopefully, as something smaller and less invasive than it was initially. We work on our self-esteem, issues of trust, insecurities, and fears so that we recognize the trauma as a part of our history but have gained the skills and knowledge to overcome or lessen the symptoms. It is our history that built us. We learn that in spite of our history and what happened to us, treatment helps us understand that we still have value, and trauma-inducing events do not define us. We are living kintsugi, if you will.

Resilience and resourcefulness are two essential keys to a person while navigating the world post-trauma. Tools for both are available at the end of the book. Resilience is what helps us get through the initial trauma. It gives us the ability to maneuver our way through the quagmire of emotions and fears brought about by (and during) the trauma. Resilience guides our capacity to navigate the social, psychological, and cultural resources that will help us in the moment and, later, to recover our strength and determination. It continues to serve us in the future in the event our stronger places break.

Resourcefulness is our tool for living in this world with post-traumatic stress. It allows us to find alternative approaches, gather our resources, manage life's stressors, and choose a path toward healing and recovery when we are working to make our way through the day. Most importantly, resourcefulness is what helps us when we experience retraumatization—when our stronger places break and we are lost in the darkness and confusion of renewed adversity.

The traumatic experience you went through will always be with you. If you have PTS, it may not go away, but the effects can be ameliorated through evidence-based treatment or, in my case, ignoring it and stuffing it deep down inside. This can result in PTS lying dormant, sometimes for years or decades until the day a retraumatizing experience happens that brings it up.

PTS treatment can be highly effective in helping survivors manage their PTS and life. It is constantly changing and evolving, so if you are considering treatment, know that there are options.

The well-known American Psychological Association (APA) now has a recommended list of therapies for PTS. These recommendations have been broken into the following two categories, taken directly from the Clinical Practice Guideline for the Treatment of Post-Traumatic Stress Disorder.[xvi]

Strongly Recommended

- *Cognitive behavioral therapy* (CBT) focuses on the relationships among thoughts, feelings, and behaviors; targets current problems and symptoms; and focuses on changing patterns of behaviors, thoughts, and feelings that lead to difficulties in functioning. (also for C-PTSD)
- *Cognitive processing therapy* (CPT) Cognitive processing therapy is a specific type of cognitive behavioral therapy that helps patients learn how to modify and challenge unhelpful beliefs related to trauma.
- *Cognitive therapy*, derived from cognitive behavioral therapy, entails modifying the pessimistic evaluations and memories of trauma, with the goal of interrupting the disturbing behavioral and/or thought patterns that have been interfering with the person's daily life.
- *Prolonged exposure* is a specific type of cognitive behavioral therapy that teaches individuals to gradually approach trauma-related memories, feelings, and situations. By facing what has been avoided, a person presumably learns that the trauma-related memories and cues are not dangerous and do not need to be avoided.

Conditionally Recommended

- *Eye-movement desensitization and reprocessing* (EMDR) encourages the patient to briefly focus on the trauma memory while simultaneously

experiencing bilateral stimulation (typically eye movements), which is associated with a reduction in the vividness and emotion associated with the trauma memories (also for C-PTS);
- *Brief eclectic psychotherapy* combines elements of cognitive behavioral therapy with a psychodynamic approach. It focuses on changing the emotions of shame and guilt and emphasizes the relationship between the patient and therapist;
- *Narrative exposure therapy* (NET) helps individuals establish a coherent life narrative in which to contextualize traumatic experiences. It is known for its use in group treatment for refugees.
- *Medications*—four medications received a conditional recommendation for use in the treatment of PTSD: sertraline, paroxetine, fluoxetine, and venlafaxine.

In conversations about trauma, we often hear about "post-traumatic growth." This phrase is used as a way of describing positive changes arising from trauma recovery. Post-traumatic growth can include the following:

- Development of personal strength where you are feeling more confident, capable, or assertive, even more so than before the traumatic experience. This may come with a regaining of resilience, which helped you get through your trauma initially.
- *Relationship building*, where you can develop closer bonds with others and increase your support network, includes improving personal relationships, finding joy in connecting with people we love, and embracing new opportunities (e.g., education, career, and more).
- *Resourcefulness*, discussed above, is too often not discussed as a part of post-traumatic growth. It is our ability to adapt to life's challenges and choose an effective course of action that will help us with our reset. Survivors may not even be aware that they are resourceful, but if you are reading this, know that your decision to escape for a weekend, ask for help, connect with your support person(s), or tap into your own strength and wisdom are a result of your resourcefulness.

Broken in the Stronger Places: From Resilience to Resourcefulness

Sadly, access to important and necessary—sometimes lifesaving - treatment has become more and more strained and limited. Years ago, it was not unusual for a person to participate in therapy for months or even years. The need for therapy was based on a decision made between the client and the therapist that included reduction of symptoms and improved lifestyle. Today, however, this has mostly changed.

National Public Radio (NPR) recently released a review of mental health care and how access has changed for the worse.[xvii] Federal law requires that people have equal access to mental health and physical health care. However, in the case of mental health, the problem arises in the loophole that gives insurers the freedom *not* to uphold the same standard of care regarding the use of evidence-based guidelines or those endorsed by professional associations. Flawed laws lead to flawed outcomes.

Unfortunately, this free rein given to insurers leads to widely varying quality and access to mental health care. This harmed the mental health industry and those seeking care: with more therapists leaving networks, more people struggle to find the therapy they need.

Fortunately, two things have happened that offset this loophole:

- Most states have enacted laws that define clinical standards of care.[3]
- In September 2024, President Biden finalized new regulations that counter the loophole, holding insurers to new standards.

With these new regulations, insurance companies will be required to improve the data they collect and report regarding limiting and/or denying treatment.

In today's society, with an entire industry managed by for-profit insurance companies, patients too often no longer have access to needed care for as long as they need it.

Although the government is supposed to have oversight and, in some cases, has challenged states to change how they are doing business, it is akin to babies being thrown into the water upstream and leaving it up to two people downstream to catch them all. Sadly, people who need treatment commonly get only what their insurance companies pay for, which may be wholly insufficient for their individual needs.

A system based on money is one destined to cause harm.

Today's for-profit health-care system and insurance industry, which includes the Department of Veterans Affairs, does not fully acknowledge that we may still be broken in those stronger places when our treatment ends. Rather than being better, it is possible that our broken places are just covered with layers of all the right things trauma survivors learn to apply—the lacquer and precious metal powder called therapy, recovery steps, different types of treatment, and so on. What is too rarely acknowledged is that an incident or series of events can occur at any time after the trauma-inducing experience, including post-therapy, and those stronger broken places can shatter like finely spun glass hitting a marble floor.

I have seen this very thing happen all too frequently among women I have helped and spoken with and have experienced this reality myself: retraumatization that can break our stronger places, setting a survivor back in their recovery.

Through the Lens Darkly

When examined through the military and veteran lens, more studies are showing higher numbers of women than previously suspected who have or are experiencing some form of harassment, assault, and/or rape in the military. When considering that there are two million living women veterans, the reality of the number of survivors in this group can be mind-boggling.

But this book is not just about women veterans, so let's talk about prevalence among nonmilitary and veteran populations.

According to the CDC, family and IPV, or domestic violence, affects approximately ten million people in the United States per year. They estimate that one in four women and one in nine men are victims of domestic violence annually. IPV includes economic, physical, sexual, emotional, and psychological abuse perpetrated against a partner or spouse, whereas family violence denotes abuse against children, adults, or older family members. In the same report, it is stated that about one in three women and nearly one in six men experience some form of sexual violence during their lifetimes.[xviii]

Broken in the Stronger Places: From Resilience to Resourcefulness

In a separate national sample of adolescents, it was found that approximately one in four adolescents (24.99 percent) reported exposure to violence at some point in their lifetime, with 13.4 percent experiencing direct violence exposure and 9.4 percent indirect exposure.[xix]

Among the civilian population, young women aged 18–24 are at an elevated risk of sexual assault. Although college campuses have long been known as less-than-safe environments for young women, the risk remains lower for them than for non students in the same age group with a risk of three times all women for students, and four times all women for non students. According to the Rape and Incest National Network (RAINN) 13 percent of all students experience rape or sexual assault through physical force, violence, or incapacitation (among all graduate and undergraduate students). The risk is highest among undergraduate students, with 26.4 percent of women and 6.8 percent of men experiencing rape or sexual assault, compared to 9.7 percent of women and 2.5 percent of men who are graduate students. 5.8 percent of students experience stalking while in college. Among transgender, genderqueer, and gender nonconforming college students, **23.1 percent** report having been sexually assaulted.

Workplace violence is also a considerable issue. A recent global study of 74,000 workers in 121 countries found that nearly 23 percent of workers experienced some form of workplace violence, which includes insults, threats, and bullying and sexual violence/harassment, as well as physical violence.[xx] More importantly, 39 percent reported multiple or recurrent episodes. Women are more likely to be victims of psychological and sexual workplace violence, whereas their male counterparts experience higher rates of physical violence in the workplace. People who experience discrimination or harassment based on gender, race, ethnicity, disability, and religion are most likely to experience workplace violence, and for migrant women, the likelihood of experiencing this violence is higher than for non-migrant women.

Why is all of this important? Because workplace violence negatively and sometimes severely impacts a person's mental and physical health and contributes to interrupted career paths and job loss. For those in the military, there may be no escape. You do not have the luxury of simply avoiding the person who is harassing, assaulting, or raping you, especially if it is someone

Trauma—Broken and Healed

in your chain of command. It is frequently the same for women in civilian employment, who may feel trapped and unable to leave. Remaining in a job because of the lack of other employment, fear, and shame is too often the reality, especially for those in low-wage and male-dominated fields. Worse, if they tell someone, they risk retaliation and not being believed. Ongoing experiences like persistent harassment can and do lead to post-traumatic stress.

Part of being in the military is the notion that you are "family" and can trust the people you serve with. They are supposed to always have your back. Yet, when you report an incident, whether it is harassment, assault, or rape, what you are too often faced with is a request to let it go, a denial that it exists, or some form of coercion, retaliation, or punishment. And yes, this persists even in 2024. I spoke with women who received death threats or were raped by their superiors as a punishment for telling. This is too often the reality for people in the military. There is no place safe and no safe place.

This institutional betrayal, discussed in chapter 3, was identified by Jennifer Freyd, PhD, as a problem in institutions such as the military, universities, and workplaces. She found that this betrayal exacerbates the trauma experienced by victims and is associated with more severe symptoms of PTSD, depression, anxiety, and suicidal ideation.[xxi]

Of course, none of these numbers factor in community gun and other violence that can also lead to post-traumatic stress, as well as other psychological or physical conditions related to trauma exposure. Race and LGBTQ status increase risk and exposure to violence, but for the sake of this book, we will not delve into community violence (e.g., gun violence, hate crimes, aggravated assault, and the like) but rather focus on interpersonal violence (IPV and/or sexual assault).

---

iii   US Marshals Service, Resources. https://www.usmarshals.gov/resources/forms/lautenberg-amendment. Viewed 01/02/2025.

iv   Maureen Murdoch, Melissa A. Polusny, James Hodges, Diane Cowper, The Association between In-Service Sexual Harassment and Post-Traumatic Stress Disorder among Department of Veterans Affairs Disability Applicants, Military Medicine, Volume 171, Issue 2, February 2006, Pages 166–173, https://doi.org/10.7205/MILMED.171.2.166.

v   Equal Employment Opportunity Commission. April 2022. Sexual Harassment in Our Nation's Workplace. Equal Employment Opportunity Commission Data Highlight. https://www.eeoc.gov/data/sexual-harassment-our-nations-workplaces viewed 08/24/2024.

Broken in the Stronger Places: From Resilience to Resourcefulness

vi   World Health Organization. Intimate Partner Violence Study. https://apps.who.int/violence-info/intimate-partner-violence/. Viewed 08/24/2024.

vii   Benjet C, Bromet E, Karam EG, Kessler RC, McLaughlin KA, Ruscio AM, Shahly V, Stein DJ, Petukhova M, Hill E, Alonso J, Atwoli L, Bunting B, Bruffaerts R, Caldas-de-Almeida JM, de Girolamo G, Florescu S, Gureje O, Huang Y, Lepine JP, Kawakami N, Kovess-Masfety V, Medina-Mora ME, Navarro-Mateu F, Piazza M, Posada-Villa J, Scott KM, Shalev A, Slade T, ten Have M, Torres Y, Viana MC, Zarkov Z, Koenen KC. The epidemiology of traumatic event exposure worldwide: results from the World Mental Health Survey Consortium. Psychol Med. 2016 Jan;46(2):327-43. doi: 10.1017/S0033291715001981. Epub 2015 Oct 29. PMID: 26511595; PMCID: PMC4869975.

viii   National Council for Behavioral Health. How to Manage Trauma. https://www.thenationalcouncil.org/wp-content/uploads/2022/08/Trauma-infographic.pdf Viewed 08/27/2024.

ix   National Center for PTSD. How Common is PTSD in Adults? https://www.ptsd.va.gov/understand/common/common_adults.asp Viewed 08/27/2024.

x   Cobb Scott J, Pietrzak RH, Southwick SM, Jordan J, Silliker N, Brandt CA, Haskell SG. Military sexual trauma interacts with combat exposure to increase risk for posttraumatic stress symptomatology in female Iraq and Afghanistan veterans. J Clin Psychiatry. 2014 Jun;75(6):637-43. doi: 10.4088/JCP.13m08808. PMID: 25004187.

xi   Smith CP, Freyd JJ. Dangerous safe havens: institutional betrayal exacerbates sexual trauma. J Trauma Stress. 2013 Feb;26(1):119-24. doi: 10.1002/jts.21778. PMID: 23417879.

xii   What is Post Traumatic Stress Disorder (PTSD). American Psychiatric Disorder webpage. https://www.psychiatry.org/patients-families/ptsd/what-is-ptsd#:~:text=Intrusion:%20Intrusive%20thoughts%20such%20as,void%20of%20happiness%20or%20satisfaction). 10/20/2024

xiii   Ying, K. "Female Veterans and TBI: 3 Things You Should Know." Constant Therapy Health. Viewed 07/24/24

xiv   Villalta L, Khadr S, Chua KC, Kramer T, Clarke V, Viner RM, Stringaris A, Smith P. Complex post-traumatic stress symptoms in female adolescents: the role of emotion dysregulation in impairment and trauma exposure after an acute sexual assault. Eur J Psychotraumatol. 2020 Jan 10;11(1):1710400. doi: 10.1080/20008198.2019.1710400. PMID: 32002143; PMCID: PMC6968575.

xv   Psychology Today. February, 2024. Gillis, K. LCSW. The Difference Between PTSD and C-PTSD. https://www.psychologytoday.com/us/blog/invisible-bruises/202402/the-difference-between-ptsd-and-cptsd.

xvi   Clinical Practice Guideline for the Treatment of Post Traumatic Stress Disorder. American Psychological Association. Viewed 08/27/2024 https://www.apa.org/ptsd-guideline/treatments.

xvii   Waldman, A., Miller, M. (2024, August 27). Insurers can restrict mental health care. What laws protect patients in your state? National Public Radio (NPR). https://

www.npr.org/sections/shots-health-news/2024/08/23/nx-s1-5084256/insurance-mental-health-care-coverage-legal-protection.

xviii   Huecker MR, King KC, Jordan GA, et al. Domestic Violence. [Updated 2023 Apr 9]. In: StatPearls [Internet]. Treasure Island (FL): StatPearls Publishing; 2024 Jan-. Available from: https://www.ncbi.nlm.nih.gov/books/NBK499891/.

xix   McLaughlin KA, Basu A, Walsh K, Slopen N, Sumner JA, Koenen KC, Keyes KM. Childhood Exposure to Violence and Chronic Physical Conditions in a National Sample of US Adolescents. Psychosom Med. 2016 Nov/Dec;78(9):1072-1083. doi: 10.1097/PSY.0000000000000366. PMID: 27428855; PMCID: PMC5096968.

xx   Crabtree, S. 2022. Global Study: 23% of Workers Experience Violence, Harassment https://news.gallup.com/opinion/gallup/406793/global-study-workers-experience-violence-harassment.aspx#:~:text=More%20than%20one%20in%20five,may%20not%20have%20done%20so.

xxi   Smith, C. P., & Freyd, J. J. (2014). Institutional betrayal. American Psychologist, 69(6), 575–587. https://doi.org/10.1037/a0037564.

"The time has come," the walrus said,
"To talk of many things:
Of shoes—and ships—and sealing-wax—
Of cabbages—and kings—
And why the sea is boiling hot—
And whether pigs have wings."

—**Lewis Carroll,** *The Walrus and the Carpenter*

CHAPTER 4

Broken in the Stronger Places

Retraumatization

Retraumatization is defined as happening when people with PTS are exposed to people, places, events, situations, or environments that cause them to reexperience past trauma.[xxii] It can be reliving a similar incident or an emotional or sensory trigger. Often, what we think of in considering retraumatization or a setback in recovery and healing is the witnessing of or exposure to an experience similar to the initial traumatic event (e.g., another physical assault, a vehicle crash, a mass shooting, and the like). It can also be the result of stressors that remind someone of the environment or the original trauma. Triggers can be brought on by smells, colors, music, sounds, conversations, or even people.

The idea of being broken in the stronger places is about retraumatization—some of which we can easily manage and work through, and some of which finds us right back in the gaping maw of Hell that is our trauma, undone entirely.

Treatment aside, one of the ways we manage PTS is through various support systems or avenues. For instance, we may have found a partner who is our soft place to land and helps keep our stress and trauma at a manageable place.

This may be the person who comforts us and knows how to exist within the myriad and changing emotions, feelings, and general health/mental health, helping to keep the things that go bump in the dark at bay. It may be art therapy or writing that helps us to manage our PTS. These things become, as a friend said, a nucleus that keeps us grounded.

But what happens when that person is not available to us? What if, because of death or a breakup, they disappear from our lives? What happens if we face an obstacle or event that threatens to (or does) shatter our stronger places? What then? These questions bring us to the retraumatization response.

In talking about retraumatization, there can be the types of triggers mentioned above, but there are also other types of triggers acknowledged as risk factors for retraumatization.[xxiii]

- Being emotionally disconnected from a loved one, peers, colleagues, and others
- Having a lack of economic and social supports or a lack of access to health and mental health care services
- Intense distress in reaction to triggers or circumstances you link to present or past trauma
- Feeling distant from other people. Feeling unable to control your emotions, such as not being able to calm yourself down, a decreased sense of security, and an inability to feel love

Real People = Valid Experiences

I had a conversation with a woman who has PTS as a result of an abusive relationship. Over the years, she had done a lot of work on releasing trauma and reducing symptoms. She shared with me that, on occasion, one of her family members will make a comment that judges her for leaving her abusive husband and suggests she should have stayed. When this happens, she experiences a strong emotional trigger that causes a break in her stronger places. Her response is to take care of herself by leaving town for a few days. She simply disappears from her family and home to heal the place broken by the inconsiderate comments of loved ones. It is a good example of how something as simple as a person's words can cause harm. Words matter.

The retelling of your story can also trigger retraumatization. For the women I spoke with during my career, this reality showed itself numerous times. This is one reason that advocates and professionals who work with victims and survivors have begun recording a woman's telling of the assault: so they do not have to retell their story and live through that retraumatization over and over again. For women veterans, I often heard how having to tell their story when they apply for service-connected disabilities is incredibly traumatizing and prevents them from applying. This is one reason I explained that they did not need to share details when they filed or had their compensation and pension exams. It was also why I advised them to find a good therapist immediately, explaining that this process could activate or revisit their trauma. This can be especially difficult during the claims process, when veterans sometimes encounter the VA or other personnel who may be insensitive to this reality.

And then there is what I call the "you're-OK-because-I-think-you-are-OK" lens, where we find harm when examining trauma. An example of this is how it is perceived that a person with PTS in a relationship or who is successful in their career is OK. Unfortunately, the VA is notorious for this, causing harm by making this assumption and denying a veteran's service-connected disability claim for MST because a person does not fit inside their box.

I too often witnessed the VA denying the presence of PTS disability because of their ideas as an institution or employees of that institution and not the real-life, valid experiences, emotions, and feelings of a veteran. Have you entered a healthy relationship and/or had a baby? Be prepared to have the VA decide that your PTS is better and reduce or deny your disability. Are you a successful artist, writer, or other? Uh-oh. The VA may deny your claim or reduce your disability because of your success. Do you present yourself well—showered, styled hair, nice clothes—during your compensation and pension (claims) exam? The VA may see you as perfectly fine since you were able to get up in the morning and make yourself look good. Are you speaking in a strong, confident manner? The VA may see this as an indication that you are OK because you are not sobbing your way through an exam with a compensation and pension examiner.

Broken in the Stronger Places: From Resilience to Resourcefulness

This approach, assuming that people who have PTS are clearly a mess, that we are unable to function or participate in the world, is problematic. It does not allow for the fact that a person has to get up in the morning and carry on because there are kids, bills, a job, a family, or any kind of responsibility. It does not factor in the reality that so many trauma survivors are forced to live their lives every single day with no other choice—because the other option(s) are death, homelessness, substance abuse, or other risky or negative behaviors. It does not recognize the fact that we build up stronger places on top of our broken places, but with the change of a life situation, that stronger place can break. It fails to account for the resourcefulness we employ daily.

Consider instead the reality that these relationships, your work as a writer or artist, your success as an executive who wears a suit or effectiveness as a public speaker, or whatever else may be the glue that holds you together. Your spouse or partner is the person who is your soft place to land. Your painting and writing are the ways you manage your trauma and stave off nightmares, anger, depression, and more. Your daily grind of getting up and dressing in your work clothes and going to work and saying smart things ten to twelve hours a day is what you learned to do to stay whole. That suit and styled hair are the image survivors with PTS know the world needs to see. These things: the loving partner, the art, the suit, the writing, may all be the resources we reach for to stave off our symptoms every day.

The presence of jobs, support systems, hobbies, and more are the lacquer and gold powder that help make up your stronger places every single day, and when/if they disappear, those places can become broken. If your partner dies, or if you are unable to write or paint or otherwise engage in whatever it is that helps keep you emotionally healthy, what is next for your PTS?

In light of all this, however, it is also important to understand the PTS spectrum and recognize that when a person has severe or complex PTS, they may not be able to do these things. They may be unable to exist in relationships, participate in public spaces, or work.

Trauma Informed: The Missing Link

Unfortunately, the VA and others have historically failed to implement trauma-informed approaches when it comes to the claims process.[4] Although that is said to be changing, it will be interesting to see how long it takes for a real-time shift to happen. They easily understand that a prosthetic is not a permanent solution, yet they are unable to recognize jobs, people, and more as the prosthetics that help survivors with PTS get through the day. If that PTS prosthetic disappears, that could seriously undermine your success with recovery and healing.

As an example, if you have hearing loss and need a cochlear implant, the VA recognizes that you will always be 100 percent deaf, because if that implant is removed, you will be unable to hear. Same with prosthetics and medicine: if you lose a limb or organ, or your medicine becomes unavailable, your health and well-being are reduced or endangered. A permanent physical disability is not seen differently because a person has been given a prosthetic or medicine **because that disability still exists in spite of these resources**. As therapists, benefits representatives, and policymakers, how can we do better in understanding this reality as it relates to mental health and apply that same approach and thinking to PTS? How do we implement system change, accepting that trauma and disability continue to exist, even if a person utilizes resourcefulness and resilience to live a healthier life?

To take this conversation through the PTS continuum, I want to end with this: experiencing being broken in the stronger places is not necessarily permanent. While strength, resilience, and resourcefulness can stave off or lessen PTS following a traumatic event, those are equally what help us pick up and carry on after a rebreak in our stronger places. A leading national organization, The National Sexual Violence Resource Center (NSVRC), identifies seven ways a survivor of sexual assault can practice self-care following another tragedy or traumatic event. These are simple, doable steps that can be used successfully to help survivors throughout their lives, especially in the face of new or renewed trauma. They are (as identified on the NSVRC page).[xxiv]

The 5-4-3-2-1 Exercise ✒

- Describe five things you currently see.
- Describe four things you feel right now. For example, "my sweater on my arms" or "the pencil in my hand."
- Describe three things you can hear.
- Describe two things you can smell right now or smells you like in general.
- Describe one good thing about yourself.

Call a Friend

Call a friend and ask them about their day, focus on what they have to say, and allow yourself to be carried away by the conversation. Also, don't be afraid to tell them how you're feeling as well!

Take a Shower or Bath

Let the experience of the warmth wash over you, and focus on the sensation. Maybe light some candles or play music as well and focus on the various sounds and scents.

Move Around

Take off your shoes and socks and rub your feet on the floor, do some gentle stretches, go for a jog or a walk—anything you can do that will allow you to focus on the sensations within your body. Describe them to yourself and try to stay in the moment.

Guided Meditation or Yoga

For some people, listening to a meditation or practicing yoga can be mentally or physically engaging enough that they're able to be completely in the here and now. While these types of activities aren't for everyone, for many, they reduce stress and anxiety.

Distract Yourself with a Project

Whether you paint, draw, sew, or even just like to color, engaging in an activity you enjoy and is soothing can help bring you into the present and relieve some of the pain of trauma.

Seek Support

Sometimes, we need to reach out for additional support—and that's OK! It is important to remember that there are other people going through similar struggles, and by addressing our experiences of trauma we can grow even more resilient. Check out the list of resources that might be helpful in your journey to health and happiness.

If you have a loved one who is experiencing retraumatization, the Mayo Clinic offers these steps that may help to guide you in supporting that person:

You can also help by being a supportive listener without attempting to "fix" the situation.

Here are some suggestions:[xxv]

- Be willing to listen, but do not push. Make sure your loved one knows that you want to hear about his or her feelings. But if the person isn't ready or willing to talk about it, don't push. Just reassure your loved one that you will be there if and when he or she is ready.
- Choose a time to talk. When you are both ready to talk, choose a time and place where you will be free of distractions and interruptions. Then truly listen. Ask questions if you do not understand something. But avoid any urges to second-guess, make assumptions, give advice, or say, "I know just how you feel."
- Recognize when to take a break. If you sense that the conversation is becoming too intense for your loved one, provide them with an

opportunity to stop for now and take up the conversation again on another day. Then follow through.

- Get help if talk of suicide occurs. If your loved one talks or behaves in a way that makes you believe they might attempt suicide, respond calmly but act immediately. Make sure the person is not left alone. If it is safe to do so, you as the friend or family member may want to discreetly remove pills, firearms, or any other objects that could be used for self-harm and get help from a trained professional as soon as possible (for instance, by calling a crisis or helpline).

Following my own breaking while working at the VA Center for Women Veterans, I despaired, thinking I would not be able to get past that, but through work with my therapist, engaging with my support system, and writing, I did. My resourcefulness was what got me through that dark year that followed my escape from DC. Am I 100 percent OK? Not even close. The PTS is permanently embedded in me because of the combination of my own experiences and my vicarious trauma gained in working for the better part of thirty years with victims and survivors. But my life is not as dark as it was in the time following September 2022. Part of what helped with the immediate mental health crisis I experienced during that time was (1) my conversations with my mental health provider, (2) support from friends and family, and (3) a one-year road trip, which you will be able to read about in the last chapter.

---

xxii Substance Abuse and Mental Health Services Administration. Tips for Survivors of a Disaster or Other Traumatic Event: COPING WITH RETRAUMATIZATION, 2023) Viewed 08/27/2024 https://store.samhsa.gov/sites/default/files/sma17-5047.pdf.

xxiii Ibid.

xxiv National Sexual Violence Resource Center. 7 Ways Survivors of Sexual Violence Can Practice Self-Care When Retraumatized During Tragedy | National Sexual Violence Resource Center (NSVRC). 7 Ways Survivors of Sexual Violence Can Practice Self-Care When Retraumatized During Tragedy. https://www.nsvrc.org/blogs/seven-ways-survivors-sexual-violence-can-practice-self-care-when-retraumatized-during-tragedy#:~:text=For%20some%20people%20listening%20to,journey%20to%20health%20and%20happiness. Viewed 10/21/2024.

xxv Mayo Clinic. Post-traumatic stress: How can you help your loved one? https://www.mayoclinic.org/diseases-conditions/post-traumatic-stress-disorder/expert-answers/post-traumatic-stress/faq-20057756#:~:text=Whether%20your%20loved%20one%20has,if%20talk%20of%20suicide%20occurs. Viewed 10/21/2024.

Women cannot lead without men, but men have to this day considered themselves capable of leading without women. Women would always take men into consideration. That's the difference.

—**Vigdis Finnbogadottir**, *President of Iceland*

CHAPTER 5

I Do Solemnly Swear

In 1977, at the ripe age of nineteen and with one year of college behind me, I deemed I was quite smart enough, thank you, and left college, moving from Colorado to Oregon to find the rest of my life and career (not thinking that the career I wanted really needed a college education). I was living the dream, hanging out with my sister and her husband, getting to know her friends, finding my own friends, and making my own way.

I had a good job, bought a badass car (a 1976 Nova SS), and did what I wanted. There was no stopping me! That is until I gave notice at my job after finding a better one. Just a few days before I was to start my new job, I was told that he had decided to hire his best friend's daughter, who needed the job, leaving me jobless during a recession.

Gas prices were crazy, businesses were laying people off, and the country was in an economic crisis. Finding a job was proving impossible, given that no one was hiring. Even government offices were giving people their pink slips. What's a girl to do?

One day, my roommate came rolling in proclaiming that she had discovered the solution to our problems (she, too, was unemployed): Join the Army! My response was, "Hell, no, I'm not joining the Army." But if ever there was someone as convincing as me, it was her. Next thing I knew, we were down at

Broken in the Stronger Places: From Resilience to Resourcefulness

the recruiter's office listening to how great it would be to join under the buddy system and travel together, how much money we would earn, the benefits we would have, and what we would learn. And, ooph, the travel! Did I mention how amazing our lives would be with the travel opportunities we would have?

Oh yeah, we got sucked right in. Until my friend, who was a single mother of two children, was told by the recruiter that she would have to relinquish custody of her children in order to join. They did not care to whom she signed over custody (it could be an ex-husband, grandparent, or other), just so long as she did. This Man's Army could not have single mothers.[5]

"What about single fathers?" I asked. "Well, we don't worry about them. The moms take care of the children, so we don't have to worry about men having custody."

Oh, hello, sexism in the '70s. So, my friend was out, but I had a car payment coming up, no job prospects, and nothing else to do, so I signed my name on the dotted line and prepared to raise my right hand to swear my oath to our country. Just two weeks later, I was off to basic training in Ft. Jackson, South Carolina.

Family and friends had varying schools of thought. My mom was cautiously proud (proud but a bit nervous and with questions). With the exception of my sister Ritha, who I was living with at the time, my siblings offered no commentary. When I called my dad, a World War II veteran, it was different. He said, "The Army is no place for a young woman, and before you get pissed off and call me a chauvinist, I say that because I know what men do to women in the military. It's not a nice place. Call them and tell them you changed your mind." It was at this point that I reminded my dad he had forfeited all rights to tell me what to do when I was six years old and he left us.

My sister Ritha, of the Vietnam War generation, was distraught, firmly on our father's side, insisting I go back to the recruiting office and tell them I changed my mind. She got angry at our friend for influencing me to do this. I did not even believe in war, she reminded me. People *died* in the military, she exclaimed. What the fuck was I thinking? The rest of my family and friends either shared my mother's cautious optimism, wondered what the hell I was thinking and why I would do something so batshit crazy, or were somewhere in the middle.

I will never forget the day I was to take the bus to Boise, Idaho for my indoctrination ceremony. Ritha said she could not go, that she would say goodbye there at the house. My brother-in-law drove me, and I remember looking out the back window to see her sitting there, crying. I never forgot her there, sitting sentinel for me. I knew she would have my back if I needed her, and as it turned out, I would.

This Man's Army

"Get your God damn lazy, goat-smelling asses off the bus now! Get off! Get off! Get off! Get off my bus!"

That was my welcome to the legendary Ft. Jackson, South Carolina, with five drill sergeants yelling at us, the young men and women crowded on the bus that had brought us to our company unit. You can bet we were tripping over each other to disembark as quickly as possible. We knew instinctively the last persons off were doomed in some horrible way that we still did not understand but feared, which is how basic training is designed (or was at the time). That bus ride and disembarking challenge was our formal welcome to our new life.

On this crisp day in January 1978, we came to our company area from the Welcome Center at Ft. Jackson. There was nothing at that center to prepare us for the shock we would encounter when we got to our companies and faced a team of drill instructors whose one job was to make us the best that we could be. The Welcome Center at Ft. Jackson was officially your last vestige of hope that it is not *that* bad before you entered the fray that is the US Army.

I was among the second wave of women to go through coed basic training in the US Army during the dismantling of the Women's Army Corp (WAC). For those of you squirming and itching to correct me: yes, the official date of the discontinuation of WACs was April 26, 1978, but they had begun recruiting women as Regular Army in 1977 and placing women and men together into coed units at Ft. Jackson. One group of women had already graduated, and we were next. Prior to this time, women in the Army had attended women-only basic training at Ft. McClellan, where they experienced a different style of

Broken in the Stronger Places: From Resilience to Resourcefulness

training than men. Here we were now, all figuring it out together: the women, men, drill instructors, and the US Army at "Relaxin' Jackson."[6]

Training was now mixed-gender, and the angst was at an all-time high. The women recruits may as well have been wearing big red targets on our backs.

It was shortly after the new year, and we were all together in one company, women residing on the top floor and men on the floors below. What the men did, the women did, with the only change in training requirements being the number of pull-ups required for women and that we had the option to do pushups and sit-ups from the bent leg position. However, the woman who opted for that altered position would hear no end of the chiding and disrespect for her choice. For that reason, many of us chose the standard positions.

We early women at Relaxin; Jackson had something to prove.

So, on that afternoon in January 1978, the drill sergeants continued to yell at us to get off the bus and into formation. Of course, it was our first minute and a half, and we had no idea what a formation was, except what we had seen in movies, but we sort of figured it out in a half-assed kind of way. They spent a good deal of time yelling at us and calling us names (*goat-smelling asses* was a favorite) before introducing themselves as the drill sergeants and telling us that for the next eight weeks, we were family: "Look to your front. Look to your back. Look to your left. Look to your right. These are your brothers and sisters. They have got your back and will always be there for you. They will do what you need them to do. They will take care of you. You can count on them for everything. You are all one unit, and it is your *job* to help each other out. If one fails, you all fail."

With an irony I am fairly certain they neither understood nor gave a damn about, what they said in the next breath was, "For you **'fee-males'** out there (there was a particular way that "females" was used in the military, with an emphasis on "feee" and a voice full of derision), we do not believe there is any place in This Man's Army for *girls* (again, said with derision for emphasis). We do not think you belong here. We do not want you here, we do not want to have you in our company or on our base, and we are about to spend the next eight weeks showing you all how much we mean that. If we have anything to do with it, at the end of this time, not one of y'all will be here."

Hello, misogyny, come in and get comfortable. You like that chair? No? I'll get you a new one.

An added note: the use of **feeemale** as a pejorative during my three years in the Army is why, to this day, I despise the phrase "female veteran." Also, it's grammatically incorrect, but that is a different conversation.

Early Decisions, Late Mistakes

So, how did we women get here? Because 1973…

Because of falling recruitments following the end of the draft in June 1973, the Department of Defense, by necessity, had to examine recruitment through a wider lens, which meant expanding recruitment in the 51 percent of the population that had been mostly excluded since the American Revolution. They recognized the value of adding more women to the military, opening up additional roles, and lifting any percentage or rules that limited our enlistment.

In 1977, then Secretary of Defense Harold Brown ordered a study titled *The Use of Women in the Military*.[xxvi] Following the end of the draft after the Vietnam War, it became apparent that an all-volunteer military was going to be problematic as far as numbers. One of the purposes of this study was to understand how women could contribute to the military. Our government came to understand that including the other half of the population (women) could be the answer to a declining enlistment. As stated in the paper, "Use of more women can be a significant factor in making the all-volunteer force continue to work in the face of a declining youth population."

The paper's findings, in a nutshell, were as follows:

- The number of women on active duty from 1971–1976 more than tripled.
- More highly qualified women were willing to enlist than were being accepted.
- Different branches had successfully expanded nontraditional roles for women.
- All branches except the Army were planning on an increase in recruitment of women from 1978–1982.

- Disallowing women on Navy ships was having a negative impact on how many women they could allow in unless the law changed.
- Expansion of the number of women serving could be an important contributor to a successful all-volunteer force.
- As the career potential for women is expanded, their recruitment and retention will continue to increase.

Findings also showed that the military could recruit "quality women and low-quality"[7] men at a lower cost than men because it did not take the same level of marketing and recruiting effort to get these two groups to join, compared to their quality male counterparts. Also, because of the well-known civilian pay gap, they estimated that women would be more likely to join the military since men and women received the same pay at the same rank and for the same jobs. However, do not confuse this with equity. Women were still being discriminated against as far as jobs they could hold, partly due to how many jobs were excluded because of concerns about women being engaged in combat.

What it came down to was this: choosing between low-quality men and high-quality women. The answer was clear: high-quality women. As they stated, women, although smaller and "weaker" (yeah, they used that word), were also brighter, better educated, scored higher on the aptitude tests, and were much less likely to become disciplinary problems. As stated in the study, the recruitment of women was associated with substantially lower recruitment costs and higher quality recruits. In the end, they needed us more than we needed them, just so they could keep the volunteer force alive.

This study also identified a higher retention rate for women compared to men (once the pregnancy rule was changed). But times have changed when it comes to retention. Interestingly, a 2020 Government Accounting Office (GAO) report showed that women are leaving the service at a 28 percent higher rate than their male counterparts. Culture and sexual assault are two of the reasons women give for discharging from the military.

Why is this important to today's military? Women are now enlisting at a higher rate than men, with Black and Latina women enlisting at the highest rate. Given this knowledge, wouldn't it make sense for the US military to be more serious about efforts to improve retention of their fastest growing group by stopping sexual harassment, assault, and rape and to work more diligently to change the culture?

What I always say is that when women can, we do, and we did this in great, increasing numbers. In 1967, Congress removed the 2 percent cap on women in the military and removed the prohibition of women in permanent commissions above grades 0-5. This change led to President Lyndon B. Johnson opening general and flag-rank promotions to women. With the limitation on the number of women who could serve in the military lifted and the academies opened to women, we began to enlist in higher numbers.

In 1972, women were allowed to command units that included men, and in 1975, thanks to a lawsuit led by Ruth Bader Ginsburg, pregnant women were allowed to remain in the military.[8] In 1975, President Gerald Ford signed a law allowing women into military academies. Today, the share of enlisted women has increased from 2 percent to 14 percent, and the share of women commissioned officers has increased from 4 percent to 16 percent. This growth has been most noticeable since 2013, when the combat exclusionary policy was lifted and 100 percent of jobs across all services were finally opened to women.[9]

This move toward an organization that was more inclusive of women mattered, both then and now. At the time, this integration that came in on the silent tails of a fog bank—with no fanfare, newspaper articles, interviews, or plans, just moving in and attaching to everything—gave us an opening. The draft was stopped after the Vietnam War officially ended, giving men, for the first time in our country's history, a new outlook on military service. They still needed to register for Selective Service, but they became less concerned about the draft. However, for the women who had been volunteering since the American Revolution, this integration expanded our opportunities to serve. The smart recruiters saw their future and began targeting us.

But not all changes or decisions made by military leaders are beneficial. While in graduate school, I accidentally discovered a paper written in 2009 by an officer at the US Army War College and came to understand that similar "manning" issues (a shortage of people enlisting) had arisen in the early years of the Global War on Terror, with a different solution altogether.[xxvii]

Broken in the Stronger Places: From Resilience to Resourcefulness

They were already recruiting women in growing numbers, so they had to shift gears again on who they allowed in.

Lieutenant Col. James Manico, the author of the paper, wrote about "manning" issues becoming a rising problem in the US Military. To assist recruiters in doing their jobs bringing in the recruits, the DOD once again began to dust off waivers issued for those who could not qualify for the military. He gave an honest assessment of the detrimental impact, both then and in the future, of using the "waiver" approach to recruit military members who not only were high school dropouts but who had sexual assault and other criminal records, were gang members, and had low entrance exam scores. This was the population to which the US military turned their eyes and efforts. Isn't it ironic that people concern themselves with the myth of standards being lowered for women, but they never talk about the US military digging in the bottom of the barrel to bring in people with behavioral and potentially criminal histories?

According to LTC Manico, waivers for criminal activity increased by 38 percent from 2001- 2007 (the time period examined in his paper). Most of you will not be surprised to read that with this upswing in the admission of this category of recruits came an **upswing in sexual assaults** in the military. These crimes increased by 35 percent from 2004–2007. Criminal cases involving confirmed gang members in the Army quadrupled from 2003–2007. To add fuel to the fire, administrative rules were changed as to how much authority battalion commanders had to remove these service members. In 2005, they were stripped of their ability to make these decisions, with authority remanded to those further up the chain of command.

Although sexual harassment, assault, and rape in the military was not new to this era, the numbers show how it dramatically increased. Because of poor policy decisions made in order to staff up, the US military intentionally endangered tens of thousands of women and men by inviting sex offenders and other criminals into their houses; and we continue to pay for those decisions today.

If you would like more information on the (continued) issuance of waivers today, you can Google "enlistment waivers" to gain an understanding of how deep this issue goes in all branches for both enlisted and officer recruits. Suffice it to say, if the military decides they need someone's skill, they will issue a waiver for anything, including felonies that involve violence, to hell with the potential damage that can be wreaked by that person.

If the military wants to reduce sexual harassment, assault, and rape in their ranks, one way to achieve this would be to stop issuing waivers to sex offenders—including (potential) officers—regardless of their skill set.

Although it may sound like I am suggesting that waivers are the cause of sexual assault, please do not make that inference. The point is that waivers add to the prevalence of a dangerous environment by bringing in sex offenders; but make no mistake: sex offenders who never had to obtain a waiver still exist in the military just as they do elsewhere. The environment of toxicity that breeds and supports sexual offenses has been in place since the first formation in the first military unit. It was certainly an issue in 1978.

The Indoctrination Is Strong

As previously mentioned, our group had ridden from the Welcome Center at Ft. Jackson to the company together. We were a collective of young men and women just fresh from mommy and daddy's house or not long separated from them. During that ride, we were just a bunch of boys and girls out of high school (maybe college), and we had been getting along the same way young men and women of that age get along. There had been camaraderie, joking, and laughter.

But at that moment, when those five male drill sergeants said what they said about *girls* in This Man's Army, they drew a line in the sand between us, and that line ended with an arrow pointing straight at the red targets they had just drawn on the back of every young woman there. That camaraderie we had known on the bus and in the Welcome Center disappeared into the mist of the day as if someone had turned on a fan. We could almost watch it dissipate into the air like dandelion puffs in the wind.

The drill instructors gave those young men an entirely new message about how things were going to be: it was the message that we women were not as good as them, we did not belong, and we were unwelcome intruders into their clubhouse. The drill instructors made it clear that they did not respect us, we would not get the same treatment as the men, and as women, we were intruders into the entitled man space. As such, those young men who had moments before been our friends were given a pass to mistreat us just the same as the drill sergeants.

We were officially "the others." At that moment, we could feel those young men, whom we had just been told were our brothers, our family, shift and change. We could see the sneers on their faces. We could hear the chuckles and smirks and hear, "Yeah, bitch," under their breaths.

It had begun.

What I realized decades later, only recently in fact, was that basic training was not just the place where we learned to shoot, throw hand grenades, understand military strategy, break down a weapon, read a map, and all the things required to be a good soldier in the US Army; it was also a training ground for sexual assault and harassment in the US military. It was the foundation for the maltreatment of women, and the message from day one was, 'Girls, you need to understand this is where bad shit is going to happen to you, and, boys, you get to do this bad shit, and nobody is going to give a fuck that you do it. In fact, men, go on ahead and get started because that is OK. You belong here, but the *girls* do not, and we do not care how you take in and use that information.' Whereas they were shrouded in the entitlement of belonging, we were interlopers and fakers.

Phrased another way: basic training is a breeding ground for sexual assault and harassment in the US military.

I remember one of the strategies used by the drill instructors to simultaneously get the men to perform while taking the opportunity to sexually harass every woman in the company. For this, they used the male soldiers as their weapons of war.

For those of you who have no military history, one of the things that happens (or used to happen, is this still a thing?) in basic training is when you do something wrong—or deemed wrong—you do push-ups, sometimes as an individual and sometimes as a whole company. I will not lie; I did plenty, with the demand generally following my asking a question, usually starting with, "But, Drill Sergeant…"

"Get down and start knocking them out. Stay in that position pushing up the earth until I get tired" was something we frequently heard. Sometimes you do them individually; sometimes, you do them as a company. Now, this by itself was not and is not a bad thing. It is about discipline building, and it builds great upper-body strength. I did not have a problem with it at all as a form of discipline, structure, and physical training and still do not. It sets you on the path to understanding what you are capable of enduring.

But here is how group push-ups sometimes went down when the men were in the company area. They would be gathered into the inner courtyard, and we—the women—would be instructed to gather at our third-floor windows and look out while the men's platoon was down below, bumping and grinding their way through the push-ups. It would sound something like this:

"Come on, boys, you can do better. Think of those girls you have back home, pining for you right now. Think of when you are home on leave. You haven't had sex with your girl in eight weeks, and now's your chance. I know your arms are stronger than that! You don't have to give up yet. Don't disappoint her. Those girls upstairs are watching. Come on, you got this. Keep going. What? You're going to wear out that soon? This is why your girlfriend got herself a new man to fuck who doesn't give up while you are here. You want those girls upstairs laughing at you for being pussies? Show them what you got!"

On and on it went, and if we turned away, we were instructed to get back to the window.

"Where the fuck do you think you are going, soldier? I'll tell you when you can step away from the goddamn window. Now get your ass back there." If we were embarrassed, we were mocked for blushing and being embarrassed. And those men down below doing those push-ups knew they had to perform for us or get chastised and demeaned. We all had roles to play by acting in the part we were given in this sexual harassment segment of our training.

This was basic training at Ft. Jackson, South Carolina, in 1978. The men learned how to sexually harass the women, and the women learned they had to stand and take it. We learned that we had no one to turn to when it happened because, in This Man's Army, our leaders were happy to lead the way in demonstrations of sexual harassment. Later, I would come to understand that drill sergeants were not just allowing acts of sexual assault and rape, but perpetrating it as well, a fact frequently acknowledged in research and interviews with women veterans. I cannot count the number of women veterans I met who were sexually assaulted either by a recruiter or drill instructor.

Eyes Wide Open

"Training activities" like the one above were common occurrences. When we were marching, some of the chants involved marching past other platoons and having their drill instructors yell out, "Eyes right (or left)!" to stare at us while they made comments or made up something new in the chant that was derogatory or sexual about us. They took every opportunity to demean us with their sexual and misogynist statements toward women service members in general. The message was we were weak, not as good as them, unable to keep up, and did not belong. More importantly, they used us as insults, accusing the men of being weak like us if they did not keep up, that they belonged in the girl platoon and would wash out with us, and, of course, that they should be angry they were being forced to train with us because we were holding them back.

Some of you may be asking yourselves, *Why is this a big deal? Isn't she just being a bit overly dramatic?* In answer to your questions, misogynist ideas, thoughts, behaviors, and words are not singularly harmful to women but to all others as well. Toxic masculinity harms men as well, including those in the LGBTQ+ community who are targeted because they do not meet the "male" standard, as defined by society, and, for the same reason, harms heterosexual cis-gendered men. The pejorative terms used against men who are sexually assaulted, harassed, and raped often include things like calling them girls, pussies, sissy, gay, homo, and more. As I said above, there's a certain way "female," used in the military turns into a pejorative and sounds something like, "And you *feee-males*."

LGBTQ+ women and women of color experience increased harassment because of the intersectionality around their identity, not just as a woman but as a Black, Indigenous, Latina, or Asian woman, and/or being bisexual or lesbian. For the record, men who were suspected bisexual or gay also experienced harassment and bullying for not being macho or manly enough. Sexism, misogyny, racism, and anti-LGBTQ+ hate are real, and they affect a broad spectrum of the US armed forces. If we are to make the military a safer place for service members, breaking down the culture that perpetuates these types of hate is required.

The drill sergeants frequently reminded men that women had parts to play in the Army, but it should not be serving *with* them—it should be *serving them*. It went on relentlessly, and every time it happened, the attitude of the young men changed and hardened toward us. They went further away from being the boys on the bus who were potential friends laughing and joking with us to marching in a straight line toward the changed status of men who looked at us with derision and disrespect, believing they were above us and knowing absolutely that they could get away with anything.

It is important to understand how this misogynist attitude follows men when they leave the military. Women (I have experienced it) are often targeted by veteran men on veteran pages or in veteran groups with threats of assault, statements that we were nothing but "mattress hags" while serving (a recent comment from a veteran man when I disagreed with him about a hot topic), and/or various other sexual comments, which is one reason we choose not to participate in what men see as safe spaces for camaraderie.

As an example, a few years ago I signed up for an Army veteran page, only to discover that their pronouns and references were all male: he/him/his and brother were used to address their audience. When I wrote an email asking them to reconsider and be more inclusive of women, what I received from the man who managed the organization was a hostile message that told me men were the majority, they were not interested in the feminist viewpoint, and I should stop being so sensitive.

Just as it was in the military, no safe place and no place safe.

Ft. Jackson became a place where women recruits were not sure we were safe, where if it was necessary to do night duty on the perimeter, we stayed close to each other and tried not to be separated, understanding that there was potential danger out there for us. Although none of us put words to the imminent danger, when a woman was separated from other women, I wondered for her safety, as I suspect others did.

As I look back, however, I realize that what happened at Ft. Jackson did not stay at Ft. Jackson. Not only were the men trained to be superior to us,

Broken in the Stronger Places: From Resilience to Resourcefulness

but we were also broken down and trained to understand that this was our lot in life as US soldiers. These lessons are what we—both the women and men—took with us to our advanced training[10] and, later, to our duty stations.

In doing my work with women veterans over the years, I heard so many stories from women in all branches who had been sexually assaulted in basic training, mostly by the drill sergeants and commanders, who separated those young women out during bivouac, night security perimeter checks, or driving somewhere and raping them.[11] I heard stories about the men of rank, those in the chain of command we reported to, who called the women into their offices and sexually assaulted or raped them, not just at regular military bases but at the academies as well. Do not fool yourself into thinking military academies are all about honor. The allowance of sexual harassment and assault by men in the academies trains tomorrow's officers that this is how things are done in the military. Their rank protects them like a shield.

These are the men and their peers who, on day one, said that we were safe there—that they had our backs, we could trust them. What we learned was that not only was this a lie, but there was no one we could turn to for support or protection. There was no one who was going to believe a lowly recruit over an "honorable" and respected drill instructor or person of rank.

Any complaints were generally responded to with statements like "What did you expect when you joined This Man's Army?" Our "brothers in arms" adopted this saying as quickly as they adopted the ability to break down an M16, and even today, many carry that attitude as veterans. We feel and see this at VA facilities, service organization clubs, stand-downs, veteran gatherings, and online veteran spaces.[12] Some of you reading this may get your feelings ruffled and insist it is not true, but it continues to be a reality. No, they are no longer allowed to be so direct with their bigotry and misogyny, but that does not mean it is not real and ongoing.

My response to the question about what we expected is that we did not expect to be harassed, sexually assaulted, and raped. That should not be the expectation of anyone who joins the military, and it should not be the expectation of the parents when they say goodbye to their children as they are boarding the bus or plane to any military base in the world.

I Do Solemnly Swear

It is OK to expect to break a wrist, to sprain your ankle, to get a sunburn or frostbite, but it is not OK to expect to be sexually assaulted, raped, and harassed just because you wanted to join the military. It is not OK to be broken by that kind of incident because you want to serve your country, and it is not OK for your country to train men to sexually harass, assault, and rape women. It is especially not OK to give noncommissioned officers and officers full rights to perform those acts, to overlook them, and to support and defend all those behaviors, which is what they have been doing for decades and continue to do today.[13, xxviii, xxix] The breaking news surrounding the assault of as many as eighty-three women and seven men during the 1991 Tailhook convention by no means indicated the first time military leaders were involved in such shameful behavior, but it was the first time it was made newsworthy, as were numerous other incidents involving officers and noncommissioned officers.[xxx] It is not their job to break women and men through acts of sexual harassment, assault, and rape. Let us be clear about this.

Someone asked me once what I thought it would take to stop interpersonal violence in the military. My answer: money. Our capitalist world has a history of making change only because they were fined and/or sued. It is what people understand. The VA budget currently bears the brunt of the cost to care for millions of veterans who were caused physical, emotional and mental harm because of sexual harassment, assault, and rape in our military. There are two ways to shift that: one, force DOD to start paying the bill for our MST-related PTSD and other injuries. Maybe if they had to bear the burden of the cost, it would suddenly matter to them, since injury, harm, and death of troops have not incentivized them to make change.

Two, a lawsuit. As mentioned, people understand money and budgets, and losing millions of dollars out of the DOD budget might get their attention. Unfortunately, for decades, the Feres Doctrine[14] has effectively protected the Secretary of Defense, the military, and its members from lawsuits by military service members or families of those injured on active duty.

The Secretary of Defense, his commanding officers, and Congress have an ongoing obligation to protect everyone who is a member of the US military. If they are unwilling to take necessary action and make prevention and intervention a priority, it is time to end the Feres Doctrine to force them to do the right thing.

Yes, I'm looking at you, all Secretaries of Defense and at your "leaders" of rank.[15] You predecessors have had every opportunity over the decades to effect real change, yet have failed to satisfactorily reduce sexual harassment, assault, and rape in the military. You have allowed people to stay after learning of their participation in harassment, assault, and rape. You have endorsed waivers for people with sex- or harassment-related charges in their history. Your complicity in taking action to change the culture and toxic environment has contributed to an environment rife with violence from the inside that harms thousands of military service members each year.[16]

No Girls Allowed

All I ask of our brethren is that they will take their feet from off our necks and permit us to stand upright.

—Sarah Grimké

During basic training, my drill sergeant nominated me for Soldier of the Week. He prepped me prior, asking questions he thought might be asked to ensure I was ready for the interview. The coaching helped, and the interview went well, or so I thought until my drill sergeant hunted me down the next day. Let's just say he was not happy when he finally got me into his office.

I broke a rule by crossing my ankles. We as women are socialized to cross our legs or ankles, a social moor drilled into our heads from the time we are young. I went to Catholic school, where the nuns were resolute in their resolve to teach us to be proper ladies, which included crossing your ankles or legs when sitting. We Catholic girls knew the "duchess slant" long before Princess Kate made it popular.[17] Of course, just going into basic training does not undo a lifetime of conditioning. You enter with your lifetime of gendered upbringing still there, and not one tells you **not** to do that—until you do it.

I Do Solemnly Swear

Unfortunately, on the day of my interview, my nerves and life training kicked in, and I shifted positions from the hips down, going from "sitting at attention" to "the duchess slant." While the latter is useful in many social and professional settings, doing it during a Soldier of the Week interview is a no-go.

I know there are some military veterans or service members reading this who may think, *You should have known.* My question is, How? This was one of those super-handshake secret things you are expected to know without being told. I was sitting at attention: straight, shoulders back, hands in my lap, but at some point, I made the error of crossing my ankles.

The next day, an ass-chewing rained down on me from my drill sergeant, who took it as a personal slight that I was denied Soldier of the Week because I was a stupid girl who crossed my ankles. He reminded me in no uncertain terms that it put a poor reflection on him, and he should have known better than to allow a girl to be sent forward for that honor, and apparently, God was punishing him for making him try to lead a bunch of girls. I should have known better because soldiers do not cross their ankles. They sit at attention. It was proof, he told me. He used it as a standard that flew over my head: I was proof that girls did not belong in the Army, no matter how good we were. He made sure everyone knew.

Not too much later, maybe about halfway through basic training, I found myself in awe of the Rangers. I had heard about this elite squad, and when I saw them, I thought, *I can do that. I want to do that. I am just as strong and fast as these men, and I have achieved everything the men in my company have achieved, even more than some. I am smarter than most of them. Why not me?*

Off I went to see my drill sergeant. "Drill Sergeant, I want to be a Ranger." I was in his office, and as he looked at me, I could see the anger forming on his face.

He came around his desk with a menacing look, pointed his finger at my chest, and said, "Estabrooks, what the fuck is wrong with you? Girls aren't Rangers, not in This Man's Army. Not now, not ever. Now get the fuck out of my office with that bullshit and don't you ever bring that shit up again."

So, that's what happens when you dare to assume there is no sex discrimination in the military, as I had done prior to joining.[xxxi]

Broken in the Stronger Places: From Resilience to Resourcefulness

Eventually, basic training graduation came, and I will point out that most of the women made it. Hard as they might have tried, the drill instructors were unable to make good on their promise to see us all flunk out. I was excited to move on to Ft. Lee, Virginia for my twelve-week advanced individualized training (AIT) at quartermaster school.[18]

Because it was not basic training, there was less discipline there than there was at Ft. Jackson, so we walked around base freely, but at a cost. We no longer had gender-specific platoons, so although platoon sergeants did not have the same opportunities to instruct their troops to stare at the women coming toward them, the comments and chants were still there in other ways, embedded throughout the base along with the fencing, signage, and old, peeling paint, but more permanent and less useful.

The men would hang out the windows and yell obscenities at us while we walked past. Those standing or walking would whistle, grab their crotches, and make sexual comments. No noncommissioned officer (NCO) or officer would stop them. No one said to them, "You're out of order." There was no discipline against it: it was just what it was, and we were expected to simply deal with it: our dues for daring to enter the clubhouse with the "No Girls Allowed" sign.

One day, my friend Julie and I walked past a line of men whose heads—like dominoes falling—turned one after the other as they started whistling and yelling at us. Of course, when you are in the military you "aren't supposed to" behave out of order like that, but no one would stop them, so it became just another thing that happened to us.

When faced with this, I and other women generally just ignored them and kept walking, but this was not that day. I will never forget Julie's reaction. She went stiff as a board, fists balled at her side, and just started screaming at them at the top of her lungs. For the first time in my life, I witnessed what it looks like when a person snaps from trauma, and this was it.

Julie was an adult survivor of incest who had worked hard to get through the hellish memories and feelings forced on her by the assault she had experienced in her youth, committed by her brothers and their friends. That day, everything in her that she had carefully lacquered and repaired and painted with gold to make strong again broke into a million pieces, brought on by the egregious behavior of the men who constantly harangued us.

What happened next was typical of what happened when a woman got angry and began yelling or, god forbid, even complaining about how she was being treated by men. An observing NCO came over to us and dressed her down, barking orders at her to move along or he would make sure she got called up in front of the company commander. There, in front of the men energetically shoveling their onslaught of harassment in our direction, she got into trouble with a noncommissioned officer—who had witnessed the men's behavior—for her reaction and response. The men got the standard perfunctory glance and "carry on" before the NCO walked away.

No one wanted to hear that her actions were a direct result of being treated like an object with no value except what she could provide to the men. No one cared how the constant jet stream of harassment constantly in our path affected us when all we wanted to do was simply get from Point A to Point B without being the target of harassment. The US military did not care that these were the kind of events that happened with frequency if you were a woman in uniform on a base: sexual harassment or worse came with the territory.

When I think about this now, I think about the many women veterans I interviewed over the years who, when asked if anything happened to them, started the conversation with "just the usual, you know."

"Tell me what 'the usual' is."

"Oh, you know, the things they say about us, sexual stuff."

"Mm-hmm."

"And, you know, grabbing. Getting grabbed and groped."

"Mm-hmm."

"And having them do stuff like grab you by the throat or push you up against the wall. You know, stuff like that."

"Oh, so more like sexual assault?"

"Well, yeah, but it happened to all of us, and no one cared, so we stopped saying anything."

To be clear, this conversation happened with a real woman veteran in 2018, and I have had similar conversations since.

Broken in the Stronger Places: From Resilience to Resourcefulness

When I hear people say it is better or different than it was when I served, I think of this and similar conversations, and my response is, "Is it really though?" Maybe in some places and for some people, or maybe it is not as bad, but if women veterans are saying "just the usual" as a lead-in to sharing full-on details about the harassment and assault they experienced, I say it is not better. The men may not be grabbing their junk and hanging out the windows and screaming obscenities to perpetrate their harassment, but that is just geography. It is still there. The Department of Defense should be embarrassed that they continue to allow unsafe spaces to be "just the usual." And yet, here we are.

To the credit of the quartermaster school instructors, thankfully, that behavior was not allowed in class, so we were granted those moments of peace in the one safe place afforded to us. There was discipline in the class because it was a learning environment. Me, ever hopeful and thinking that the classroom environment would be the standard once I got to my permanent duty station, made it my goal to get the hell out of Ft. Lee. All I wanted was to get away from the madness of the harassment, which I had learned was all-encompassing, so I worked very hard to get through that class and leave. In my mind, I continued to believe this could not be what it was like everywhere.

My training was intended to be a twelve-week class, but I finished in six. This was accomplished because the class was designed so that students could work at their own pace. I wanted out of there, so I took advantage of that design by accelerating my studies. I am not sure what I was thinking with the idea that it would be different on another base, with Ft. Lee proving to be the same as Ft. Jackson outside the classroom when it came to the treatment of women service members, but life does have a way of rising up and screaming in your face about just how delusional you really are.

One thing I clearly remember about Ft. Lee was encountering some troops from the 82nd Airborne. I became fascinated by them and the idea of doing what they did. Ritha (my sister) got a call:

"I decided I'm going to go airborne."

"The fuck you are. There's no way I'm letting you jump out of a perfectly good airplane!" she informed me.

I ignored her and kept going. I could not be a Ranger because I was a woman, but surely, I could go Airborne? I recalled my interaction with my drill instructor at Ft. Jackson telling me I could not be a Ranger, but then thought, *Why not try this? Why not me?* I was strong enough, fast enough, smart enough. I could learn whatever I needed to know, just as they had.

So, I went to my sergeant and said, "Sergeant, I want to go 82nd Airborne. I want to transfer or test or do whatever I need to do to be a part of the 82nd Airborne."

He stood up from his desk and came around to where I was standing, and I saw the same look on his face that I saw on my drill instructor's face when I asked about being a Ranger. He pointed his finger in my chest and said, "Estabrooks, what the fuck is wrong with you? Girls aren't 82nd Airborne, not in This Man's Army. Not now, not ever. Now get the fuck out of my office with that bullshit, and don't come back."

It's like there was a script.

Ritha got another call, this one from a sister who was disheartened and filled with anger and righteous indignation. How could it be true? How the fuck could the military, where we were supposed to be fighting for democracy and rights, be such a leader in blatant discrimination? Because she agreed, she was angry on my behalf; because she loved me, she had the sense not to say, "I told you so," or, "Come home."

I was a different person when I was nineteen years old. I was not the person who fought, advocated, and spoke up when there was injustice. I was just a nineteen-year-old girl who believed people when they spoke. I had been told that there is no arguing when you are in the military: you just followed orders, and my young self accepted that. So, I walked away, and I did not cry, because soldiers don't cry, but when I got to my room, I was so angry, thinking, *I am in the Army. We are supposed to be fighting for democracy and rights, and yet here I am being discriminated against just because I am a woman. Tits and a va-jay-jay lose every time.*

The crack in the facade spread.

I was so unclear about that when I joined. Even though I was a budding feminist, I was unaware that gender discrimination still loomed large and women had fewer rights than the men in the US military, on top of it being more dangerous for us. The recruiter had left out the part about thousands of jobs being closed to women in the Army, which I came to understand in time.

Broken in the Stronger Places: From Resilience to Resourcefulness

It never ceased to amaze me that military women were disallowed thousands of opportunities just because we were women.

Here is a gun, here is a uniform, here is the same oath to the country, freedom, and democracy, but you are just going to have to pretend these things do not exist. If you were a woman of color, indigenous, or part of the LGBTQ community, it was worse yet. As we had since the American Revolution, we had sworn to protect and defend that thing we were not allowed to have for ourselves, and as far as everyone seemed to be concerned, that was simply right.

Obviously, recruiters then and now do not give you a warning sign that says, "Caution, gender discrimination and danger of assault ahead." As part of the war machine cog designed to enlarge the machine, recruiters either ignored it as if it did not exist or, worse yet, were perpetrators in assaulting and raping the women who joined. Oh, how ignorant I was about our limited rights, that we were not allowed the same jobs as men, and that democracy—ours or someone else's—had little to do with it. The truth was we had only as little or much as the men deigned to give us while they stood with their boots on our necks.

Decades later, I met a woman who was 82nd Airborne during the same time I served. *How*, I wondered, *did she get what was denied to me?* She said that she had a mentor who fought for her. She was able to get in, pass all the tests, do all the work, make the required jumps, and get her Airborne patch. However, she said, there were things she was not allowed, like any duty that involved jumping, even as an 82nd Airborne soldier, just because she was a woman, so she rarely jumped. What I learned after investigating was that in June 1978—the same time I was at Ft. Lee—that First Lieutenant Bennis M. Blue arrived at Ft. Benning, Georgia, to attend airborne school and become the first woman to earn her airborne wings.

As she should have been, she was proud of that patch and her belonging, but she was also aware that she was seen as less, as different. This is how discrimination works: when you are othered, for instance, as a woman, person of color, non-Christian group, or LGBTQIA+ community, all of whom exist under different laws, rights, policies, and social structures, doors are closed. This "othering" presents the opportunity for people to treat you differently, as though you do not belong and are simply taking up space.

Onward, with Hope

My permanent assigned duty station after leaving Ft. Lee was Harvey Barracks in Kitzingen, Germany. However, following my AIT, I was asked to spend a month in Oregon recruiting women. Even with my experiences, I was still willing to recruit women because, were it not for the sexual harassment, I liked being a member of the US Army. Part of me continued to believe it would get better at the next base.

Just before the month ended, my father died, so I was given additional time at home before leaving for my duty station. When my time was up, I took my letter of commendation for having recruited so many women and went on my way. On July 3, 1978, I was dropped at my company headquarters: 66th Maintenance Company, 87th Maintenance Battalion, Third Infantry Division, where I would spend the next two and a half years.

The Cold War was still alive and well, and the Wall was still in place, meaning the focus was on threats coming from the Eastern Bloc (Communist) countries, like Russia, Czechoslovakia, East Germany, and others. American troops stationed in Germany at the time fell under the US European Command, which coordinated with other commands to ensure defense of the border and the allies. At 66th Maintenance Company, our job was to serve as a primary supply station for military vehicle parts, from the smallest passenger vehicle to tanks, coming into and leaving Germany.

We were also a tank cannibalization unit, which is to say we got tanks in, broke them down, and then shipped off the parts, in addition to managing the shipment and receipt of parts for all military vehicles and conducting service and evacuation on equipment in the field. Our shipments came not just from other military units but also from Sea-Land trucks shipped over from the United States. Most surprisingly, I later discovered that we also moved small arms. Arms aside, my job was to receive, log, and distribute automotive parts, and I was very good at doing that.

When I arrived, my platoon sergeant, Sergent First Class (SFC) Brown was waiting. He was one of those guys who was big as a tree with an even bigger voice, the combination of which can be intimidating upon the first meeting. However, he sat me down and explained that I was the first and only woman

Broken in the Stronger Places: From Resilience to Resourcefulness

in the company and one of very few on base, and if I had any problems, I was to tell him. He also shared that they were working on getting more women in but he had no idea how long it would be. In a fatherly way, he advised me to be careful, but he also gave me the "boys-will-be-boys" talk. This included the standard excuse-making for male behavior: they are far from home, they do not have their girlfriends or wives, most were really harmless, yada yada yada. He said he could not really do anything about how men in other companies behaved, but he had set expectations for the men in the company, and they were aware.

I hate to imagine how it would have gone had he not set expectations. Over the next two and a half years, I and other women who arrived at Harvey Barracks were subjected to sexual harassment and assault daily from the men in our company and on base.

The Wheels of Harassment Grind Slowly

As the years dragged on, I made some friends at the company, and I pissed off a lot of men and some women. The harassment and assault were never-ending, and so I learned how to live and move in that environment. SFC Brown was the only person who disallowed it, but he was rarely there to address the situation, so his words of warning to the men went mostly unheeded.

My way of managing was to become more assertive and aggressive and to use my voice in addressing what was happening. Sometimes, that meant yelling; sometimes, it meant striking back. Sometimes, it meant shutting myself in the outhouse and having a good cry. The environment forced me into a type of personal growth that, I believe, was a double-edged sword I carried with me throughout my life. I learned how to stand up for myself and others, but I also began to learn and adopt the philosophy that men were pigs and could not be trusted. Before you clutch your pearls over this statement, remember where I was and what I said were my negative experiences with men.

A decade later, thrust willingly into the field of domestic violence and sexual assault, my life became a constant series of "see-I-told-you-so" moments. Frankly, the male behavior I have witnessed over the years has not given me pause to believe otherwise. My VA psychologists have been confounded by this, but as a woman who works with survivors of harassment, assault, and rape, I have also witnessed some of these same psychologists coming to a place of understanding my core belief system.

In fairness, it was not just the male officers and NCOs who were useless in stopping sexual harassment and assault. My company commanding officer (CO) and the executive officer at 66th Maintenance Company were both women, yet they did nothing. The executive officer, a woman lieutenant, chastised me one day after I complained about some men who were harassing me while she looked on, stating that really the problem was that I was not handling it correctly. Her advice to me was, "You can catch more flies with honey than with vinegar," and that I should "try just being nicer to them." You cannot make this shit up.

She expressed her disagreement with the way I handled the men, cursing and yelling at them, even trying to reason with them when they did not, as she put it, "act the way you want them to act" and, again, told me that I should try just being nicer to them. "Maybe if you are nicer to them, Estabrooks, they'll be nicer to you." This age-old advice given to girls was as useless in the US Army as it was in seventh-grade gym class. Also, I may have expressed that hell would freeze over before I tried her approach and quickly learned that complaining got me nowhere.

My job took place at a remote Quonset hut about two kilometers from our company, on the opposite side of the base and off-post.[19] I was the only woman out there for about the first six months or so, a situation that kicked open the door to nonstop sexual and gender harassment. Unless SFC Brown was present, the men out there, and the men who came through with their truckloads, saw me as an easy target. Unfortunately, SFC Brown was rarely there, and his second lieutenant, who was almost always there, chose to be blind to events that took place when it came to me, eventually the other women, or our physical and mental/emotional safety.

I found myself constantly on guard, listening to the men talk about their sexual prowess and what they had done before the Army, what they would do once they returned home, and what they did here that they believed their girlfriends and wives back home would never know. There was no one to care about the inappropriateness of what they did or to interrupt their behavior, so it was simply part of the work environment, sitting there alongside the pencils, staplers, and coffee cups with day-old dregs that sat on some desks.

I was not a prude and had heard these sorts of conversations before, but never in this type of situation where I was *required* to sit and listen to it with no way to leave and no one to make it stop, while frequently being the target of their conversations or looks. My pre-Army life had included working alongside men, but then I had been able to choose not to be present, to excuse myself, to walk away and avoid those who made me uncomfortable, or to report it to someone who cared (although in the late '70s no one, not even HR, cared very much). But the point is that when you are in the military, you are forced to stay where you are, sit at your desk, and work next to the men who are assaulting and harassing you. Quitting your job, or even having a human resources department you could file a complaint with, was never an option.

There, wearing that uniform, it was my duty to remain at my desk, have discussions about incoming shipments and the like, and walk through the office to the sound of their comments, whistles, and sex noises. There, in Kitzingen, Germany, there was truly no place safe and no safe place if you were a woman in uniform.

Some of you may be thinking, *What, she just did nothing? She let it happen? I would not have put up with that.* Allow me to enlighten you: like every woman in the world who has had similar experiences, we did not *let* anything happen. We had no control when it came to their behavior and their decisions. I tried every approach: reasoning with them, talking to them, asking them not to do it, yelling and cursing at them, ignoring them. I remember one time asking how they would feel if someone was doing this to their sister, mother, or girlfriend. Their response was that they did not have to worry about that because mutherfuckers knew better. Right asshole, you are the mutherfucker who doesn't know better then?

People *choose* to behave inappropriately, badly, harmfully, and/or dangerously. They *choose* their actions intentionally, knowing they can get away with it. They *choose* their targets, knowing they are powerless to stop them. That is why they are doing it. We are not to blame for the horrible behavior of others. Hard stop.

I Do Solemnly Swear

It was not just there at the remote workplace where this happened either. When I first began working there, we often had a ride out to work in a personnel carrier truck.[20] Those are the large trucks you see with the canvas over the back, usually filled with soldiers. Sometimes, I was able to sit in the front with the driver, but if not, boarding and disembarking off the back of that truck meant more opportunities for the men to comment and grab or attempt to grab me.

For those who have not experienced a ride in a deuce and a half, I will explain. When you are climbing on, you are in a physical position where you are pulling yourself up and must bend over to enter. You then walk hunched over to get to a seat, the seats being benches around the front and two sides where you all sardined in. Out of necessity, there is touching of shoulders and legs in close quarters.

On those days when I could not ride up front, it was my effort to try to be the first on the truck. Why? If I had to get on when the men were climbing in, it was a less than pleasant experience. They would stand behind me and share a string of commentary about my ass and/or the way I was climbing up and into the truck. At the same time, there would be hands reaching from inside the truck and from on the ground, "offering" to help me. When you are a military woman outnumbered in a company of men, "help" is not what you are getting when they are reaching for you.

Once I was on the truck, I would usually find that they had "saved" me a seat somewhere up front, which meant I had to walk through their imposed gauntlet, hunched over, to get to the front of the truck. It was hands grabbing, words reaching out to me, and feet to trip me so someone had to "catch" me, and they could make "offers to help" as if they were not harassing me.

Eventually, because the motor officer began refusing dispatches, which meant the trucks were not moving, others and I frequently found ourselves walking to work. By this time, more women had come into the company and were assigned to our unit, so we walked as a small group of women (usually three or four). Our walk took us from one side of the base to another, forcing us to walk through the base and directly through the 164th Armored Division: our near-daily gauntlet from hell.

Broken in the Stronger Places: From Resilience to Resourcefulness

As we approached, the men would exit or move away from their tanks and line up, the better to sexually harass us. Eventually, though, they grew tired of simply yelling obscenities, sexual innuendos, and body commentary and began moving—as one—nearer, getting closer and closer to us as we made our way through. By the time we got to the end, the bottleneck of the gauntlet had become so small that they could have reached out and touched us, and many acted as though that was their intent.

So, when people question why I and other women veterans have issues or problems with men in groups or male veterans, perhaps it is because of incidents like this that so many of us were forced to endure while serving.

We spoke up, but nothing happened. Our feelings of insecurity and fear of assault meant nothing to those in charge—not at our company, not to our CO, not elsewhere. We were continually told there was nothing that could be done, to be nice, and/or to ignore them.

This went on until about three or so months before my enlistment ended. One day, my two girlfriends and I had just left the area where the tanks and infantrymen were located when we heard someone yelling and turned to see an officer's car coming toward us. We stopped and stood there watching until it came to a stop not far from us. Soon enough, we saw the rank of the person who exited the vehicle and came to attention. We saluted the General as he approached.

"How's it going today, soldiers?" He asked.

Now, here is the part where every person on the planet who is or has been in the military knows the answer, which is (with a snappy salute), "Just fine, sir! Things are great. Thank you for asking, sir!"

Which was the answer given by my two friends.

I, on the other hand, had fewer than six months left in This Man's Army and was sick of the harassment and discrimination, so my answer was different than theirs or what it should have been.

"Not so good, sir!" I retorted with just the right amount of respect, tinged with "I have something to say" in my voice.

He and his aides looked a bit surprised about this soldier who dared to go off script. But, to his credit, he looked at me while his aide dutifully wrote down our names, rank, and company and asked, "What seems to be the problem, soldier?"

So, I told him about the men in the tanks and our near-daily harassment. I explained that we had no choice but to walk from our company because there were no trucks available to take us to work, and this was the only route to our parts yard (pointing to the building). I went on to tell him that it was not just here where we were at the mercy of the men but all along our route from our company, no matter the route. I even mentioned to him that I had not joined This Man's Army to be subjected to harassment, assault, and discrimination, but it seemed as if we had no choice but to put up with it, and we were tired of it. He shook his head while I was speaking, his aide writing furiously, then thanked me, saluted, and gave us the "carry on" order.

We went on to work and forgot about our encounter until we were called into the CO's office with Sgt. Brown. Of course, he looked directly at me when he explained the requirement for command attendance and questioned, "What did you do, Estabrooks?" So, I told him.

Sgt. Brown was renowned for his booming voice and the fact that he was a screamer, and what came after was a string of expletives from the top of his voice. "Why the fuck did you go to a General with this instead of coming to me or anyone else in your chain of command?[21] I know you know better than to jump the chain Estabrooks, goddammit!"

I explained to him that we had, in fact, told him and others in our chain of command numerous times. I also explained that we frequently encountered men of rank who were, purportedly in a chain of command somewhere, and they either engaged in or ignored what the men were doing. We did not go to the general, I explained—he came to us. He drove his car into the field, got out, and asked us questions. All I did was answer.

Of course, that led to a lecture on what "How's it going, soldier?" means and that no one actually gives a fuck how you are doing. Nevertheless, the die was cast and into the CO's office we went, which led to a conversation with the First Sergeant and CO from the 164th.[22] Although they were exceedingly angry with us, they also assured us that the order had come from the General that actions would be taken against anyone accused of harassing us in the future. We were assured that the next time we walked through that unit we could expect complete silence.

This small victory was life-changing for the women because it made us feel just a little bit safer as we walked to work. It also felt like a change that would help future women service members on base. Two things happened: one, future walks did not include words or a gauntlet from those men in the tank unit, and two, suddenly, rides to work picked up again.

Saying the Quiet Stuff Out Loud

From the time I entered the Army until the time I left the VA forty-two years later, here is what I learned: *Every man who wears a uniform is not a hero*, and many of them cannot, in fact, be trusted around your daughters, sisters, mothers. As parents, let's instill better values in our sons When giving them lessons on behaving as a decent human being, remind them to always behave as if the person they respect the most is watching because if they choose not to do it in front of that person, then it is most likely the wrong thing to do.

The military stories you have likely heard from your male friends and family members do not include tales of them engaging in or witnessing sexual harassment and assault because all those men know what was happening was wrong. They know that even if they were not actively engaged in these things, they stood by, ignoring it, watching it, which makes them complicit. I say this with assurance as to its accuracy because I can tell you firsthand that there was not *one* man who did not, on some level, participate, even if that meant standing and observing quietly while other men did it. Or, because they are men, they just did not notice or did not see anything wrong with it. In my time in uniform, every man did harm, either actively or passively. This is the reality that breaks with the "not-all-men" and "male-as-protector" myths.

My experience in the US Army was one of daily, unrelenting, unending sexual harassment, assault, and discrimination. If I was on a military installation, I had no place safe and no safe place for the three years I served, and *that* is the story that defines my service—the story that defines so much of who I am and how I now see the world. It is the steel bar that caused so many of my broken places, wielded by men who committed the acts and the leaders who stood by and literally gave it a wink and a nod. There was no honor to be found.

How do we, as a country and as citizens sending our beloved children into this quagmire of danger from within, make change? Good question. One answer: we make it a priority to make it our business. If you are an elected official or employed by one, make it a priority. Do not ask the officers and leaders what you need to do: ask the survivors and victims. Ask them in a safe setting, not in the presence of cameras, microphones, and unfriendly elected officials who berate and deny the truth of military dangers that come from literally every direction.

Look back at the long history of US congressional hearings on the topic and ask yourself why they have continued to overlook the failures of the DOD while concurrently giving them control. Ask yourself why they have continued to allow the fox to guard the hen house, knowing that the research and data show they cannot be trusted with the safety of their troops. Make sure that when writing a bill to make change, you add in safeguards and expectations and then ask hard questions. Bring in consultants from national sexual assault and domestic violence organizations to lead the way and provide evidence-based training. Hold the Secretary of Defense responsible when the numbers do not change or when a high-ranking official is found guilty and then given a pass. Ask to see how many Officers and NCOs have been allowed to stay after they themselves committed an act of violence, and then demand to know why and demand change.

Seek the truth and then act on it when you discover its ugliness.

---

xxvi   Office of the Assistant Secretary of Defense. Director, Resources and Requirements. 1977. Use of Women in the Military, Background Study. Washington D.C. Viewed 08/31/2024, https://apps.dtic.mil/sti/tr/pdf/ADA047118.pdf#:~:text=Within%20that%20context%2C%20the%20use%20of%20women%20in%20the%20military%20is%20a%20question%20of&text=1977%20will%20cost%20$54%20million.

xxvii   Manico, JL (LTC). 2009. Ethical Imbalance: How The US Army Overcame Its Manning Crisis. US Army War College, Carlisle Barracks, PA.

xxviii Calkins A, Cefalu M, Schell TL, Cottrell L, Meadows SO, Collins RL. Sexual Assault Experiences in the Active-Component Army: Variation by Year, Gender, Sexual Orientation, and Installation Risk Level. Rand Health Q. 2023 Jun 16;10(3):10. PMID: 37333672; PMCID: PMC10273889.

xxix   Estabrooks, E. The US Military Culture: Why Current and Recommended Policies are not enough. Columbia University School of Social Work Journal. 2013

xxx   Ibid

xxxi   In 2013 Defense Secretary Leon Panetta discontinued the combat ground exclusionary policy and gave the branches three years to enact changes that would allow all women to serve in all positions, including infantry and other fields that were specific to combat. In 2016 the first two women, Capt. Kristen Griest and Capt. Shaye Haver, graduated from Ranger school.

Terrible things are terrible. Let's just acknowledge it.

—Paris Hilton, *Paris (2023)*

CHAPTER 6

The Order of Things

Home Again, Home Again

While I was stationed in Germany, I exchanged letters and tapes with my sisters and mother, but mostly I spoke with my sister Ritha. We spoke when we could, which for me meant going to the special phone office, putting my name on the list, handing over however many Deutschmarks I wanted to spend on that day's phone call (generally limited so everyone had time to use the phone), and then both of us rushing to say everything in our allotted time.[23] It was the late '70s, so that is how we rolled when it came to international calls.

Because of the difficulty in making calls, most of our communication was via cassette tape recordings we sent back and forth. Because Ritha was my person, I told her everything too, sharing my experiences in every correspondence with her—the good, the bad, and the ugly. She heard about the sexual harassment and the stories of being grabbed on the ass, breasts, waist, arm—whatever they could grab. I shared my complaints that fell on deaf ears and the lame excuses provided by the men: "I was just playing around with her, Sarge. You know I didn't mean nothing." Then they would apologize, as they were instructed, and move along. As women, it was our duty to accept the apology and suck it up, knowing it would happen again. Accepting was not an option but a direct order.

Ritha would respond with concern and frustration: "Why was nothing done?" "Was I OK?" "Could I come home?" I always assured her I was fine and could last it out, but the constant vigilance it took to maintain any modicum of real safety and healthy mentality was exhausting and stressful. When I was there, in the thick of it, though, I had no real idea how it was cementing itself into the very core of my being. When I thought of it, I simply assumed that when I finally got out of there and back to "the world" (as we called the United States and home), it would all just be left behind me there, on that Army base.

Ritha kept these confidences, as far as I know. She was the keeper of my secrets then and when I returned home. Interestingly, it was not until after she died that I realized what I had asked of her—to hear and keep the secrets of pain and brokenness from her younger sister and know that she could do nothing. While I grieved her loss, it occurred to me that part of what I grieved was the loss of the person who had held my secrets so close for so many decades.

As they say, hindsight is 20/20. After her death, I thought a lot about her and our history together. It was at this time that I began to really think through my social worker/advocate lens about the information I had given her and the effect of that on her. I began to wonder if I had been unfair to her, handing her all these trauma packages and asking her to hold on to them for me. I contemplated how hard it might have been for her and how she had dealt with all of that or if she had eventually just let it go. I also recalled that some years before she died, when I filed for military sexual trauma PTS as a service-connected disability, she was the one I called for support, and I was surprised by how quickly she opened to the conversation.

When I asked her during that call if she remembered, she said, "How could I ever forget? I saved those tapes and letters for a long time, Liz, wondering if you would ever talk about it." She went on to say more about how she wondered out loud why and how I had managed to stay in the field of violence against women for so many years. She mentioned how difficult it had been for her to do that work, which was one reason she did not stay, but she had concluded that staying was how I dealt with what had happened to me.

The Order of Things

She asked if I was doing OK and what prompted the call. Was there something I needed that she could help me with? I asked if she felt comfortable writing a letter to the VA about what I had told her while in the Army, and she said she would. She talked about some of the things she remembered I had said and conversations the two of us had while I was serving. She mentioned how she had noticed I was different—harder and angrier—when I returned and asked if I wanted her to include that.

As much as it was a relief to have this conversation with her, it was not until years later, after her death, that I really thought about her and the years she spent not just listening but holding that space for me. It occurred to me that the natural process for her, as someone who listened to my trauma, would have been to figure out how to manage and store what she had been given by me. I will never know how she dealt with that over the decades, but I frequently wish it was a conversation we had shared. What might I have learned from any conversation about this with her: How it affected her, whether it had long-term impacts, and, mostly, whether there were any questions I could answer or a discussion that she would have liked?

Trauma Is as Trauma Does

This unrecognized trauma experience is what I brought home from Germany with my one-year-old daughter on December 8, 1980. In the months that followed, I meticulously rid myself of all my military-related items, except my dress uniform (only because Mom threatened me if I disposed of it). Unfortunately, what I did not realize at the time was the amount of mistrust, anger, and pain that remained tucked in those dark corners of my duffel bag like strings and lint shed from clothing, staying with me no matter how many times I changed bags, towns, homes, or men.

Goodness knows my own trauma colored my lens and impacted my ability to choose a kind man instead of those who easily lived up to my negative expectations of men. The further I went down the road of helping survivors, the angrier I became about policies, men, and the military. It is hard as hell to make room in even the largest bed for two people when you also add their combined individual and collective baggage.

Broken in the Stronger Places: From Resilience to Resourcefulness

The thing about trauma is that you may not know you are having a trauma response. Most people honestly do not know that they have post-traumatic stress. Sure, they notice their behaviors, and others may notice the behaviors, but unless they are erratic, everyone just carries on. So, when I was loud and aggressive, they just figured it was me. Loud and aggressive was what we did in our family. When I yelled, people attributed that to being a family thing. When I drank a lot, it was written off because I was high functioning at my job. Hell, it wasn't just "them" that overlooked my PTS—it was me. It took more than thirty years for me to even consider the possibility, even though my career focused on serving victims and survivors of trauma.

Other people experienced trauma, not me. What I experienced was not trauma-related, right? It was not even something that crossed my mind; after all, I was never raped. It was mostly just sexual harassment, and I was fine, thank you. Trauma symptoms like irritability, mistrust of men, insomnia, and depression? Check check check and full-on check. So? None of this was enough for me to recognize my own trauma.

I think Ritha knew. She never said anything, but she knew—especially when I first returned to Oregon a year after my discharge. People would occasionally bring up my military service, but Ritha became adept at changing the subject. She was especially cognizant of the need to do this when people joked about the harassment and discrimination I encountered or said, "Hey, Liz, tell that story." She was the person I could count on to stand between me and the angst and tension that arose in me because of these conversations.

In 1980, there was no such thing as transition when leaving the military, and military sexual trauma was not a phrase or acknowledged. You went through your discharge process. They handed you your final orders and put your ass on a plane or bus, and you were done. Sure, they were supposed to do physical and mental health checkups, but I missed that. My discharge process was a mess because of a combination of my arriving with a one-year-old child, the invisibility of women (and mothers) in the US Army, and sheer incompetence of those whose jobs were to manage discharges.

There were very few servicewomen with children in 1979, even though Ruth Bader Ginsburg had fought and won that fight for us in 1975.[24] Of course, we could keep our babies and stay in, thanks to her, but they did

The Order of Things

everything possible to encourage (coerce, force) you to sign the discharge paperwork once your pregnancy was announced.

When I found out I was pregnant, I informed my first sergeant[25] and my CO. My CO was clearly livid that she could not force me into signing early discharge papers, but I knew my rights, so I stayed.

Why stay if it was so bad, you might ask. Because in the military, I had health care and financial security I knew was important to me as an expecting and, eventually, new mother, and it was especially important for my child, who would have the health care she needed for the first year of her life. As a single pregnant woman, these life needs outweighed my unhappiness with the environment and the Army. My daughter was a gift I had been given, and my focus was on doing what was best for her.

What followed my decision to stay opened my eyes to just how unprepared the Army was to deal with a pregnant soldier. One of the most obvious was that there were no maternity uniforms, which meant I wore civilian clothes with my Army name tag. It also meant no more physical fitness formations or participation, even though I wanted to continue exercising, and they moved me to the warehouse on base instead of having me out at the yard. Their reasoning was that it was a safety thing.

The ability of women to continue their enlistments crossed swords with the US Army's "no single mother" rule, such as preventing my friend from enlisting with me. We did not actually have to give up our children, but we were required to complete a ream's worth of paper that instructed us on the many steps required to remain. Today, they call them *parenting plans*. I'm not sure what they were called in 1979, but it was that and more. Of their requirements, I had no real complaints, though, because they made sense.

Briefly, here is how that looked. As the mother, I had to find a babysitter who would take my daughter at any time of day or night, any day of the week, and keep her for as long as necessary. I also had to find a temporary guardian whose job it was to collect my daughter (from the babysitter or me) in the event of a war and take responsibility for ensuring she was safely removed from the country and returned to her other temporary guardian (my mother) in the United States.

Broken in the Stronger Places: From Resilience to Resourcefulness

I had thirty days after my daughter's birth to ensure everything was in order, or I would be discharged. It sounded relatively easy, but it took nearly six months to locate the women who would do these things for me and my daughter while I was stationed in Germany and then get the paperwork signed and notarized by everyone, including my mother in Texas. It's a good thing I started when I found out I was pregnant because it took about six months to accomplish (snail mail, no Internet or email).

I no longer remember the names of the women who provided such support and care for my daughter and me while I was in Germany, but I will be eternally grateful for those women who adopted me and my daughter as family and held us in their safe embrace, prepared to do whatever necessary in the event of war.

The closest we came to having to consider if we would need to enact the conditions of the guardianship was when the Iranian hostages were taken, and we went on alert[26]. Of course, when I dropped her off at daycare in those wee hours, I did not know why we were being called out, as they were keeping the details dark. We knew only that this time it was different—more real—than previous alerts. There were no cell phones then, and the only access we had to news was what was delivered through military sources: the newspaper and the Armed Forces Network.[27] Having those two media sources removed kept us clueless, which is what they did during that alert. Consequently, it was a good two days before they told us what had happened and why we were on alert.

Fortunately, we did not go to war or engage in conflict, so I was not required to enact the steps necessary for my daughter to be removed from me and the country, but because of the incident, the reality of that happening came home to me in a very abrupt way. Like many who served during peacetime, I am abundantly aware of how fortunate I was not to have to worry about leaving a child behind for war. To the women out there who handed their children over to others so they could deploy, sometimes only six weeks after childbirth, I say, "Thank you, sisters, for your sacrifice."

Fast-forward to December 1980 and the end of my three-year enlistment in the US Army. Never having gone through the discharge process and not knowing any military women who had, I had no idea what to expect and just thought there was a formal process I would go through. When I arrived at

The Order of Things

Ft. Dix, New Jersey, fresh off the plane with a fourteen-month-old child, I learned that the US Army had no apparent plan on how to handle my discharge process. There was a plan, but it did not include single mothers.

I learned that not only was there no family billet for us, coming in at midnight after an all-day flight, but there was no daycare for my daughter. So, there I stood among a group of exhausted travelers trying to get an NCO to understand that although they wanted me to be in formation with everyone else at 0600 the next morning, I had a baby and just could not accommodate them, not because I had not done my part, but because they had failed to do theirs.

After someone in charge finally agreed to put me in a hotel, since their other option was me sleeping with my child in the single-person billets so she could potentially wake everyone up in the middle of the night, I was given instructions to come back at 0800 for out-processing. Again, I held up my precious little girl and said, "But what about her? Did you arrange for daycare? Is there a daycare center I can take her to before I report? What is the plan for tomorrow?"

In-charge guy blurted out in his most "I'm-sick-of-this-shit-because-it-is-after-midnight-and-way-too-late-for-this-kind-of-bullshit-and-I-didn't-issue-you-that-goddamn-child-so-why-is-she-my-problem?" voice, "We'll deal with it in the morning, soldier. You're dismissed for the evening." So, I got into the cab they had ordered and left.

I returned at 0800, still expecting them to have a plan, but that was a misplaced expectation. Nope, no daycare option. They had a long list of offices I was supposed to visit, including discharge examinations, but because I had a one-year-old, no one to help, and no daycare, they remained unclear on how to handle the situation. Ahh yes, military inefficiency at its finest.

After a long wait that took up a good portion of the morning and a diaper full of the best a baby has to offer, they finally figured out that just making me sit and wait at a desk with a small child was not going to work. The stinky diaper and her fussing helped an officer who had just arrived determine that someone had to decide what to do with me and my non-issued dependent, so he yelled at everyone, but no one in particular, until someone finally brought all the paperwork to me. The person assigned sat with me and my paperwork and just checked and initialed everything, both of us pretending I had been to all the required offices and through the required steps. I was officially getting a short-cut version of a discharge process.

When it came to the medical part, though, I hesitated. He went over the medical section briefly. Do you have anything wrong with you that you want to claim? Yes, the Army had given me flat feet, bad knees, and a sketchy back, none of which I had when I joined. How is that handled? At this point, he looked at me and my fourteen-month-old, who was starting to squirm and fuss again, and told me that I would have to get medical checkups and opinions before leaving and that would mean staying another three days. I asked if they were going to arrange daycare and a place for us to stay during the process, but he said I would be on my own.

As he spoke, all I could imagine was the monstrous task of undertaking the necessary steps it would take for me to do this alone. With no situational bearings, no car, and no support, I understood that I would need to locate temporary housing and daycare by myself, which in 1980 would have been a very different task than today. I knew this meant leaving my daughter in a strange place with people I did not know or trust, and I could only imagine how horrible it would be for both her and me, so I said, "You know what, just finish my discharge processing and send me home." He warned me that making this decision meant I would *never* be eligible for benefits for my medical problems, yet he seemed greatly relieved by this decision, which put him one step closer to being rid of me.

Some decades later, it occurred to me that, had I had a spouse or been a spouse, this would have gone very differently, but because I was a woman in This Man's Army who had chosen to have and keep a baby, I was not entitled to the same support services as a spouse or married man.

They drove me back to my hotel with my discharge orders in hand, and the next morning, I flew home. My three years of service to our country had officially ended. Years later, I realized the extent of what I had done—the benefits for me and my child that I had walked away from. But again, no transition process, no one to care or give me advice. I was just a girl who had been in the Army and came home with a child. My service experiences were irrelevant.

The Order of Things

The reality is they likely would not have discovered my PTS then anyway because there were no sexual harassment, assault, rape, or other relevant questions asked during that time, and it is unlikely a mental health exam would have either acknowledged or recognized it as a problem. Of course, I may have received some benefits for physical health conditions, but that failed to matter.

So, life after the Army began. Instead of returning directly to my family in Oregon when I left the Army, I went to Seattle to try to see if I could make the relationship with my daughter's father, the first man who ever abused me, work, even though I knew in my heart that was never going to happen.

In the Words of Dory: Just Keep Swimming[28]

Picture this: me, in a Seattle employment office in 1980, trying to explain my work in the Army and what qualifications I was now able to add to my resume. The fact that I was a woman who had served in the Army and that my military occupational specialty (MOS) had been in the supply field, managing shipping and receiving, a job she could not wrap her head around for a woman, discounted all the work I had done for the past three years, landing me in a bank, making minimum wage, doing incredibly boring work.[29]

I was in Seattle, home to industry, warehouses, and more, but it would have been too outside the mainstream for employment office woman to connect me with jobs in supply, so she just went backward and settled on my pre-military experience as if the past three years had not happened. I was a girl, and we were not really veterans. Plus, in 1980, being in the military was really a male occupation dontchaknow? "Here, honey, go to this bank interview. I think you'll be just what they are looking for."

I took the job and was happy to have one, and I did not hate it. At least no one was grabbing me or talking about my looks, my ass, or the size of my boobs, so I stayed and added a new job to my resume.

The job was good, but the personal relationship with my daughter's father was terrible. Nothing about it had improved since we were in Germany. When I was in high school, Home Economics was a big deal that all girls took. One of our requirements was to plan our wedding. I had never been a girl who thought or dreamed about my wedding day, so that exercise had been a struggle for me. Two men (including my daughter's father) had asked me to marry them, and I had said no to both. Because nothing was ever serious when it came to the men in my life, attachment had never been a reality for me, so I was not stuck on the idea of staying with this guy, even though there was a child. I had seen women get hit, and that was not something I wanted to experience. As the threats of physical abuse grew worse, I knew that leaving was my only option. The day he pushed me to the ground and raised his fist was the day I knew it was time to go.

Although I had begun to realize while we were in Germany that he was an abuser. I had made the error of thinking it was environmental, and not him as a person. As victims often do, I made excuses: it's the military, being away from home, and stress. He will be better/nicer when we are both out of the Army and together in the civilian world. That 20/20 hindsight told me I should have listened to my intuition, but I was young and wanted to believe the best.

Ladies, do not do what I did. If you know for a fact or have a feeling that someone is not a good person, do not "give it a shot." Just leave. Leave before they become abusive in any way. Leave before they ever take a swing at you. One year into this toxic relationship experiment in Seattle, a final attempt by him to punch me, and my solid kick to his groin was enough for me to call my sister and her husband and ask for a rescue. I could not get back to my small town and family in Baker City fast enough.

Small Town, Small Ideas

In small towns across America, getting a job is often about who you know. I knew my sister, my brother-in-law, his family, and the friends I had left behind, including their friends. Despite my resume and short five years of job experience, people's friends and families beat me to every job I applied for. With a daughter to support, I started taking whatever work I could find. I had left the car with the toxic abuser in Seattle, so I had a bicycle with a child seat. If you want a good chuckle, imagine someone with limited bike-riding skills trying to balance the weight of an eighteen-month-old on the back. Let's just say there were some tipovers. Thankfully, neither of us was injured, as I had

The Order of Things

learned the fine art of falling in slow motion to protect her as if I were just laying the bike down.

I had four jobs at different times of the day and night, so I relied on my sister and some friends for transportation assistance when it came to the night job. Fortunately, I was also able to find a babysitter who was flexible. What time is it? What day is today? Am I supposed to be at the newspaper, the restaurant, the other restaurant, or the drug and alcohol rehab center? Oh shit, I showed up at the wrong place. Time to buy a Day-Timer (for those of you who are younger than Gen X, those were calendar books you wrote appointments in).

I was barely making ends meet, but at least I was working and making enough to pay rent and buy some food. A friend who worked for the Department of Human Services suggested I apply for food stamps and childcare assistance, so I did. Just the childcare assistance made such a difference! I was able to drop the daycare provider, with whom I had become ever more dissatisfied, and locate a licensed provider (required by DHS).

Fortunately, my friend's wife was just such a person. My daughter loved her, and their family loved her right back. Good daycare truly is one less stress point in a parent's life, and this definitely made a difference for me. The stress of working multiple jobs went on for about a year until my brother-in-law's aunt put in a good word for me with her best friend, who worked at First National Bank. Her reference and my resume with banking experience gave me just what I needed to get an interview and be selected. Because banks were notorious for low wages, I started at $3.35 an hour (minimum wage in 1980), earning just $6,968 a year, which, adjusted for inflation, would be $24,773 before taxes today. Living large.

But I had health insurance and a paycheck and no longer needed my Day-Timer and flexible daycare.

When I left Seattle and the toxic relationship, my rescuers were my brother-in-law Carl and a family friend, Jim Summers, who borrowed their friend's truck for the rescue. When I arrived in Baker City and met their friend, he immediately charmed me into a date. Although Ritha issued a strict warning that we were not to see each other, we two ignored her and carried on.

I remember that first date: I was sitting on the passenger side of his bench seat when he started talking about Newton's law of motion. "You know about

Broken in the Stronger Places: From Resilience to Resourcefulness

Newton's law of motion, right? An object in motion stays in motion with the same speed and in the same direction unless acted upon by an unbalanced force." He was charming and funny, with an impeccable sense of timing. At the same time he finished that sentence, he turned a corner hard and fast, and I slid over and ended up in the center of the seat next to him (no seat belt in his old truck). He smiled his big, charming smile and laughed. I was hooked.

That relationship came and went over the next ten years—up and down through our marriage and divorce and relationships with other people in between—until a year after the birth of our son in 1992. Just as my daughter was a gift, so, too, was my son. I always say that although his dad and I could not make it work, our son got the best of us both. I could not be more grateful that we produced such a phenomenal person.

During the "off" periods of our on-again-off-again relationship, I lived as a single mother to my children. Even as a young woman, I struggled with the idea that any man could truly love me, even if he said it regularly, so I spent my time working, focusing on my kids, directing my professional efforts to my career, and dating when I could. Poverty aside, life seemed perfectly normal and happy. The broken places were nicely covered, and I rarely noticed them. The fact that people (OK, mostly men) occasionally referenced that I seemed angry a lot did not seem relevant or important. I did not care what they thought or if it kept them from having interest in a relationship. I was perfectly fine with being a single mother.

When I dare to be powerful, to use my strength in the service of my vision, then it becomes less and less important whether I am afraid.

—**Audre Lorde**

CHAPTER 7
A Sea Change

By 1989, I had started working in the insurance industry and was thinking about what was next for me professionally. I had always wanted a degree, and while in Germany, I had actually taken some psychology and social work classes with the idea that I would eventually get my master's in social work or psychology. Unfortunately, there were no GI educational benefits for me because of the time that I served and the amount of time that had passed, so between living in a small town and being a single parent, the degree seemed out of reach.

By that time, social services had begun growing and changing around the nation. Governor Neil Goldschmidt decided to make a pledge toward Oregon's development potential and economics, which included a twenty-year vision focused on making Oregon a business contender in the twenty-first century, establishing the state as "the gateway to the Pacific Rim." What came from his vision was called *Oregon Shines: An Economic Strategy for the Pacific Century*. This was a good plan with strong benchmarks that, unfortunately, quickly appeared to be yet another go-nowhere study, but it was the impetus for change.

In 1990, Governor Barbara Roberts was elected in a state that was on the fast track to experiencing severe economic problems because of the passage of Measure 5, which severely limited property tax increases, generating a 15 percent cut in funding for state programs (besides education). Governor Roberts was handed an impossible task: trying hard not to destroy social safety nets while developing a 1993–1995 budget.[30] In order to prevent the destruction of these safety nets, she embraced *Oregon Shines*.

In 1993, the Oregon Legislature passed HB 2004, establishing the Oregon Commission on Children and Families (OCCF), with a county commission in all thirty-six counties. The goal of this commission was to improve health for children and families across the state, bring government agencies together with community programs and service organizations, and "identify community strengths, concerns, and opportunities," incorporating benchmarks they developed. These benchmarks included reducing juvenile crime, increasing prenatal care, and decreasing teen pregnancy

Why am I telling you this, and how is it important to my story? Because in 1993, shortly after the Commission was established, I was invited by a friend to sit on the Baker County Commission on Children and Families. They were looking for community members, and she thought of me. This "yes" was my launch into the world of social justice—particularly domestic violence and sexual assault—because the same person who recruited me to the Commission later recruited me onto the board of MayDay, Inc., Baker County's domestic violence and sexual assault crisis center.

When Yes Turns into a Career

When I later agreed to join the board of MayDay, Inc., the only thing I knew about domestic violence and sexual assault were the things I had seen, heard, experienced, or seen on movies and television. In other words, I knew it existed, but I had no knowledge of theories, laws, or practices. Like most, I was ignorant of those realities in the field. I was also acutely aware of system failures, which I had experienced since my youth. Social services in the '60s and '70s were different than today.

One giant system failure revolved around the fact that there were few, if any, laws about domestic violence or child abuse. Believe it or not, children did not have much protection then. I recall working for the Youth Corp as a student assistant to a teacher in the summer school for children of migrant workers. We began to notice that one little girl (maybe third grade?) would flinch if we lifted a hand near her, and she often fell asleep during class. There were other indicators, like bruising, that she was being harmed at home. When I asked the teacher if she was going to do anything about it, like tell someone, she informed me that she could not, lest she and the school be sued for slander. In the '70s, there was no mandatory reporting, and she went on to explain that if she accused the parents of harming the daughter, they could sue, and she might lose her license. She was unwilling to risk her career in this way, as were others.

The system failures were numerous, but mostly, they meant no safety for women, and this has remained predominantly true, even today. Over the years, I had heard stories from women of sexual assault and rape, and I had my own military experiences with sexual harassment and assault. I had seen a family member get backhanded so hard she fell out of her chair. I grew up in a small town in Southeast Colorado where the cops had opinions about women getting hit that made it unsafe for the women. When I was 18, I saw my mother get assaulted by her husband, and when the cops came, they refused to arrest him, even though he had her pinned to the hood of the car with his hand on her throat. When I insisted they do something, the cop threatened to arrest me for not showing them enough respect.

My experience with law enforcement could be summed up by the phrase "they did not give a shit."

So, I thought I was prepared when I joined the board. Maybe not so much. Saying that MayDay had some serious problems when the new board and director came on board is like saying traffic is bad when the freeway has been a parking lot for an hour. There was almost no money, with the threat of closing our doors looming. Staff were doing the best they could, given the nightmarish "leadership" of the previous director and board. Essentially, the board consisted of people who did not really care and had never bothered to learn about these issues but whose interest was being able to brag at their cocktail parties about being on the board. The director was a man who slept at his desk, wrote no grants, conducted no outreach, and mismanaged to a frightening degree. Although there were guidelines and policies, they were treated more like recommendations than requirements.

Broken in the Stronger Places: From Resilience to Resourcefulness

We found ourselves having to triage everything: grant writing, volunteer recruitment, training, and outreach so that we could stay alive to serve the victims and survivors coming through the door. Which comes first, the chicken or the egg? Our priority had to be the victims and survivors, but we could not do this if our doors were closed.

Our solution was to do both: the new director would manage the organization, and one of the Board members would focus on grant writing. Fundraising was also necessary, so I stepped into the role of public speaking and asking (begging) people to donate. Planning a fundraiser with no money was a challenge, but we all began working on this as well. As the public face of the entity, recruiting volunteers was part of my fundraising goal. But first, all board members received advocacy training on domestic violence and sexual assault intervention so that we could begin staffing the twenty-four-hour crisis line ourselves.

Speaking about the agency and the topic meant immediately and thoroughly educating myself. I reached out to other agencies around Oregon and the Oregon Coalition Against Domestic and Sexual Violence for help on this. Simultaneously, I was doing a deep dive into research while reading book after book on the subject, which included books written by survivors and subject-matter experts in the field. All of this while working a full-time job, arranging my schedule around my new volunteer schedule, and raising a one-year-old and a fourteen-year-old.

It never occurred to me that my negative experiences with abusive men, combined with my experience of witnessing violence and my own military experience with sexual harassment and assault was informing my work and passion.

Passion, Anger, and a New View

The more I learned about domestic violence and sexual assault, the deeper my anger and my passion for change. I absorbed this information like a sponge while people began to speculate that I had an abusive ex in my past. I said neither yes nor no, but the truth was that my experiences with men were a catalyst for my becoming a board member.

A Sea Change

One day, walking through a local building that housed multiple offices and stores, a poster caught my eye: "Are you a victim of domestic violence?" I stopped to read the poster and was surprised (maybe not a lot) that I was able to answer yes to all but one of the seven questions. It was a long time ago, and posters have changed, but for readers asking what those warning signs looked like, here's a short list, which now includes technological/digital abuse. Even if your partner has never physically assaulted you, consider these questions, taken from the Love is Respect website[xxxii]:

- Does your partner control or limit where you go, forcing you to ask permission to do anything, including seeing family?
- Does your partner withhold affection, criticize, gaslight, or humiliate you?
- Are you prevented from spending money, or does your partner control your spending?
- Does your partner accuse you of having an affair and/or go through your things?
- Are you afraid or concerned about your partner's temper, jealousy, or possessiveness?
- Are you prevented from spiritual or religious practices?
- Does your partner use technology or social media against you or to stalk, harass, or harm you?

I read somewhere once that the best predictor of divorce is not whether a couple has fights but how those arguments or fights look. Arguments happen between couples, and during those arguments, people sometimes say things they should not say. Neither I nor any other advocate in the field of domestic violence or sexual assault includes "normal" relationship interactions when we talk about domestic violence. It crosses over into domestic violence when these behaviors become a pattern intended to manipulate—to gain and maintain control of a person. These behaviors are meted out as punishment, and they change with regularity. The abuser is in control, with a bar that is constantly changing. What you say or do today may end up with your abuser punishing you tomorrow.

So, yes, when I saw that poster, the realization hit me: domestic violence had been part of my life beyond what I had witnessed my mother and other women experience. I had always thought that abuse meant getting hit, so this awakening had a sudden, irreversible effect. The shock when it sank in was palpable, and I understood that I could never un-know what I now knew.

In one relationship, the threat of physical assault was ever-present. This was an easy relationship to leave because I recognized this as abuse. The harder part for me was recognizing emotional, financial, and mental abuse. When in a later relationship these abuses existed, where the silent treatment and humiliation were favored forms of punishment, I recognized the accompanying pain and confusion, but still, I blamed myself, not him, as is always the intent of the abuser. In that situation, I justified and tried to rationalize. I told myself the lies that if I were just a better partner, this would not happen. I was the one who had to change.

During the frequent periods where he did not speak to me—sometimes a day, sometimes weeks—I willingly went along with his assertion that it was my fault, and if I truly cared about him, I would know what was wrong. And, of course, there was the unspoken rule that once he started talking to me again, I was not allowed to ask what I had done. I was just supposed to know and be grateful he had forgiven me.

To this day, when someone withdraws and just stops speaking to me, the devastation and depression hold their epoxy-like grip. I find it impossible to accept that I did nothing wrong. Surely, it must be my fault, right?

During these times, the pain and angst from that past abuse remain real and raw for me.

Lacquer Up and Keep Going

So, I said yes to joining the board of MayDay. Our business and operation plans were moving along. Staff morale improved. We were able to get enough donations to continue inching by, in part because the staff began calling people they knew, including past donors, and asking for money. I was thrilled and surprised at how many people said yes.

There was a $30,000 grant opportunity coming up through the Commission on Children and Families, and we knew we had to act, so one of the board members, a seasoned grant writer, volunteered to write the grant. She got a major start on it before she was called away on a business trip, a trip that ended up being longer than originally expected. Her plan was to take the grant and work on it while she was away, but she soon realized that could not happen, so she called to ask that I finish the grant.

"I have no idea how the hell to write a grant!" I pleaded with her, so she finally agreed to help me all she could. She reminded me that I had been reading grants for some time while with the Commission on Children and Families, knew the local nonprofit organizations, and knew enough about MayDay and domestic violence by that time. "You got this, Liz."

So, I wrote the grant and sent it off to her. She called immediately, "Liz, this is great. Amazing. I cannot believe this is your first grant. I just have one piece of advice."

"Of course, please, what do I need to do? "Ask for the amount, Liz!" she yelled into the phone. Turns out I had given them every bit of knowledge they needed in order to approve a grant but had never quite gotten to the point where I asked for money. I adjusted the grant, fitting in the request, and we turned it in with literally minutes to spare.

The grant was with Baker County Commission on Children and Families, which I had resigned from in order to join MayDay. They invited representatives of each organization to come and speak, and because I had written the grant and I was the public-facing representative, it was on me. Knowing all those commissioners did nothing to allay my fears or nervousness, but get through it, I did, and spectacularly.

They had advised when the meeting opened that they had learned of deep funding cuts, so the amount they had available to dispense was greatly reduced. Consequently, that would impact how much each organization could receive. When the Commission announced the grant recipients, we were toward the end. Every single organization had received a much lower amount than they had requested. Then it was announced that MayDay had received

Broken in the Stronger Places: From Resilience to Resourcefulness

$30,000—the full amount requested. I was filled with pride and relief over this announcement, both because of the work we had put into it and what it meant to our organization.

We had invested all our time into that one grant, and our only grant writer had left and, we had learned, not returning. I was new and at the steep end of a learning curve, and we were out of money and had exhausted every avenue. The importance of this grant was that if we did not get the money we needed, we would likely close. Saying we were relieved is an understatement. We were jubilant (although aware that we had to keep going).

Then shit hit the proverbial fan.

---

xxxii   Love is Respect: Types of Abuse. https://www.loveisrespect.org/resources/types-of-abuse/ Viewed 10/24/2024.

We have to be hopeful. I don't think you can change the world, I don't think you can do justice, if you allow yourself to become hopeless. And so, your hope is your superpower. Your hope is what allows you to stand up when other people say "sit down." It's what allows you to speak when other people say "be quiet."

—**Bryan Stevenson**, *social justice leader and attorney*

CHAPTER 8

Into the Deep End

A Woman's Voice

Generally, it is easy to speculate that the majority of people do not expect to hear certain phrases during their careers. One of those phrases would be, "Little lady, it'll be a cold day in hell before a goddamned woman tells me how to do my goddamned job." Yet there it was, out there on the table, a gauntlet slung at me with vehemence by the Baker County Sheriff at a meeting that included, besides myself and the executive director of MayDay, Inc., the city manager; supervisor of the Oregon State Police (OSP) Eastern Region; and Baker City police chief.

The impetus for this meeting was a brutal, violent assault against a woman by her boyfriend on a public street. He had not been arrested, and the truth was that this incident was not an anomaly but rather the norm in the city and county. I do not know who said it, but I have heard it said that when faced with the decision to get involved, it is a choice between doing something or doing nothing at all. To the detriment of the victims of Baker County, MayDay had done nothing for too long.

Broken in the Stronger Places: From Resilience to Resourcefulness

However, we were a new board with a new director, and we knew we could not choose to do nothing. As a result, we had called the meeting under the agenda of engaging in dialog to promote improved law enforcement services to victims of domestic violence through increased arrests, as mandated by Oregon statute. At the time of the assault, I was the chair of the MayDay board of directors, and my sister Ritha was the executive director, hired by the board following the dismissal of the previous director.

This assault had not been the first nonaction event by local law enforcement. They had been refusing to follow Oregon statute about mandatory arrest for some time. Their approach was most often to blame the woman, say, "Well, he said he didn't do it," and walk away. We learned through conversations with the attorney at the Oregon Coalition Against Domestic and Sexual Violence that Baker City had been on their radar as non-actors in protecting victims of assault and rape for some time. They, including the attorney, offered to support us in every way possible.

Our goal in calling the meeting was simple: discuss how we could facilitate system change that would affect overall long-term response by local law enforcement. Our objective was to improve the response, intervention, and arrest rates by law enforcement in arrests of domestic violence and sexual assault perpetrators in Baker County.

As new members of MayDay, we had been briefed on these problems. It was made clear to us by existing staff and previous board members that our organization had long recognized that victims of Baker County had no expectation of protection. The sheriff and police chief had made it clear over the years that they did not believe the victims, did not believe the mandatory arrest law was just, and they would provide little assistance. Although this extended to all women, and not just victims of domestic violence and/or sexual assault, our focus and concern was on this particular population. In the previous year, we had served over two hundred victims of violence, but local law enforcement had made only fifty-three arrests. They simply walked away from or ignored the majority of calls. To put the numbers into context, there are fewer than ten thousand people in Baker City and just under nineteen thousand in the county. While we had the second lowest rate of domestic violence-related arrests in the State of Oregon, we knew the arrest rate had little to do with actual occurrence, given the nonresponse and arrest rates by local law enforcement agencies.

The sheriff's words in that meeting began a two-year battle for change in Baker County. During the meeting, we presented photos and records to illustrate the problem as well as explaining Oregon Statute 133.055.[31] Our request was that the law be followed for the protection of victims in Baker County. The response of law enforcement at the table was anger at us for asking them to simply do their jobs.

As I looked across the table that day, I realized that the length of the table between us, with my executive director and me at one end and him and the others at the opposite, symbolized the reality of the existing divide between us and them. He was in collaboration with the most powerful people in that small rural community—all of whom were men. We had a small band of women with little power and almost no influence. Nevertheless, we possessed several factors in our favor.

The women on our team of staff and board members had varying levels of education, both formal and informal; we had advocacy values, held a strong sense of professional responsibility and interest in advocating for the victims, participated in other organizations and coalitions, and we had or made the time. Our skills to undertake a major advocacy project may have been limited, but our deficits were nothing insurmountable.

The Measure of Misogyny

Arrest records for the previous years showed that local law enforcement failed on nearly every occasion when they received a call, in spite of state laws and associated regulations that mandated them to make arrests in cases of domestic violence and sexual assault. Victim reports told us that police officers and deputies made regular and frequent derogatory comments about and to victims of rape and domestic violence and that law enforcement had no intention of helping. In that small community, it was also common knowledge that the Sheriff and Police Chief held women in very low esteem.

Following the meeting with the sheriff, police chief, and city manager, what became clear to us was that there was little hope for us to achieve change through collaboration, and we were dealing with full-blown misogynists. Indeed, the sheriff's statement had placed us immediately onto the adversarial square of the game board.

However, just days after that meeting, the captain (supervisor) of the OSP who had been present at that meeting came into my office and apologized. He made it clear that he did not share the attitudes or positions of either the chief or the sheriff. More importantly, he pledged his support, advising me that he and his officers were at the service of MayDay and the victims of domestic violence and sexual assault in Baker County.

His apology and pledge of commitment to MayDay were important because of territory. City police officers can legally operate only within the bounds of the city. The sheriff and his deputies could operate only within the confines of the county, and they may not respond to calls within city limits without specific invitation from the police department. However, at their discretion, Oregon State Police have full authority to respond to any call anywhere within the state. This offer of support by the supervisor was a turning point for us in obtaining protection for victims in Baker County.

Understanding the issue required educating ourselves on several levels. In learning about municipal, law enforcement, and judicial authority, one fact we learned was that police departments and sheriff's offices are entirely autonomous. That is to say, they have no one to answer except local officials and voters, and if there is no directive or backlash from these groups, there is no consequence. For us, this meant that we were completely on our own in addressing the problem. Our only hope lay in getting the voters and citizens of the community to understand the problem and apply enough pressure for the power groups to choose change.

We developed a two-pronged strategy. The plan would address how to deal with law enforcement and how to engage the community. In dealing with law enforcement, we accepted that we had no choice but to adopt the adversarial strategy, but we had OSP on our side. As for the second, we chose to focus on educating the community about the issue of domestic violence and the law. Our approach would include appealing to the emotions of our audience and their sense of justice and fairness. I had developed very strong connections within the community, and we had some board members who were well-known among higher circles. It was my intent to begin the collaboration process using my connections and those of the board.

We began advising law enforcement and city and county officials that Oregon statutes mandated arrest in domestic violence cases. The city manager, police chief, and sheriff had insisted that their efforts were stymied out of fear of being sued for false arrest, so I made sure they had copies of the laws that protect municipalities and individuals from false arrest lawsuits in domestic violence cases.

I reached out to the district attorney and judges, the state sheriff's association, association of police chiefs, Oregon Supreme Court Justice Wallace Carson (a known ally of the domestic violence movement in Oregon), the Oregon Coalition Against Domestic and Sexual Violence (OCADSV), and the Oregon Bar Association. I sought the advice and support of staff at the state's other thirty-five crisis intervention centers, and a known feminist attorney in the state stepped forward and offered her guidance and support. She also volunteered to lead a lawsuit if we could find a victim willing to participate in the ordeal that such a suit would engender. We made certain elected officials knew that we were contemplating supporting a domestic violence victim in a legal proceeding but expressed hope there could be a resolution, anticipating that these moves would widen the gap with local police and sheriff personnel. Unfortunately, they cared not at all about the potential for a lawsuit and had no interest in changing their approach when it came to domestic violence and sexual assault incidents.

If Not Me, Who? If Not Now, When?

Over the course of the next two years, I would spend an inordinate amount of time stumping for change. I was the official voice of MayDay, charged with the step of advocating through education, negotiation, and persuasion, and focused on presenting my information as effectively as possible. Following the death of her husband, my sister decided to step down as the director. I left the insurance business and became the full-time executive director, allowing me to fully embrace the work. I spoke locally, regionally, and statewide and worked diligently to gather resources and allies, both via speech and the written word.

Broken in the Stronger Places: From Resilience to Resourcefulness

We developed quarterly newsletters, and I made certain there were monthly press releases and/or letters to the editor in one of the two local papers.

My approach was one of simple facts combined with stories of the humans affected that touched people both intellectually and emotionally. Intellectually, I wanted them to be made aware of laws around violence against women and why the safety or danger posed to another woman impacts community safety and health. Emotionally, I wanted them to feel empathy and concern enough that they asked, "What can I do?" instead of "What should the victim do?"

My presentations included simple, brief, educational, and awareness-building information on domestic violence. I worked to get people to be empathetic to victims and understand the complexity of domestic violence, shared our organization's role and function, and reported our numbers, comparing them to the rest of the state. I frequently shared how many crisis calls we received, how many women we put into temporary shelter; the number of children involved, how many women and families we sent out of town, and how many restraining orders were obtained by women. These numbers were large and shocking to folks in our small community but not nearly as shocking as finding out that fewer than 25 percent of calls led to arrests.

To be clear, 75 percent of cases that did not include arrest were not because the cop did not have evidence but more likely because they did not want to. In the case of the woman who had been badly beaten on the street, they chose not to arrest him because she had stayed with him throughout the abusive relationship. They felt it was her fault.

In one case, a woman had called the police, but when they arrived, the abuser instructed her to get out there and tell them everything was OK or he would kill her. She did so, and the police drove away. She had a bloody towel wrapped around her head when she spoke to the police. Then there was the case of the medical provider who beat his wife. Law enforcement said they would not arrest him because he was a good doctor, and they had to think about what would happen if their child was injured and they needed him to provide care. The excuses piled up.

In order to have evidence against law enforcement, I had developed a questionnaire that we asked every client to complete. It was simple in its design. Our purpose was to determine if the police had been called, if they had responded, and if the abuser had been arrested. If the answer was no to any one of these questions, we wanted to know why. We also collected a brief description of her experience with law enforcement (either via phone or person-to-person contact), and that officer's name. Every victim and survivor who called or came into the office was presented with the chance to complete the questionnaire, and all said yes. As an independent nonprofit organization, not connected to any municipal or state office, we had complete autonomy in how we managed our own affairs, which means there was nothing they could do to stop the questionnaire.

We chose this approach because both the police and sheriff's office had told us when we asked for records that they did not keep records of calls, only arrests. The importance of this is that the initial number we had—two hundred responses, fifty-three arrests—did not include the numerous calls law enforcement chose not to respond to. This questionnaire helped us get a picture of how many women had made calls to law enforcement and how the response rate and arrest rate compared to each other, in addition to the number of women who called or came into our agency without ever having called law enforcement. The summary of findings from the questionnaires was informal and could not have been used as valid research, but it was telling.

I shared the results of these questionnaires each time I spoke before a group.

At the end of my presentation, people would be empathetic, sympathetic, outraged, and ready to help. An unexpected outcome was that there were people who wanted to share their stories of how they had called the police to come to a neighbor's house but got no response. They had noticed, and I gave them a way to talk about it. My wrap-up always included a plea to them to contact city and county officials, talk about the lack of responsiveness from the police in cases of domestic violence, and write letters to the editor demanding change. We placed the national awareness-building slogan, "Domestic Violence, it is your business," on book markers, bumper stickers, and stickers and handed them out. I helped people understand the issue and how they could be a part of the solution.

Four things happened that helped sway things in our favor. The first was that donations to MayDay more than doubled the first year, serving as matching funds and organizational support for grants and helping us pay for another staff position and additional programs. Second, more women started calling, and we saw our numbers double as well. Victims became more aware that we were a strong, viable organization there to help them, and they began to trust they had someone to call who would listen and help. Third, the arrest rate began to increase. It did not go up much: in the first year, it only increased by about thirty arrests, but it was a start.

Oregon State Police had several times been admonished by the Police Chief and Sheriff for intervening, as I had been for calling them. I remember one day when a woman called our office. She had called the police because her abusive ex, whom she had thrown out, came to her house. She had put his belongings outside to pick up, and when he got there, he picked up the TV and threw it through the bedroom window, barely missing her as she lay in bed. She called the cops, but they refused to come. I found myself standing between two desks, a phone at each ear—her on one, the OSP captain on the other. The captain assured me he would send troops, which he did.

Shortly thereafter, the DA called us to his office for a meeting with him and the other agencies, where he proceeded to chew both of us out: me for calling OSP and OSP for responding. The captain stood his ground, informing the DA that his job was to protect and serve all residents of the state, and he had no intention of doing less. That mattered because what followed was that the district Attorney reluctantly began to show his support. There was, after all, an election approaching.

Finally, an investigative reporter from *The Oregonian* got wind of a story of police corruption unfolding in the county and walked into my office one night. That first meeting lasted several hours, but my story confirmed what he already knew: local law enforcement agencies were violating numerous laws against citizens. I agreed to give our clients his number, and he was besieged by calls from victims who wanted to tell their story. His investigation lasted four months and included him dumpster-diving outside the police station. In the end, he had evidence against the police department and sheriff's office that went well beyond my office and included incidents of harassment, cover-ups, racism, and sexism and went to print with a breaking story about law enforcement in Baker County. The article went out on the AP, and my mother called me from Colorado the day the article came out, both excited and curious about everything that was happening.

Following the article and the immense amount of public awareness being conducted by our organization, we began to see evidence that small steps were being taken. The number of women using our services was climbing, our budget was positively impacted, programming was increased, and our support base had grown dramatically. However, we also knew that our work was far from over. There had been many incidents that showed us the police and sheriff's office were not giving up without a fight, and they bore much resentment toward me. For instance, we had collaborated on a grant with the DA to hire a domestic violence/sexual assault investigator. It became clear that his services were being used by the county for other purposes. The final straw was one day when we called him about a particularly awful case involving a woman being beaten, and he told us he could not respond because he was working on a non-DV case, advising that it would be a day or two before he could come in. My complaint about this led to a wider gap in communication between our office and county/city officials. Ultimately, this animosity by city officials and law enforcement was wearing on the board, and I had to work harder to convince them we were doing the right thing.

Political Winds and Breaking News

During this period, the nation was seeing a movement to more fully recognize the social, legal, and political ramifications of violence against women and to more completely embrace the idea that intimate partner violence demanded a higher level of attention legally. Sadly, the critical event for this movement came from the murder of Nicole Brown Simpson and Ron Goldman and the exposure of the violence she had suffered at the hands of O. J. Simpson. This national story landed domestic violence in everyone's living room, adding power to our small-town movement.

The signing of the Violence Against Women Act (VAWA) by President Bill Clinton in 1994 granted millions of dollars to domestic violence organizations across the country. It addressed the very problems we were facing and targeted law enforcement education. In collaboration with a retired OSP officer and five of us from OCADSV, the Oregon Department of Public Safety Standards and Training developed a comprehensive domestic violence

Broken in the Stronger Places: From Resilience to Resourcefulness

awareness curriculum to add to their basic law enforcement training program. Locally, in a collaborative effort, the district attorney agreed to be the neutral party to manage our VAWA grant and hire the domestic violence investigator who would take the lead on all calls. Our Request for Proposal was successful, and we were, again, one of the few organizations in Oregon to receive the full amount requested.

When the *Oregonian* story broke, it went out on the Associated Press and made news in seven states. This story served as the final straw. The Oregon Department of Justice (DOJ) could no longer ignore what was happening in their state—especially when they were positioning themselves to manage hundreds of thousands of dollars of federal VAWA grants—and they were forced to respond. They opened an investigation, coming to interview me and a long list of victims, and when I handed them a box of questionnaires as evidence, they were overwhelmed. They also issued an invitation for me to speak in Salem before a special committee on services to victims of domestic violence.

An interesting story about that: before it was my turn to take the podium in front of the committee, I was called out into the hall by a representative who asked me to scale back my testimony and not be too detailed. I told him I had not spent years fighting for justice, only to be silenced when the chance for truth came. When they called my name to speak, I gave them all the details of what had been happening in the county. I also made sure to issue a warning not to assume this was just small-town politics in one community, reminding them that women in communities all over the state experienced noncompliance by law enforcement and courts.

It took approximately six months, but eventually, the police chief resigned. The city spent seven weeks in a job search and found a veteran officer from Portland. Although they had not involved me in the search, he insisted on speaking to me before agreeing to take the job. He wanted to know what he was up against on the force and in the community. As a final victory, in November, a new sheriff was elected. He turned out to be a fabulous addition to our community when it came to fairness and justice meted out by law enforcement.

The Places We Belong

As executive director, I had begun to realize that our ability to provide services to victims and survivors was hindered by the fact that we had no shelter. Our solution in sheltering victims had always been to put them up for three days in a hotel. If they needed additional time, we sent them to a shelter elsewhere. So, in 1996, I began the process of working longer hours and more days, committed to raising the money necessary to purchase and stock a home that could be a shelter. This led to a battle with community members, who were concerned that such a shelter in their neighborhood would be dangerous.

Interestingly, they used the lack of law enforcement response as a reason for the city not to approve the zoning, insisting that since this was—by our own account—a problem, it should not be allowed. Funny how no one took the position that law enforcement should be forced to do their jobs.

There was literally a group of men in town who, in backroom meetings, decided which women had stepped out of line, were too messy and too nosy, and came after our jobs. When they targeted me, there was no saving my job. Those men in their little club were coming after me in full force, reminding me that powerful people do not forget. As mentioned previously, there were problems with the domestic violence investigator not doing his job for us, and the board blamed me and my battle with law enforcement. In a meeting of the DA and MayDay board, one of the board members shared with me that the DA had said, "The problem is Liz just doesn't know her place."

That meeting culminated in the head good ole boy (yes, it was a real committee), who happened to also be the editor of the local paper, calling my board and threatening them: either fire me or risk having the organization smeared in the paper. They caved, and I was fired. This firing coincided with the news that we had received a $300,000 grant for the purchase of a home. My concern at the time was less about my firing and more about how this would be managed by MayDay, given that I was the only one who really understood the grant, the requirements for opening the home, and funding. Fortunately, the funding was cemented for the purchase, and they were able to follow through. This accomplishment is a great source of pride for me all these decades later.

Broken in the Stronger Places: From Resilience to Resourcefulness

If you are asking yourself: *Wait, isn't that illegal?* The answer is, yes, it is. In a call to the Oregon Bureau of Labor and Industries (BOLI) and an attorney, I found out that what the editor had done to have me fired was, in fact, illegal. However, the best BOLI could do was interfere with the board's threat to block unemployment, and the best advice the attorney would give me was, "I'll need a $15,000 retainer." Coming up with money I did not have to fight a battle that would suck energy and life out of me made a legal battle a no-go

The firing had been public and messy, and I was exhausted. I had spent more than two years fighting a tough fight, reading about myself in the paper, traveling the state, shrugging off the name-calling, and ignoring my life. I had lost a tremendous amount of weight and was the picture of unhealthy. Years later, I was able to look back on that firing and recognize how I had benefited from this change. I would never recommend anyone endure that kind of attack, but sometimes it turns around.

After being fired, the employment office qualified me for an educational program by determining that since I had no college degree, finding a job at the same level would be nearly impossible. I started college under the displaced worker program and took a nice, quiet job in a dress shop where I had time to study and contemplate whether it was all worth it and if I wanted to return to that work. More and more often, I began to question what I was doing in the social justice field (and especially in the field of domestic violence and sexual assault) and whether what I was doing really mattered.

My degree was to be a Bachelor of Science in Liberal Studies with minors in political science and gender studies. My intent with this degree was to continue focusing on the field of violence against women and social justice, but still, I questioned why and if it really mattered. The question became, why? Why would I go back? What good did I do? What difference did I make? What change could I really make? Would it matter if I just didn't?

In pondering this one day, I said to myself, "If I knew that it mattered to even one person, I would stay in this work." Not too much later, a woman walked in, and again, I heard a phrase I never expected to hear: "You're Liz Estabrooks. You're the reason I'm here." I did not remember her, but she shared with me that I had helped her when no one else would. Her husband had gotten custody of the kids because he had the money and the power, but my fight for her gave her the courage to stand up to him and fight for her children, so she was back to do just that.

I wiped my tears and remembered at that moment what I had said: that if I knew I had made a difference to just one woman, it would be worth it, and there she was, standing in my dress shop, proof some battles are worth the fight. Sometimes, the words you least expect to hear are the words that help you decide the place you belong.

Activate Life: Phase 2

My daughter, thirteen years older than my son, had left home after her high school graduation, making it just me and my son at home. Starting university with a five-year-old was difficult, but I knew it would be a better life for us in the end, so I pursued my courses toward the goal of early graduation and a higher, steady income.

My undergraduate program was everything I wanted. Eastern Oregon University had just decided to offer a minor in gender studies, which, when combined with political science, fit perfectly with my bachelor's of science in liberal studies. Sounds cool, right?

But you know what they say about liberal studies degrees. You want fries with that?

It was not really that bad, though, because, during my degree, pursuit a friend who had become the Executive Director of the Baker County Commission on Children and Families called and asked if I would be interested in a contract with them leading the development of a five-year strategic plan to improve services to women and families and reduce teen pregnancy, substance use, violence, and juvenile crime in our community. The Office of Juvenile Justice and Delinquency Prevention had money and wanted to decrease these issues to improve community safety. Ruth wanted me on the project because of my expertise. She also knew I needed the money and had this particular skill set. I said yes.

This work was an excellent way for me to sharpen my skills and expertise while laying the path for future work. Family violence is a huge risk factor for each of these behaviors and problems. Baker was chosen because we had

Broken in the Stronger Places: From Resilience to Resourcefulness

active nonprofit organizations working individually and collaboratively in each of these areas, and we also had the highest rate of juvenile delinquency in the state at more than 150 percent of the average rate. Not a good look.

So, I adjusted my lens and started working on research, writing, presenting, and helping make change in the community, making sure that those doing the work in social justice understood the need to rethink their approaches and how they were working with women who had experienced interpersonal violence; how they were working on matters of safety for families. I also worked with communities, tribes, nonprofits, and governments to implement programs that addressed workplace and school violence because that was where I saw the potential to make a difference. That work continued for years while I kept listening to and reading stories of women and girls who had seen and experienced violence and abuse in their families. The stories kept coming; my work continued because it mattered.

This contract helped me secure future contracts as a consultant, including developing and implementing statewide training for Oregon Department of Human Service employees. In collaboration with the state, my training partner and I developed what we called the "domestic violence intervention and prevention 101" training. We traveled the state, training classrooms of people, exposing myths and facts, and addressing best practices for intervention when working with victims and survivors.

This was a difficult year, personally, as my son was only about ten, and the constant travel became a custodial issue with my ex. While I was able to retain custody of my son, it was not without difficulty. I missed him intensely, but my work was training thousands of employees on such an important topic, knowing how it would improve services for victims and survivors of domestic violence statewide. I needed the work and to feed my soul, so I pushed through the work and those times I was separated from my son, making sure I had conversations with him to explain why it was important and that I missed him terribly. I believe—hope—he understood.

As a single woman, my primary focus needed to be on the financial stability of my household, so as political winds shifted and funding was lost for consulting work, I took a four-year break to work for a network and internet security company. During that period, I also continued to work independently to help women who were in violent relationships or who had left and were trying to get help. Continuing this work on the side helped assuage the guilt I felt for what felt like abandoning all these women.

I remember having a conversation with a woman I met during that time who had been deeply involved in working with abused children. She spoke frankly about how it had gotten into her soul and stayed, eating her from the inside. One day, her husband asked her to come to work with him. She struggled with the decision because she felt like she was abandoning the children, but she told me she believed it saved her life.

"Maybe," she said, "the time has come for you to save your own life, and this is your message to do that." Of course, I could have listened, but I did not. The work continued to call me.

You fall, you get up, you keep moving.

—**Michelle Obama**, *The Light We Carry*

CHAPTER 9
A New Path

A New Old Decision

Fast-forward to 2011: "Oh my god, Ritha, they accepted me" is how I started the call with my sister when the acceptance letter from Columbia University School of Social Work came. Sure, I applied, but I did not actually think I would get in, and when I did, I sobbed. When I collected myself, I called my big sister and shared the news. She was the first person I told, just as she was the first to find out when I joined the Army and when I was pregnant with both my children. Truthfully, however, it did not go well. She became upset, "Why New York City? You were accepted at the University of Washington and the University of Southern California; why New York?" followed by a terse "I gotta go" and the silence that follows a hangup.

I was devastated, began to cry, and called my other favorite sister, Theresa, who said both congratulatory and soothing words, and then called Ritha and explained to her she had hurt my feelings (as sisters do). Ritha phoned back, apologized, and said she was proud of me—but, in the typical Ritha fashion that I will always miss, stated she did not have to love the fact that I was moving across the country,

Broken in the Stronger Places: From Resilience to Resourcefulness

Theresa was only eighteen months younger than me and had moved to Baker when her two children were young, leading to a closer relationship than we had in our youth. Although we were close in age, we had our own friends and lives. I left when I was seventeen and she was fifteen, and from that time until the time she moved to Baker, we saw each other only occasionally during family get-togethers. Once she moved to Baker, my appreciation of Theresa as a sister and a friend grew into an adult relationship that was not just about being sisters but about being friends and confidants. Although we have had our arguments like all siblings, our relationship became more cemented in friendship and loyalty to each other.

There was never too much fun for us to have, and she was always supportive in ways that even Ritha was not because she never let her personal feelings get in the way. Theresa has always had my back, even when I am not in the room, no matter what challenge I faced or change I sought, and I hope she can say the same for me. A person could not ask for a better sister or closer friend. I knew that even though she would be sad that I was leaving, she would support me 100 percent in this. She did not disappoint. Just as she had supported me through the firing and my undergraduate program, she supported me fully in obtaining my graduate degree, a dream I had put off for years.

My daughter had already turned eighteen and was out of the home during my undergraduate college years, so it had no noticeable impact on her. However, I knew it had been hard on my son. My goal had been to complete my schooling in under four years so I could be done with it. The only path to this success was taking twenty-hour terms, so that was what I did. My secondary goal of summa cum laude was only possible by working toward straight As. As an overachiever, school also meant taking the hardest classes that involved a ton of reading and writing. To avoid my son losing more time than necessary, much of my work was done after he went to bed, a behavior that also exacerbated the sleep disorder that had begun while I worked with MayDay.

So, I knew that my schooling and work had been difficult for my family. My son was only five when I started my undergraduate program and had just turned nine when I completed my degree in January 2001. I had initially intended to go on to graduate school afterward, but that changed during a

A New Path

conversation with a friend that shook my son to tears. She had asked what was next, and I mentioned applying to graduate schools.

When he heard more school, his stress of the past nearly four years landed hard, and he burst into tears. In the hugs and soothing that followed, he tearfully said, "You promised that when you graduated, you would be done with school!" Looking at his young face and wiping his tears, I promised to wait until later, which came when he graduated from high school.

When I announced my acceptance at Columbia University and impending move to New York, my family ran the gamut from angst to pride and cheer to angst, and before I moved, they had a farewell and good luck barbecue for me. They all showed up, even Ritha, who by that time had become a hermit and rarely went anywhere.

Two years later, when I graduated, they threw a graduation party. Someone asked me if that meant I was returning to Baker City to work. I quickly put that idea out of their heads. Theresa had already let me know that people were asking if I would return, and she had been working to dispel them of that myth, as she did again that day. Ritha, however, quickly excused herself and left the party. I came to understand that she was intensely proud of me, but she also realized we would never live in the same town again. Just as she did when I drove away from her in 1977 when I left for Basic Training, she stayed on the porch, waived, and said goodbye tearfully.

This was repeated when I was offered a job in Canada and again in Washington, DC. Theresa would give me a big hug, say tearful goodbyes, and do something goofy for me so that she would not cry. At my going away party before leaving for DC, she presented me with a large black poster with a compass in the center that said, "Home Is Where Theresa Is," signed by family members. That poster has stayed with me since that date and is now in the office of my new home. It felt important to me, so when I wanted to take it on my one-year van journey, I had it made into a small curtain that was a constant reminder that I had people who loved me and a home to go to. Funny how, without even knowing it, Theresa has been my true north for decades.

Every time I left, though, Ritha would come and say goodbye, but with a hint of irritation shining through her sadness, knowing that although these jobs meant great things for me, they took me further from her. We were linked, she and I, in a different way than I was linked with the others. I loved her immensely, no more than my other siblings, but because of the trauma that she held for me, the bond that linked us went beyond our childhood.

There's Nothing to See Here

During my time at Columbia University, my entire body of work was on women in the military and sexual assault, harassment, and rape, where I did a deep dive into the research and stories. Those stories and the research found their way in through the cracks, seeping out unbidden because of an incident or occurrence. It was here that I learned about what the Department of Veterans Affairs coined MST, which covers the trauma held by service members who experienced harassment, assault, and rape while serving on active duty. It was there and then that I began subconsciously stocking up on my lacquer and gold supply and began regular applications.

During this time, I was immersed in researching, learning, and writing about military sexual assault. Some might say I was obsessed. With the permission of my professors (except economics), I found a way to use that topic in every class where a topic was not assigned. My new career goal was to be an expert in the field, and I have never met a goal I did not love.

One thing that I did not realize was the depth to which that research and learning was getting inside of me, tearing at the fabric of my own trauma from so many years ago. Whatever feelings were brought up, I quickly lacquered over. No time for feelings or pain—just work. Once I get past the degree, I will think about it, I assured myself. There's nothing to see here.

This was a pattern I clung to for the remainder of my career, which even-tually took me to the VA.

No Safe Place, Still

The very first VA I received care from was in Boise, Idaho, in 2005. They had long been known for being one of the best VA hospitals in the country. However, even the best has problems.

A New Path

Because of when I served, I was priority level eight with the VA, which means I was not eligible for care until I received my benefits establishing me as a veteran with service-connected disabilities. I had heard stories from women veteran friends who used the VA about being called "Mr." (a too-common occurrence, even today), difficulties with care, and sexual harassment at VA facilities; but being new, I had not experienced anything firsthand until I started using the Boise hospital.

They (the VA) had asked me to go to an initial appointment to establish care and provide some baseline health information. Their instructions were "Go to women's health on the third floor." So, the day of my appointment, I rolled up to the Boise VA and went up to the third floor. When the door opened, I was greeted by a hallway filled with janitorial equipment: mops, brooms, buffers, and the like. Down at the furthest end of the hall was a woman at a desk. I also took in three doors with curtains on them.

I stood in that elevator, holding the door open, wondering where I had gone wrong. I checked, and, sure enough, I was on the third floor. The elevator began the obnoxious dinging sound that happens when the door is being held open too long, and the woman's voice echoed from the desk down the hall said, "Ma'am, can I help you?"

> **Me:** "Yes, I think I'm on the wrong third floor (stupid thing to say, I know)."
> **Her:** "What are you looking for?"
> **Me:** "Women's Health"
> **Her,** with a sigh I could not really hear so much as understand and see: "Yes, ma'am. This is women's health."

Me, as I looked at the doors with curtains and the janitorial equipment, still holding the elevator door, still making the obnoxious sound: "Let me get this straight. I served in the same Army as the men, yet they get an entire fucking hospital, and I get the janitorial closet?"

> **Her:** "Yes, ma'am, I'm sorry."

Broken in the Stronger Places: From Resilience to Resourcefulness

So, I got out of the elevator and walked down the hall. In all honesty, though, it was good care I received from them, as far as the care went. Today, Boise has one of the best, most modern VA Women's Health Clinics in the nation. But that is not to say everything went great. Care for women in the VA system was limited for women when I first began using their services. Additionally, we were frequently called "mister," and the sexual harassment was constant. I had heard of this happening to women, so I was somewhat forewarned when I first began using VA health care. However, when I had jobs that offered health insurance, the sexual harassment and disrespect for women led to me opting for care outside the VA for a long time.

Like so many other women veterans, sexual harassment was something I had to steel myself for whenever entering a VA. Whether it is due to my age or changes in the VA, I no longer contend with sexual harassment, but that does not mean it does not happen. Women still complain about it happening nationwide.

My worst experience happened one day at the VA in Washington, DC, while there for a physical therapy (PT) appointment. There were four veteran men in the waiting area. I waited in that room with my shields up, or so I thought. When going to the VA, like many women, I tried to remain vigilant of my surroundings, not focus on the men, and make it appear that I was not paying attention. A book and headphones were standard gear to give the illusion that I was involved in my book and music and could not hear what was going on around me. The truth was that there was no music or reading happening. I was alert to every sound and action around me, alert to the possibility that a man would come up to me and intrude on my space or send sexual harassment hurtling my way.

This is too often the reality for women visiting the VA. We must monitor the space to look out for men who harass us, usually verbally, sometimes physically. For women of color and LGBTQ+ women, that reality is multiplied. When women enter this space, it is with the awareness that it is unsafe for us. So, I really was not reading or listening to music. I was just protecting myself, on high alert, waiting. Shields up.

That day, as I sat in the physical therapy waiting room, there was a man directly to my left, one to his left, and two men across from me. I had taken note of the room and their placement when entering the room, so I positioned myself in a way that allowed as much visual scan as possible while remaining alert. The man farthest to my left was an old guy with a cane.

Right after I sat down, I heard him. "Hey. Hey, beautiful."

I ignored him. "Hey, you want coffee, beautiful? Want to go get a cup of coffee with me?"

I continued to ignore him and pretended to read.

He got louder. "Hey. Hey! I'm talking to you. You want to go get some coffee with me?" As my heart began to beat faster, I continued to ignore him.

Directly to my right was the window for the waiting room, staffed by two employees who were in earshot. At that time (2013), there were no glass shields on the windows such as you find today, because there was no COVID or concern about anything crossing that barrier. So, anything that happened in the waiting room they could hear—especially a man who was yelling at someone.

Giving the illusion of ignoring his comments, I continued to look down at my book, but I could see out of my peripheral vision that he was approaching my direction, and then I saw his feet and legs in front of me, facing me. He said, "Hey bitch!" My legs were crossed, so when he swung his cane, he hit my foot with the bottom of his cane and said, "Hey bitch. I'm talking to you."

I looked up, took out my headphones, closed my book, and very calmly (which was deceiving because my heart was racing and I was anything but calm) said, "Mutherfucker, you touch me again, and I will kill you with that fucking cane."

It was dead silent in the room as my voice rang out. I was as good as alone with him. Nobody had said a word to him about his behavior. No one said, "Stop, don't do that. You are out of line." No one said anything to him while he was accosting and then attacking me. Not the veteran men in the room, not the staff behind the window.

It was not until I threatened to kill him that one of the employees behind the glass came bursting through the doors into the waiting room and called my name. The woman ushered me inside, and once we cleared the doors, she said, "Are you OK?"

I looked at her and, shaking and in tears, said, "*No*, I am not fucking OK! I'm *not* OK. I was being sexually harassed and ended up being assaulted

Broken in the Stronger Places: From Resilience to Resourcefulness

by that man, and you all just sat there, and you would have continued to sit there had I not said what I said. Your only concern is that I threatened to kill him with his own cane. Let's be clear about that. You all do not give a shit about women being harassed or assaulted in your VA by male veterans, and I am sick and fucking tired of it."

After my appointment, I got off the bus near my home, and my boyfriend at the time called. As I was walking home, I shared with him what happened. I was so angry and distraught, and I was sobbing while relaying the incident. He was saying all the right things and working with me to help me calm down, and when I had settled, he said, "I just want to suggest something—maybe you have thought of it, maybe you haven't—but you know you have shared with me what happened to you in the Army, and I just wonder, Liz, if you have thought about your own military sexual trauma (he had learned that phrase from listening to me speak). I wonder if the deep dive you are doing on military sexual trauma for school is starting to bring up your own trauma from the past?"

He was right. I had been doing so much work on military sexual assault and trauma and other women veterans that I had not considered my own at all. Even then, I did not think about my years of work in the private sector, or in the MST field.

I said, "It's something to consider, and thank you. You might be right." But I was so wrapped up in graduate school and getting everything done that I needed and wanted to do that I put it off until later. 'I'll deal with that later. Right now, I have to get through graduate school."

I continued to do more, and more intense, work on military sexual trauma in women veterans, and published a paper in the Columbia School of Social Work journal.[xxxiii] Then I deepened and broadened my research, reading more and more about women veterans, their health conditions, homelessness, suicide, substance use, and military sexual trauma, writing more papers. I got through graduate school, but I remember during that time how angry I felt while I was doing my research: anger toward the DOD for ignoring the problem, toward the VA for allowing it to continue in their own institution, anger toward all the men who actively participated in perpetrating harassment, assault, and rape, and those who stood by complicity while it happened.

Life Happens Upstream

Following my graduation from Columbia in 2013, I spent some time in Canada with my then boyfriend and, while there, went on some job interviews—one with Edmonton Police Department (EPD) in Edmonton, Alberta, Canada, that was especially promising. Unfortunately, their immigration and hiring rules interfered with my ability to get hired, but they were able to offer me a temporary contract. Although the contract was on the opposite side of the sexual assault spectrum— working with the offenders—EPD leaders felt I was the best consultant to do the job. Their rules for permanent hires were different than their rules for contracting, which is how they got around bringing me on board.

The work was a completely different approach to addressing sexual assault than any I had taken in the past. My task was to work, over the next nine months, with community partners in Edmonton to develop a housing plan for what Canada refers to as "high-risk and violent offenders" in an attempt to reduce recidivism. This population is exactly what the title implies.

For me, this required putting aside preconceived notions on this topic, which, in a nutshell, was primarily the belief system that sex offenders cannot be treated and have the highest recidivism. Before I began my work, though, there was an abundance of research to be examined. This was initially a struggle for me because of my own deep feelings about offenders. However, I also understood that stopping violent crimes was not about just jailing these people but stopping them from offending. Throughout my years working on intervention and safety, I had always understood that prevention was key, yet that is the one thing countries do less of in this field. Pretty much everyone is prioritizing fishing babies out of the river over going to the headstream and stopping it there (see below). That is not a judgment but a reality.

I was grateful for that opportunity because, in the research needed for me to succeed, I learned much of what I had known about offenders, especially sorting myth from fact. However, the realization that people loved and respected me when I did the work as a victim advocate and activist, some of those very same folks got pissed off that I was doing work on the offender side. What they could not (would not) seem to understand was that there must be efforts on this side if we want to reduce or stop violence against women.

While working on community safety in the late '90s, I attended a meeting with some men who had gained recognition for stopping the skinhead movement in Northern Idaho during the '90s. One of them used this anecdote in discussing the main approach to change: get it at its source.

Two men were fly fishing in their favorite river one day when they spotted a baby floating toward them. Naturally, they hurried to its rescue. As they pondered how this baby was floating down the river, they saw another, then another. Soon, they were unable to catch all the babies, so many were coming at them.

One began wading toward the bank as the other cried, "Where are you going? I can't catch all these babies by myself!"

The wading man replied, "I'm going up river to find out who the hell is throwing in all these babies so I can stop them."

This story perfectly illustrates that the work we do on the victim side is not enough because there are more victims and survivors coming at us, and we cannot save them all.

There is an overwhelming belief that offenders cannot be rehabilitated and will always continue to offend, no matter how much prison time they serve. As I discovered in my research, recidivism among sex offenders is neither hopeless nor meaningless. The idea behind this (pilot) Canadian project was to offer a way of overseeing and providing services to those who, once they left the system due to expired parole or probation and could not be legally monitored, with an end goal of public safety through reduced recidivism.

The research shows one of the biggest problems with high-risk/sex offenders is that, once they reenter society, the system designed to protect the victims also prevents the offender from living in safe environments where they can have access to support systems that help prevent re-offense. By virtue of their crimes, they are legally barred from living and working in numerous jobs and locations because they cannot be around children and/or women.

A lack of housing may prevent them from staying in touch with mental health providers, support groups, and more. The classes they attended often also failed to accurately and effectively hold them accountable. I learned that if and when this group of offenders are safely housed and provided with appropriate and ongoing safe access to care services, including support systems, their recidivism rate can actually fall below that of property crimes and drug crimes. As a longtime advocate for reducing violence against women and children, I was intrigued and worked diligently to work with community partners and the Edmonton Police Department to complete the work.

What the Edmonton Police Department, along with the Alberta Government, intended to do was provide housing and services to these offenders. With the community partners on board, we built a structure of housing and wraparound services that also meant informal oversight once they went off their probationary period. In my research, I also learned that the United States, at that time, was one of the few first-world countries that did not conduct this type of effort on some level.

While doing my work in Canada, I had put out of my mind my graduate school conversation with my boyfriend about seeking care and services for my own MST, yet here I was, working in a way that kept offenders in the front of my mind, and shoring up my own inner strength so I could make a difference. I also found myself in frequent arguments with him over the work I was doing.

He resented that I was "helping" these offenders and often exclaimed that the best approach was simply a bullet to the head, insisting that it made no sense for me to be helping these men when I had for so long been focused on helping women and children harmed by such offenders. I realized that while it was easy to be proud of me when I was helping victims, he found it less so when my work was benefitting offenders. When I asked him one day if his position would be the same were one of his sons found to be a violent or sex offender, his response was simply to be angry and assure me his sons would never do such a thing.

Ultimately, my passion for my work—which he had insisted from the beginning was one of the things he most respected and loved about me—led to relationship degradation. I returned to the United States after the contract and, within a matter of days, received a text from him that he just could not continue being around someone who so forcefully voiced their opinions and thoughts.

This is important to the story, as he helped me during those times when I was suffering emotionally and mentally in graduate school. He had helped spread the lacquer on the broken places, adding the precious gold metal powder so the scar was stronger and made more beautiful. He had become one of the few men in my life that I actually trusted and believed.

The breakup was surprising and traumatizing, snapping the broken place he had helped to mend and make stronger. Not to be dissuaded from carrying on though, I began the hard work of once again lacquering over my broken places, making them ever stronger, adding an abundance of gold powder over the top, making sure the scar was strong and, on the surface, beautiful.

The work in Canada was my first and only foray into working with offenders, but those lessons remained with me and added to my expertise. What was more surprising was that working on this side of the fence had no discernible impact on my PTS. You see, I was not hearing the stories of the things these men had done. It was all numbers and impersonal research. I did not need to know the details of the crimes they had committed, only that the goal was to improve post-release services and reduce recidivism (reoffending) among this population. This time, it was not the work that added to my trauma, but betrayal by my boyfriend.

The Things We Live With

Pain doesn't go away. You only learn to live with it. Music is how I manage it.

—Sinead O'Connor

Because I could not qualify for Canadian immigration because of my age, I asked my then boyfriend to sponsor me. He was unwilling to do so, and only after I returned to the U.S. did he tell me via text that he was unin-terested in pursuing a relationship. Yep, he broke up with me by text. I was devastated. He had pursued me hard from the first day we met, and with that pursuit came assurances that he was different than previous men and would never betray or hurt me. He was easy to look at and be around, and he made it easy to believe him. The text felt like an immense betrayal.

Months after returning to the United States in September 2015, I came face to face with the realization that deep depression had set in, and I needed help. There was no longer graduate school keeping me busy, nor was I working much, which opened all the doors to allow the demons I had been fighting to come together and settle in. I looked in the mirror one morning and, as they say, saw someone I did not recognize. I never left my home except to shop for groceries, did not go anywhere or see anyone, and spent my days mostly watching tv, drinking, or laying in bed, yet rarely sleeping. When I looked in the mirror, I realized that the lack of sleep and sunshine, combined with the excess alcohol, had reduced my skin to a pallor. The general lack of self-care was evident.

I contacted the VA asking for help and was fortunate to be assigned a therapist named Betsy, a caring, knowledgeable psychologist who began the process of using her skills to heal my broken places. However, her work was focused on my current situation—the depression from the breakup. Underneath remained the military sexual trauma I had so carefully ignored for more than three decades, and which I was beginning to suspect was an issue.

When my therapy with her ended and we were in our termination session, she asked if there was anything else. I said, "You know, Betsy, over the past decade, I've been asked the MST screening questions by various VA providers.[32] I have answered yes to most of the questions, but not one person has ever, ever, paid attention to it, asked me about it, or asked if I needed support." She was aghast, even at herself, apologized profusely, and connected me to a counselor for MST-related PTS, a Marine veteran, Jaimie, whom I greatly respected.

By this time, I had started my job at the Oregon Department of Veterans Affairs working with women veterans and had begun listening to the stories of women veterans who had experienced sexual harassment, assault, and rape. One day, Jaime got into my personal experiences with men and how that crossed into my professional work—all the way through my current circumstance.

During this session, she asked, "What is the percentage of men you would say, in your belief, would do harm to a woman if given the opportunity, with no consequence."

Broken in the Stronger Places: From Resilience to Resourcefulness

Without hesitation, my answer was "98 percent."

She seemed shocked and said, "That's a very high number, Liz," asking how I arrived at that number.

Because I understood that, according to her, I was wrong, I said, "Okay, maybe as low as 93 percent, but I think it's at least 96 percent."

My response was to ask her how she did not get high numbers. She is, after all, a psychologist and a Marine who specializes in post-traumatic stress related to combat trauma and MST. She has worked with many women and men who have been harmed by sexual harassment, assault, rape, and other forms of violence over the years. My own experience was such that, except for a handful, the men I had met in the military had participated in committing some act of violence, harassment, or abuse against the women with whom they served. Those who did not perpetrate just stood by and watched it happen without doing anything or speaking out against it happening.

Over the decades, I watched and listened to friends and family members talk about their own experiences of abuse and violence. I had worked in a crisis intervention center with women who experienced some of the worst acts of violence one can imagine, sometimes with the knowledge or participation of their own or their partner's family members or friends. I had seen my own partners, boyfriends, and male friends ignore the abuse their male friends perpetrated. One ex told me he would not do anything because his friend, the abuser, "knew all the good hunting spots," reducing my girlfriend, who was victimized by him, to less value than the deer and elk those men loved to hunt together.

Every day it had unfolded before me personally, professionally, or in media—women harassed, raped, assaulted, beaten, and murdered by the men who were intimate partners, bosses, coworkers, friends, and, of course, relatives who said they loved them. How, I asked her, was I supposed to believe that what I was seeing was not true when the sum of my life experience was that the majority of men were willing to bring harm? I wanted her to tell me how her experience as a psychologist and Marine kept her from seeing the world through *my* lens? Over the next six years, three other VA psychologists would ask me the same question, always with the same answer. None were able to answer my question: How do you *not*?

xxxiii   Estabrooks, E. 2013. In Search of the Arc: The Path to Justice for Women in the Military. Columbia Social Work Review. https://www.academia.edu/4274373/In_Search_of_the_Arc_The_Path_to_Justice_for_Women_in_the_Military?source=swp_share.

When I dare to be powerful, to use my strength in the service of my vision, then it becomes less and less important whether I am afraid.

—Audre Lorde

CHAPTER 10

Work Now, Heal Later

In January 2016, I landed a job that seemed as though it was designed, if not destined, for me. The Oregon legislature had just passed Oregon HB 3479, which established the permanent position of Oregon Women Veterans Coordinator at the Oregon Department of Veterans Affairs (ODVA). Since it was a brand-new position, they left it to me to design what it would look like. They literally instructed me to build the program based on the verbiage in the legislative bill and what I felt was best, and so I did.

I embraced the job and put aside my therapy. Who had time for healing when there was work to do and women to save? Besides, I was fine. Fine! I'm fine, thank you.

One of the certainties we all shared at ODVA was that although we knew there were an estimated twenty-six thousand women veterans in the state, they were a mystery to us. Most had simply faded into the background upon returning home, too often not seeking their benefits or care at the VA—benefits and care to which they were entitled. Most did not even recognize themselves as veterans.

What this meant was that few women attended veteran events (and if they did, they were not identified as such), and few stepped forward for their benefits. Others may have had negative experiences with the VA—experiences that happened because they were women, the VA had done a poor job of providing care and benefits for women, and the VA was not a safe place for women. One reality we faced was that while some county veteran officers were doing a good job for women veterans, too many were not, and some had never written a claim for a woman veteran, while others had, but with less success than the men they wrote claims for.

The VA's history of approving benefits to women had left many women with a sour taste. The approval process for conditions like military sexual trauma was emotionally and mentally painful and frightening, and too often, women were denied for lack of "proof." Additionally, many women had experienced the sexist culture and design that was the Veteran Benefits Administration, as well as the bias sometimes held by claims developers and veteran service officers[33].

You will often hear veterans say there is not a lot of difference between the VA and military, and they are not entirely wrong, since military policies can affect VA benefits and services. This truth was evident in working with women who had attempted to obtain benefits.

For instance, in spite of the fact that women during the post-9/11 era were engaging in combat situations and had historically, when they attempted to obtain benefits for injuries and conditions related to combat or deployment, including PTS, they were denied based on the fact that military policy clearly banned women from combat via the combat exclusionary policy. Therefore, the VA's position was that they could not approve combat-related benefits for women since women were not officially engaged in combat. One woman I met told me how she and her husband had served together in Iraq and had very similar experiences and disabilities. His disability benefits had been approved before his discharge was final. Years later, she was still fighting for hers.

Whether this was a legitimate VA policy or not, I do not know, but what I do know is that women were being denied by the VA. Women were also contending with VA employees and veteran service officers who allowed their own sexist belief systems to interfere with providing equitable care for women. Consequently, many women had historically negative experiences when it came to the VA, so they had just stopped trying to get their earned benefits and health care.

Work Now, Heal Later

One of the first things I did as the Oregon Women Veterans Coordinator was establish the need for a change in our language. Early on, I met a woman veteran who had served as a Marine for twelve years, but when I asked her if she was a veteran, she said no. I came to realize that our words were a barrier to care and services for women veterans. Why? Because too often, women do not identify with the word "veteran," even when they've served for decades. It is the constant messaging that tells women we are not "real" veterans. Part of that has to do with combat, but part is the internalization of a culture that "others" women and diminishes our service. With this understanding, ODVA worked toward a language change across systems: stop asking women if they are veterans and ask them instead if they served in the military. While the first usually got us a no, the second would get us a yes even if she had a nightmarish experience or had received a less-than-honorable discharge.

We wanted all the women veterans and knew that getting them to identify was a first step. Our work included encouraging community partners to change the wording on their intake forms, and as they did, almost without fail, they found they had more women identifying as veterans.

Because I had an unlimited budget and two astounding bosses until 2018, there was complete freedom to go and do what I needed to go and do, and I moved forward like a woman possessed, working sixty or more hours a week, driving from one end of the state to another with the sole purpose of finding women veterans and hearing their stories, sometimes not getting off the road until 10:00 or 11:00 p.m. If we were to locate these women and help them, they needed to know about me *and* their benefits.

The plan I gave my bosses was that, in the first year, my goal would be primarily outreach to every county of the state while also conducting speaking engagements and training veteran service officers in order to increase the knowledge base around women veterans. The outreach would consist of attending all events targeting veterans (and those that did not), as well as conducting "listening sessions" for women veterans. I made it clear that these were not round tables or forums. My most important task in year one was to find and hear from as many women veterans as possible—to hear their needs, issues, experiences, and concerns—and to convince these women that they had earned and deserved their benefits. It was a grueling schedule that I kept for the four and a half years I worked at ODVA, slowed down only by COVID.

These listening sessions were exactly that: me listening. No men, no reporters, no other ODVA or VA representatives allowed. Just me with my yellow pad and pen and a table full of women veterans (and their service animals if they had them), many of whom had never had a chance to talk about themselves or their experiences. There was no computer, no last names, and everyone got the chance to speak, no matter how many women were in the room. There was no interrupting, except the occasional statement of support from another woman or my asking her to elaborate.

My conversations started a lot of confidential sharing within the groups, and I remember one of my first groups. I sat with maybe fourteen or fifteen from their early twenties to one woman in her eighties. The women were going around sharing their stories that ranged from broken bones to cancer and military sexual assault.

I would have these listening sessions so I could understand the plight of women Veterans: what were their issues, complaints, and experiences—in the military, in the VA, and in their lives in general? What were the issues that had affected them and continued to affect them, including problems with the VA: services, care, and benefits? The only rules I had were no interrupting, no "shoulda-woulda-coulda" stuff. In other words, people in the meeting were not allowed to tell the woman speaking what should have, would have, or could have been done. Additionally, there was no dominating the conversation. I wanted every woman to have the chance to speak.

In these sessions, women would talk about the fact that they had worked hard to be strong because they are women veterans and are expected to be strong, yet they had these broken places that occasionally opened up. They would talk about the guilt and remorse they felt over their inability to hold on to a relationship, how they felt like they may not have been good mothers, the anger they felt. I often heard my mother's regret in their voices.

In one of my very first meetings, the conversation turned as it did toward their experiences of harassment, assault, and rape in the military. Many of the women stated it was the first time they had ever shared what happened to them—they had never talked about it before. As mentioned previously, it was a common outcome of these meetings for women to talk about how they had kept their assaults to themselves because they did not feel safe having those conversations, even with loved ones. I began to understand the value of just sitting and listening to these women and giving them that safe space. So, I would always start these meetings with the fact that everyone had their story, and this had to be a safe place for everyone to share.

During this day's conversation, a woman mentioned that it was fascinating that every woman in that room alone had shared experiences and had carried them inside of them since it happened. The eighty-plus-year-old woman sitting to my right said quietly, "Maybe it's because no one ever asked, or she never had the chance to tell." I turned to look at her, and she almost imperceptibly nodded her head, and I nodded back in understanding.

Over the years, I worked with a few women in her age group who acknowledged what happened to them. One thing I learned in my time is that those who are over sixty are often overlooked because there is a prevailing assumption that sexual assault in the military is a new thing in the past thirty or so years. I want to emphasize that there are women veterans from WWII who were sexually assaulted during their service. I am the person in the room who says the hard stuff, so I am going to say this here: your heroes of WWII were doing this shit, just like they are today, but these women are tied to the silence that turns his actions into her shame.

How many of those old veteran men were sexually assaulting and harassing women on active duty? Those beautiful women we see in photos and at events likely have their own broken places, which they had to bury because who would believe it happened or who would support them, especially if they were women of color? Who would stand up and call out veterans the world called heroes? These women came home from WWII, Korea, and Vietnam with the trauma of having been in those situations, in addition to the trauma of sexual assault they tucked away. They added lacquer and gold, put on a smile, and showed the world their stronger places. In doing my work, I came to understand my father's warnings when I joined and why he did not want me to enlist.

Women veterans often shared with me the lives they lived upon returning: the relationship struggles, problems parenting, inability to hold a job—realities

Broken in the Stronger Places: From Resilience to Resourcefulness

made more difficult by the secrets they had to keep locked up inside of them because it was not something that was discussed, and there was no one to tell without them being shamed, or possibly left by their partner or spouse.

I began to wonder how I, just one person, could help twenty-six thousand women whom, I came to understand, had been waiting for someone like me. To answer that question, I worked more hours, slept little, relaxed almost not at all, and drove longer distances.

Oregon is over ninety-eight thousand square miles with a distance of 663 miles from Brookings to Enterprise, and there is no way to drive across the state without going through a snow zone. Travel had to be planned carefully. One week, I logged over three thousand miles driving to meetings, conferences, and listening sessions. The constant travel and long hours in the car, combined with the constancy of hearing the stories of trauma and discrimination, began to take their toll. Getting home from that three-thousand-mile trip, I tipped over, so to speak. I called my boss and told her I had to cancel my upcoming appointments and stay home for a few days of recovery. She was very supportive, but it did not come without personal guilt over the cancellations. With one exception, the people I had to cancel with were all very understanding of my need to take care of myself.

Because of the vast distances, there are four different VA health systems that serve the needs of Oregon veterans, depending on where the veteran lives. Parts of Eastern Oregon use the Boise VA system; a small part of the Eastern/Central area utilizes the Walla Walla VA; most of the Willamette Valley, the Oregon Coast, and Central Oregon use the Portland/Vancouver VA; and Southeastern Oregon, Southern Coast, and part of the Willamette Valley/Cascades uses the Roseburg VA system.

Like all state veteran agencies, ODVA works in partnership and collaboration with the VA on local, state, and National levels, connecting them to veterans in similar and different ways. One of the things the VA does not like to admit is that their "veteran" is, by default, a white male, and it is for this segment of the population that virtually all care has been developed and prioritized for more than 150 years.[xxxiv] Similarly, ODVA had also historically focused on the default male veteran since its inception in 1945.[34] Fortunately, in 2016, Oregon became a state that recognized marginalized populations such as women veterans, LGBTQIA+, tribal, and incarcerated veterans and set out upon the path of moving toward equity for all. Prior to that time, these populations were lumped in with default male veterans, to their detriment.

The importance of this move toward working specifically with these groups was that, historically, they have received fewer benefits, and the care has not always been appropriate or accessible. For instance, the majority of military members come from rural communities, yet until the last few years, most of the VA offices, clinics, and providers were in cities, making care less accessible for rural veterans. Because women have been invisible as service members and veterans, their needs have been overlooked for decades. Then there was the culture, mentioned previously, of women being harassed and demeaned inside VA facilities, all of which led to reduced quality and accessibility. LGBGTQIA+ veterans, tribal veterans, and veterans of color have faced greater immense barriers to care over the years.

Sometimes, it's the little things that matter, like the fact that until the past few years, Black women could not get ethnically appropriate wigs, and people of color had to wear white prosthetics. One women's health provider explained to me how not having the full spectrum of women's health services can lead to problems in diagnosis and treatment. Her example was in pelvic floor treatment. She explained that in this case, there is generally a team of providers, from the doctor to the physical therapy specialist, who work together, which is necessary for the best outcomes. For women, the VA did not have this combination of specialty treatment entirely inside the VA, which led to disjointed and less effective care.

My job was to connect everybody, with women veterans being at the center of things.

The women veterans of Oregon began learning about and trusting me. I never made promises that things would work out—only that I would help. "I promise I will do my best." They feared repercussions by the VA or a VSO, so they had to know I would not use their name or any identifying information if they spoke about something negative anywhere. They trusted that when I spoke with the hospital director for their area about the various complaints coming in, I would strip out unique conditions or diseases that might identify an individual. They knew I would be writing down the complaints and taking them to whichever agency person was in charge, whether that would be VA, state agencies, or nonprofit organizations. They also knew that I would not use their name unless they gave permission. The end goal for all of them was not just about them but also to improve services in a system designed for men. This is why they allowed me to share. That, and sometimes they were just flat pissed off, and who could blame them?

Abiding by the ODVA commitment to shift the language, the title on flyers and email blasts said, "Are you a woman who served in the military?" When I had my way, the duration of the listening session was not listed with a start and finish time, but only a start time. I did not want the women to feel rushed.

And so they came. In four and a half years, they just kept coming, either to those events, by email or phone, or through a referral from a community partner. They came saying, "I saw the flyer… my friend/social worker/housing person said you could help me… I read about you in an email or article." Some said, "My husband/wife met you at the stand-down and suggested I call you."

At the end of my four and a half years, I had asked over two thousand women to "tell me what I need to know to help you."

So they kept telling me.

Breaks, Deep, and Wide

What I did not realize at the time was the depth to which these women's stories sunk into my soul. I listened as they gave me the details. They did not see me cry, noticeably crack, or show emotion or shock. Instead, they saw me listen without judgment, heard me say I was sorry these things happened to them, and watched me do everything to prove my statement that while there were no promises, I would do everything possible to help them. It did not occur to me that this carefully planned strategy of sacrificing my needs to help others would aggravate my mental health condition as I ramped up my work.

Everything was fine (nothing to see here) until one day, after a particularly hard listening session, I had a reaction that made me realize there were cracks inside of me that maybe were starting to make their way to the surface. So, I began to stock up on lacquer and gold, adding it daily as part of my makeup and dress-for-the-day routine, examining myself carefully to be sure every spot was covered. Sleeping pills, check. Makeup, check. Stylish outfit, check. Big smile, check. Wine, check. Mindless movies and television shows, check.

I assured myself every day that nothing had a negative effect on me. The stories—bury them deeper. It's all good here. I'm good. I'm great. Check, check, and check. When my bosses expressed concern about the amount of work I was doing and the fact that I just kept going and working and talking and writing, I assured them I was fine. "I'm fine. I'm great. I'm good. No worries at all!" Nothing to see here.

After all, there were things to do, women veterans to help. I did not have time to fuss over things like looming PTS and my own history born of issues with men in general and male veterans in particular. More lacquer, more gold. A guy challenges me because of something I said. More lacquer, more gold. My boss shows concern and asks me how I am. "I'm fine, thank you. See my shiny gold bits?" I sit down across from a woman, "Tell me what I need to know to help you." More lacquer, more gold.

This day, though, after this particular listening session, it took more than the usual efforts to cover the breaks. One of the women talked about the truly horrific story of her rape experience and how she continued to be not only emotionally but severely physically impacted every day because of what had been done to her. I left that session and knew that this time was different. I could feel myself struggling as her words continued to press into my psyche. *Just get to your car and you'll be OK*, was all I could think.

On the way to my car, I passed a man sitting on the street who said, "Hey beautiful, smile." What happened can only be described as a violent vision that flew through my inner eye in the few steps it took me to pass him: I was so filled with rage from hearing her story of what those men who were supposed to be her brothers and have her back had done to her, I envisioned myself kicking out my foot and striking that man directly in his throat while screaming, "Don't you *ever* tell another fucking woman to smile, you smarmy piece of shit, do you understand?" It was like a movie scene where someone has a flash of a memory, but it was me, having this flash of a thought that was so real I could see it.

When the flash was gone, I was still walking past him, and I just looked at him and kept going without a word. I am not sure what my face must have looked like, but what was clear on his changed expression told me he saw that vision inside of me. I said nothing, knowing inside that if I said anything at all to him, everything that had been bottled up for all those decades would come unleashed in primal fury.

I got to my car as quickly as possible and started driving. Within about fifteen minutes, something I had never experienced happened. I began shaking and crying so badly that it was necessary to pull over and collect myself. It was just raw anger and hatred toward the men who do this. This is not admitted to give you as a reader fodder to say, "See? She hates men," but to help you understand how someone who has had a trauma experience and then spends years supporting women who have been (sometimes violently) traumatized, can have this visceral reaction that is, in her circumstances, completely normal. Somewhere inside, I was able to acknowledge and be grateful for the fact that I had not kicked that man in the throat for sexually harassing me on the street.

This is what trauma looks like. This is what I call being broken in the stronger places. I was the strong person who sat and listened calmly to these stories from these women because if they could live through these horrific acts and then live through the memories and constant medical problems associated with them, then, goddammit, I could sit there and listen so they could get the help they needed, so their voice and truth could be heard. I made sure I was strong in order to do this work, but on occasions like this, something would snap. It was invisible to the world, something I never shared with a soul, but those moments took a lot of fucking lacquer and titanium powder to fix the breaks.

Lessons Learned—Sort of

It was not until I had been working as the Oregon Women Veterans Coordinator for some time that I applied for my own service-connected disability for my experiences of harassment and assault, and it was not my idea. But we'll get to that. For those of you who read the words "harassment and disability" in the same sentence and are tempted to think that harassment does not justify applying for and receiving service-connected disability, I'll stop you there.

Work Now, Heal Later

I was sexually harassed by the men in the Army every single day, all day long, while I was on base and in uniform, and that harassment was just as likely to be supported or conducted by noncommissioned officers and officers as it was lower enlisted ranks. It was only when I was away from the base and in civilian clothes that they were not verbally and mentally coming at me. I assure you that ongoing, never-ending sexual harassment has a harsh, negative impact on your mental health. But do not just take my word for it. Studies have shown that harassment can cause post-traumatic stress, depression, and anxiety. It can lead to trauma and is a risk factor for substance use, suicide, and homelessness. It is the foundation for sexual assault in the workplace, including the military.

No one tries to stop it from happening, even when you complain, and the worst part is that you are forced to go to your workplace and work with the perpetrators of this harassment every day. When in the field, you are also forced to live with/around them. In the military, when you are being harassed, there is no place safe and no safe place. It was in my office, at my company, in the cafeteria, in transportation, and on the street. Ever-present harassment is no small thing.

So, while I was helping all those women get their benefits, I was not thinking of me or my own disability benefits. I had made a point of being strong in my broken places so that I could support women veterans and do my job. My friend Gus, who was the lead trainer for veteran service officers in Oregon, was working with me on a woman's claim and talked to me about filing a claim for military sexual trauma myself. He had heard me stand in front of groups and talk about the experiences, challenges, and barriers faced by women veterans, speaking about sexual assault, harassment, rape, and intimate partner violence and their short- and long-term effects. I would encourage women to file, and I would encourage everyone else to understand and see MST and do their part in encouraging women to file for their benefits. They were conversations I had without even thinking of the words coming out of my mouth, so used was I to the script.

On this day, Gus said to me, "Liz, I want to gently bring something up that I think is important, and that is us filing a claim for you for your own military sexual trauma." We had quite an involved conversation about it where

Broken in the Stronger Places: From Resilience to Resourcefulness

he spoke to me about my insomnia, lack of relationships, trust issues, and more—all of which he had heard me casually mention. I started thinking and realized, *Yeah, yeah, that was it over all these decades. That is what it was that I had been feeling and experiencing and what had been interfering in my life.*

After returning from my three years in the Army, I stopped talking about my military service because, when I did, it led to jokes about the experiences I had—even the experiences of harassment and assault, and my complaints were oftentimes fodder for jokes. People wanted to hear stories, but these were not just stories: they were shitty fucking experiences I had, one after the other, these experiences of harassment and assault, of being grabbed, pushed, backed into corners, blocked from getting off the truck, and more.

I had never thought about my own experiences as being connected to military sexual trauma until my boyfriend brought it up during grad school and then again when Gus made his statement. While supporting me in working with and helping so many women, my friend Gus helped me get my service-connected disability for MST. He saw me, and that helped me begin talking openly about my own experiences, which I had done only with a select few in the past. For all of this, he will always hold a special place in my heart.

Over the four and a half years I was at ODVA, I heard so many stories, and it was different than sitting and listening to the women I had listened to over the previous years when I was working in the field of domestic violence and sexual assault and community safety. It was different because it was so often a reflection of my own experiences and a reminder of how lucky I was that I was not actually raped while serving. My understanding and desire for change became greater, but I found myself having to strengthen my resolve and my broken places even further when interacting with women veterans.

But at some point, those broken places they had made stronger would break. That moment could be the moment they said the words the very first time they talked about it, when they first admitted it after twenty, forty, or sixty years of keeping it tucked in the large pocket inside their soul. Like the woman I met who was seventy-nine years old and called me because her claim with the VA had been put off. Her claim had been dragged out to the point where it had been almost a year, inciting her to contact Senator Wyden's office to find out what the hell was going on.

Work Now, Heal Later

When something went to an elected official from a woman veteran in Oregon, it came to me to attempt resolution, and that was how I came to know this wonderful seventy-nine-year-old woman veteran. I phoned her and found out she had hired a scum-sucking attorney who had done nothing at all for her. Literally nothing: yet he would end up getting his fee anyway because that is the way it happens when a veteran hires an attorney. Scum suckers. (Side note to veterans: please do not hire an attorney to work on your claim. In the vast majority of cases I worked on, they did nothing except take a veteran's money. You can get free help from county veteran service officers and volunteer veteran service officers.) This wonderful elder of a woman veteran ended up receiving her claim solely because of the work I and the veteran's liaison at Sen. Wyden's office did. That bastard of an attorney did literally nothing for her, but the lawyer got his portion of the first check.

To this woman's story, though, she had carried what happened to her with her for the many decades since leaving the military at the age of twenty, telling no one. Fast-forward to 2018, when she was in a women's group and the topic of military sexual trauma came up. For the first time in her life, she uttered the words of what happened to her, and a young post-9/11 woman veteran sitting next to her said, "Ma'am, that's military sexual trauma. What happened to you is sexual assault, and you have what's called military sexual trauma. That's what you have." That group and the young woman sitting next to her were the impetus for this woman filing her claim. This is what women do for each other: we hold each other up and say the hard things and help our sisters through it, whatever "it" is.

When we were talking, I could hear her anger when she said, "Goddammit, they're the ones who told me. The psychologist in that group confirmed that it happened to me. The VA people are the ones who said I have military sexual trauma, and I have been seeing a psychologist for it since then. I was in groups before then, trying to figure it all out. I understand now after all of this. I understand why my kids are angry at me for the way I parented them and why I could not keep a marriage or even a relationship. I could not parent my children properly. I was not able to keep a job throughout my life. I could not keep my husband, all because of what happened to me in the military. I'm angry. You bet I'm angry! It destroyed my life. I filed my claim for MST, and

Broken in the Stronger Places: From Resilience to Resourcefulness

now they are denying it. I'm seventy-nine years old, and I've waited all these years, and they are denying my claim after telling me I have MST? You bet I'm pissed. I filed a claim because they told me I had military sexual trauma, and I want my claim resolved!"

This woman had tried to shore up her broken places for almost sixty years. She had hidden it all those years, adding band-aids and then lacquer and gold so she could be a mother, a wife, a friend, an employee, but those places kept breaking. They kept breaking, and at the age of seventy-nine, she was able to be angry for the first time in sixty years, putting words to what made her angry.

Broken in the stronger places can be so many things. It can mean going along the path when you put on a bandage or cast or whatever so you can keep going, and then it breaks again when something happens—a word, a behavior, an incident. Sometimes, it sneaks out there, and sometimes, it is a sudden occurrence of something that happens, but it does break again!

I met one woman in her forties who had suffered a heinous experience in the military and then covered it all with layers and layers of bandages covered in lacquer and gold. It was during the claims process that everything she had diligently covered over throughout the decades suddenly began to come out with a vengeance. All those stronger places she had spent twenty years covering suddenly shattered, and she began having a breakdown. "I don't understand," she said. I thought talking about it would make it better. All these decades, I've been fine, and now I'm not. Everything keeps coming back to me, and I'm struggling everywhere—in my marriage, and my job and with my relationships. I can't sleep. I'm a wreck."

Because we were both from rural locations and from similar climates, I used an analogy that I knew she would be able to understand and said, "You know how, when you were a child, there were all those large dirt areas, and after it rained and the sun came out you would see the cracked earth, but if you stuck a stick down inside of them sometimes water or mud would bubble up because the soil was cracked and dry on top but there was still water underneath? If you put the stick back into the hole, though, the water continues to come out, and the hole gets bigger."

She said, "Yeah, yeah, I know about that."

Work Now, Heal Later

I said, "Well, that's what you have done. You've poked a hole in it with a stick, and now it's going to keep coming out, and you cannot stop it. You cannot stop this by yourself. Get a support system. See a therapist. Know that, throughout this process, it is going to keep coming out because you broke open that cracked earth in your soul, and you cannot stop everything from coming out like the water from the ground. Now, for yourself, find people who can help support you. Find a woman veteran's group, a psychologist, a social worker, and keep that until you feel as if you no longer need it. Do not let the VA decide when your therapy is done: you stay with that, because all the way up until the end of this claim process, and even after, it is going to be raw, and it is going to bubble over. Take care of yourself, sister."

These are the types of conversations I would have with the women I helped. Making connections and giving analogies, encouraging them to get support. I was always honest with them about the fact that it was going to be harder before it was easier. Sometimes, I would sit and listen as they told me again about what happened to them. After a woman's compensation and pension exam, she would sometimes call me, angry, distraught, or crying because of how the appointment went.

Sometimes, I would go with her to the appointment, and then we would sit outside and talk until she felt better. I remember one time, sitting on a bench outside the office where she had her exam, her service dog came to me and laid his head on my leg. He stayed there for a long time. She looked at me and smiled, then said, "He knows there's something wrong. He knows you need him more than I do right now, and that's OK. I'm glad he is here for you."

I was the post-session counselor, and most of the time, I was the only one she could talk to about this stuff unless she had women veteran friends she could call or was working with a therapist. If her claim was denied, I would sit and listen some more as she completely broke down, and then I would promise we were not done, and I would keep helping her until the end.

One woman who had been violently assaulted in the military and continued to suffer serious physical, emotional, and mental problems from the assault came to me after her claim was denied by the VA and went into appeal. She had waited through multiple suicide attempts and twenty years to file her claim and was still denied by the VA, in spite of the mounds of evidence from the investigation, the trial of the rapist, and the diagnosis of her MST-related PTS and injuries that she submitted. Ultimately, after going through the reconsideration process, she finally received a 70 percent rating. She called and said, "It feels like they only believe my story 70 percent! I know that's not real, but that's what it *feels* like. I can't work, I'm suicidal, I'm losing my relationship with my husband, I meet all of the conditions of 100 percent, and yet they say I'm only 70 percent service connected." After listening, we talked about the next step and the work we would do to get her to 100 percent.

To clarify, the percentage of service connection disability for the VA represents the severity of a veteran's disability and how much it impacts their overall health and ability to function. Ratings range from zero to 100 percent. A zero percent rating means the disability exists but does not affect the veteran's ability to work or perform daily activities, while a 100 percent rating means the veteran is unable to work or perform daily activities. The amount of disability rating is what determines how much the veteran receives in service connection compensation.

From the day she filed the original claim until the day we finally helped her win a 100 percent service connection, she would reach out through regular, sometimes weekly, calls any time her strong places broke. I had her number in my phone, so anytime the phone rang, I would steel myself, knowing what was coming. I would answer, and she would immediately begin yelling at me until she was completely spent while I sat and listened. What I knew, though, was that she was not yelling at me. She was yelling at injustice, but it was me who answered the phone. I was the person who would listen and the person she could trust. I already knew all the details of what happened to her, but I learned much about her and from her during our association. My lesson was that she needed to keep telling the hard parts because those were crucial to her story and her life.

Her calls were a weekly reminder that sometimes people just need to get it out of their system: they don't need you to give advice or fix it. I learned over and over again how the pain of something traumatic can be just as real decades later and that claims are not about money but the validation of a veteran's experience.

As with my mother when she first shared her story with me, I sat silently in support until she was done, telling myself that if she could endure those things, I could bear witness and listen with no evident shock or tears. After about a year, she received news of her 100 percent service connection. My phone rang one day, and it was her. What I heard was a calm, quiet woman who said, "Liz, it's ___." Chuckling, she said, "I know I have yelled at you every single time I've called you and that you thought you were going to answer and hear me screaming at you again, but I'm not yelling today. I feel better today because I got my letter for 100 percent service connection, and you helped me. You helped me over this past year, and I don't know what I would have done without you. I may have killed myself. My husband probably would have divorced me. I want to thank you so much for sticking with me, for answering my calls, and for being there for me with no judgment over this past year. I thank you, my husband thanks you."

It All Matters

It never occurred to me that I could possibly do it any other way, that I could never listen to a woman or fight for her. It was my job, and it was the right thing to do, so I did it with fervent passion. If I did not do it, who would? Had I not taken the time to help these thousands of women veterans over the time I worked as the Oregon Woman Veteran Coordinator, who would? What would have happened to them? If I made their lives just a little bit better, it was worth it. I gave them someone they could trust, helped them file their claims, went with them to appointments, and connected them with people who could provide mental health services and/or claim support. I would often just sit and listen when no one else would.

This work did not stand alone, however. It came on the heels of nearly two decades of work with nonveteran women who had been physically, emotionally, and sexually assaulted and abused. Since my mother's story, I had sat and listened over and over and over again, and when I was not listening, I was reading, researching, writing, and talking about violence against women. It had become one with my soul, adhering like mesh to a healed wound.

Broken in the Stronger Places: From Resilience to Resourcefulness

I did not fully grasp over the years what the work meant to me and my own mental health, my soul, and self. I kept listening to their stories, as horrible as they were, and saying, "You're welcome. I'm so glad I was able to help. Thank you for trusting me."

I remember one time, years earlier, when I had first begun working in the field, one of my sisters asked me how I was able to sit and listen to all these women speak and not cry. How was I able to just sit and listen with a stoic face and not be affected or become personally involved? She wanted to know. My answer was, "You know, I can't answer that. I don't know how I learned to do this; it is just something I have done from the beginning. I knew instinctively that these women needed me to just sit and listen. It was their turn to cry, not mine."

Had I shown pain, horror, sadness, fear, or shock or shed a single tear when any one of these women spoke with me, it would have shut them down. Women do not want to make other women cry. Had I started crying, they would have said some version of "I'm sorry I made you cry." They would have apologized and stopped so that they did not make me cry, and then they would have felt bad.

Like my mother, the women I listened to over the decades, those whose stories I heard, needed someone to sit and hold space for their truths, someone who made it not about themselves but about the victim/survivor. It is hard for people to hear this truth, whether they are "helpers" or lovers, family members or friends. Survivor and victim truth that sounds like a red, oozing raw wound is too much for most people, so they are uninterested or unwilling to listen, leaving those of us in the field who are. We are the few.

It was my job to help them move forward, not stop them in their tracks or, worse yet, push them backward. So, from day one, I lacquered and lacquered and lacquered and held in the tears no matter how horrific the story, from the first to the last, my tears began to dry up until I got to the point where I did not have to force myself. Eventually, I did not even have to try not to cry: it just became second nature to listen without allowing their stories to cause me pain or emotion. I flat lined. With the exception of a few instances, I had no affect as they spoke.

This is not to say I never felt a thing. I felt compassion and empathy. The anger, sadness, and pain I learned to bury. There were some cases, though, those worse things imaginable done to women that it took me several days to recover. These were stories that I found I was unable to shake: stories that got into my soul, and they stayed there. But it was something I had to get through for them, that I had to help these women get through. Eventually, though, as the years wore on, it became ever more difficult. I was headed for a crisis point of my own, one where my desire to help others with their trauma became the breaking point of my own.

---

xxxiv Explore the Rich History of the Battle Creek VAMC. US Department of Veterans Affairs website. https://www.va.gov/battle-creek-health-care/about-us/history/#:~:text=The%20first%20National%20Home%2C%20now,Homes%20continue%20at%20VHA%20today. Viewed 07/29/2024.

What counts in life is not the mere fact that we have lived. It is what difference we have made to the lives of others that will determine the significance of the life we lead.

—**Nelson Mandela**

CHAPTER 11

Dreams and Nightmares

The End Game

I am proud of the work I did, and I am glad it was me. Nothing in my life will ever make me regret this path. My broken places are my own.

After I had my breakdown in DC, in one of my sessions with my psychologist she said, "My god, I cannot believe you lasted almost thirty years. Even after having your own experiences, you went into this field on purpose, and you were able to sit and be the receiver of so many stories. It is no wonder you are here, at this place in your life. Frankly, I'm surprised you lasted thirty years. That speaks to your resilience. Thirty years and thousands of stories; there are psychologists who have not been through your personal experience and have not made it that long."

My response: "Please don't talk about me like I'm a hero. I don't know how I did it, I just did, because that was my job, and it needed to happen." Early in my career my focus and passion was on making change—for one person, two people, a hundred, thousands. Whether I was helping one woman or was speaking at a conference in front of 400 women, it all mattered. That is the reason I did everything I did and stayed. When that woman came into my shop and said, "You're the reason I'm here" while I was at a low point in my life, it lit a fire under me, and that ongoing fire was the catalyst for the change I sought.

So, when I was invited to go to work at the VA Center for Women Veterans (CWV) in 2020, that promise of change was what drove me. I went in full of hope that I could make a bigger difference, because they were THE office for women veterans. I went into CWV filled with optimism, absolutely convinced that this work was going to make change for women veterans, that I had finally achieved a position where I could make a difference on a larger scale. This job was my opus.

Many women advocates understood that the then Secretary had little regard for women veterans. However, we also knew that the directors at the VA Center for Women Veterans knew how to work around him to get their work done. Our faith was not in him but in the women who served during his administration.

The VA Center for Women Veterans was founded in November 1994, literally as an act of Congress, who recognized that women were not receiving equitable care at the VA, we were unsafe, and we faced discrimination by the VHA and VBA. The intent of Public Law (PL)103-446,[35] Section 509, subsection 318, was to "advocate for equitable outcomes and access to VA benefits, services, and opportunities for women Veterans through education, outreach, and collaboration. By empowering women Veterans to achieve their life goals through VA benefits and services in collaboration with community stakeholders."[xxxv]

This public law is important to any woman veteran who wants to understand the role of the Center, designed to advocate on behalf of women at the VA, because it is very specific in how CWV is to operate. There are mandates and directives written in this law that are to serve as guidelines to the center director, the VA Secretary, the VA Deputy Secretary, and others as to the role and function of CWV. Nothing about the law has changed since 1994.

I will admit that during my career I did not always follow the rules precisely, but that was only in cases where it involved protecting women and children. The enforcement of rules and guidelines was what needed to happen, and sometimes, I had to force that by skirting the rules, as you read in

Dreams and Nightmares

Chapter 8. I never violated rules simply because I did not want to do what I was supposed to do.

Part of my breaking came from understanding that the new director was less inclined to follow the mandates and directives simply because she did not want to. Perhaps it was because she did not understand her mandates and directives, or perhaps it was because she was fearful of doing so, but either way, harm was done. For instance, her refusal to address the harmful policy that allows the VA to maintain medical providers who have sexually assaulted veterans so long as they hold their state medical license. When she stated that this was the information given by the Deputy Secretary, she was unable to confirm (or did not know) whether the policy covered those who were convicted or if it was just relevant to those with complaints/accusations filed against them. Either way, harm is done to vulnerable veterans through this policy, and her refusal to investigate and drive for change was counter to these three directives:

1. Serve as principal adviser to the Secretary on the adoption and implementation of policies and programs affecting veterans who are women.
2. Make recommendations to the Secretary, the Under Secretary for Health, the Under Secretary for Benefits, and other Department officials for the establishment or improvement of programs in the Department for which veterans who are minorities are eligible.
3. (10) Advise the Secretary when laws or policies have the effect of discouraging the use of benefits by veterans who are women.

Other actions that are counter to directives include failing to submit an appropriate budget required for operations; reducing outreach to women veterans, directly impacting their awareness of benefits, eligibility, and programs; failure to ensure compliance with appointing members to the Advisory Committee for Women Veterans; failure to publish research and studies significant to women veterans (or reporting incorrectly).

The relevance of her failures and the failures of the VA to this story is that they lent themselves to a toxic and stressful work environment. Despite the number of times she was advised that, under the new operations, we were failing to address PL 103-446, she refused to change her direction.

Broken in the Stronger Places: From Resilience to Resourcefulness

Prior to the appointment of Secretary Denis McDonough, there was a thorough understanding of the work required of the CWV Director in helping to establish policies and programs at the VA. This is not to imply that everything was perfect because it was not. There were occasions when the previous CWV Director was overridden or her recommendations overlooked. However, the CWV and their advisory committee were generally able to make recommendations and push through changes that mattered, ensuring that the unique challenges, experiences, needs, and issues of women veterans were in focus at the VA. Still, the Center was, unfortunately, not always consulted when an event or program was in the planning stage, which sometimes led to things going sideways and our office having to work on immediate reparation and solutions.

An example of this happened going into my second year at CWV, just prior to the administration change. The Undersecretary for Benefits at Veteran Benefits Administration worked with his team to host a national phone town hall about military sexual trauma. Town halls are popular events with the VA. They are VA-organized public sessions attended by veterans, family members in the audience, and VA leadership as panel members. Those in the audience can express concerns, thanks, suggestions, and thoughts with VA leaders. The event can be hosted by leaders in the VA Washington, DC, offices or by the leaders at state VA facilities. One of the most notable differences between a town hall and listening session is that, in a town hall, the VA representatives get a chance to tell attendees what they should have done or can do better in the future and to impart information. A listening session, however, is focused on the veterans in the room leading the discussion, without anyone expressing what should or could have been done by the veteran.

Regarding this particular town hall, we (CWV representatives) were later told that the intention was they would have veterans call in to address problems that had encountered with MST-related claims and, hopefully, find solutions they could use toward changes that needed to be made. *As my mother always said, though, the road to hell is paved with good intentions.*

They failed to include CWV or the Office of Military Sexual Trauma within the Office of Mental Health, and that failure directly impacted the outcomes of that event. Think for a minute about all the things that can go

Dreams and Nightmares

wrong when you fail to include two of the most relevant offices on the topic in your planning and implementation of a phone town hall on a massive scale. This is important not because of ego but because CWV, the Office of Women's Health, the Office of Mental Health, and Chief of Staff Pamela Powers had been working closely since the beginning of COVID on hosting multiple phone and video town halls for women veterans. This collaborative group understood that the VA could not stand by and simply wait for COVID to end. For the sake of the veterans we served, we had to pivot and continue to offer outreach and listen to what the women wanted and needed.

We had conducted at least a dozen such outreach events successfully, and each time we used our new knowledge to improve the next event. Unfortunately, when you have experts at your disposal and refuse to use them because you have an "I-am-an-island-and-want-all-the-credit" mindset, things tend to nosedive straight into hell. VBA successfully invited disaster with this town hall by excluding all our offices.

Because I have a diagnosis of MST-related PTSD, it is on my VA medical records, as is the case with hundreds of thousands of other veterans. On December 17, 2020 they roto-dialed us—all of us. I cannot remember the exact words of the auto-dial voice when I answered, but it was something to the effect of "Welcome to the VBA town hall on military sexual trauma. Please press 1 (or whatever it was) to join the event." The message gave some indication that benefits would be discussed, so because of my job and my specialty area, and because I was curious about this town hall we had not been notified of, I pressed 1.

I heard one of the hosts talking and introducing the event (the undersecretary of benefits maybe?), and after a few more minutes of "yada, yada yada, we are amazing" back-patting, they invited callers to phone in, unleashing the pain of the few into the ears and hearts of the many. Caller after caller phoned in and quickly became emotionally distraught (one near hysteria) while telling their own stories of rape. I was listening, first in interest and then almost immediately in horror, that no one was going to help the caller or stop this train wreck. I found myself sitting in my living room, saying to myself out loud, "Somebody stop this, someone do something. Where's a counselor to take over their call? *Why are you allowing this to continue?*"

Broken in the Stronger Places: From Resilience to Resourcefulness

As stated, I have decades of experience as a victim's advocate and have heard these stories over and over, but I was always prepared. I knew going into every single conversation that I might hear tragic, painful, horror-filled stories that are what nightmares are made of, so I was always ready. But this? Even I was not prepared for the racing heart, tears, and overwhelming feeling of anger and sadness that hit me, because I did not expect a town hall to consist of people sharing their stories of rape in detail. Partway through the third caller's story, I threw my phone across the room screaming, "What the *fuck* is wrong with you people!" I called my boss and gave her the rundown. She was appropriately horrified and angry.

Turns out I was not the only person on the call who had such a deeply visceral reaction. We learned the next day that the Office of Mental Health started getting call after call to their hotline from veterans who had been horribly triggered by the event. Although both women and men had been harmed, the majority of the calls coming in were from women. We also started receiving emails, and on a number of women veteran Facebook pages I began seeing post after post from women who had been on that call. All were deeply disturbed and justifiably enraged that (a) their privacy had been violated and they had been roto-dialed because they have MST and (b) they had been subjected to these detailed stories of sexual assault when what they expected was to hear useful and helpful information on VA benefits and claims. It was a nightmare of the highest order.

Meetings began to be called, and this time CWV and the Office of Mental Health were invited. We began the process of doing anything we could to help all these veterans, but it was too little too late. One thing we made clear to the VBA team was that they had thoroughly screwed up that town hall and were solely responsible for the damage. Had they simply brought us in at the beginning, such an event designed that way would never have happened.

Acting as the voice of the aftermath, CWV sent apologies to those that we heard from who had been harmed through a singular act of ignorance. Unfortunately, there was nothing we could say, offer, or do to make it better, and those who had been on the call made it clear that they were not interested in hearing from us. They wanted an apology from the Undersecretary for Benefits, but he and his team had gone radio silent. The result of this nightmarish event was that the leaders of the House Committee on

Veterans Affairs issued a cease-and-desist on further town halls and demanded answers, none of which I believe they ever received.

All the good we and others had done in outreach over the past eighteen months had been undone by one egotistical act that epitomized bureaucratic failure. We all simply waited for the new administration to take over in January and hoped things would be better. The impact on veterans was that they lost confidence and trust in the VA, too many assuring us and others that there was nothing the VA could do to get them back. When we view this through the proper lens—that of the veteran—it is easy to understand how such an institutional failure harmed the humans that counted on them.

Applying this to the administration that followed on the heels of such a failure, the saying about the road to Hell can also be phrased this way: the road to hell is paved with false hope, because the new administration was not only *not* an improvement, but they brought an entirely new set of problems. Hopes dashed.

One Step Forward, Two Slides Back

When I was invited to come to DC and serve as her Deputy Director at the Center for Women Veterans in 2020, I was honored and excited. The majority of my career has been a commitment to improving care and services for women and girls across the continuum. Since obtaining my graduate degree, I had devoted myself to women veterans. This was my opportunity to elevate my work and dedication to improving life for women veterans, so the yes was out of my mouth nearly before she finished her question.

At that time, the director had worked under three Presidents, a post-military career that spanned decades of working in both the White House and the VA. She knew how to get things done, regardless of their political leanings. For her, it was about the people and the work, not politics, but she also understood completely how she had to work within the political framework to accomplish goals and outcomes. She embraced the idea that good could be found in the work of those who came before her, and her job was to build on the foundation they had left so their efforts were not to be erased. Her approach was to expand on what her predecessors had done.

This is how she managed the Center for Women Veterans when she became Director. Her goal was to build on the successes of the previous Directors while also focusing efforts on enhancing CWVs presence nationwide so that women veterans and others not only knew we were there but saw us as a valuable resource and partner. Given that our focus was on improving services to two million women veterans—including increasing not just quantity but quality for those served, her leadership was initiative rich. She respected my expertise and saw me as a way to keep an eye toward policy, utilizing my knowledge about women veterans while simultaneously building strong outreach and addressing internal (VA-wide) change.

We got things done. We increased outreach, included the indigenous women veterans' population in ways they had not been in the past, and were making plans to expand further by connecting to women veterans in outlying territories and around the world. She made sure we were conducting round tables and forums monthly—including the partnership with other offices—during COVID when the world was shut down. The upside was that because my boss was who she was, she had people who said yes when she wanted something done, and they were more than happy to reach out to the Director of the Center for Women Veterans to fulfill expectations they had for their offices and VA. With these collaborative partners, she made sure our office was asked or invited to the table, and when we were not and she found out, she made sure we were there. Getting to a yes was something she was very good at!

I knew going in under the Wilkie administration that he was a conservative appointed in 2018 whose focus did not include underserved populations, but he also did not get in the way of those who did the work because he understood it made him look good. I knew that the CWV team knew how to fight the fight and was 100 percent involved in making change. She knew how to manage because she had spent decades doing work under different administrations and in locations. If there was a policy or guideline written that needed our input or change, she would go after it. If I brought something important to her attention, she did the same. Regardless of the president, the director knew how to get things done.

When Secretary Denis McDonough came on board, I remember clearly how I felt when he said, "I am going to prioritize women veterans. All veterans will receive equitable care under my administration. Women veterans will be a priority as long as I am secretary." I was excited and looked forward to the possibilities for women veterans with him as secretary. It was some much-needed lacquer and gold because we imagined it would make our jobs easier. False hope.

The Emperor's New Clothes[xxxvi]

With the administration change, it became clear to me that those days of hope and making a difference were over. Soon, it was apparent that making change was going to be more of a challenge because it was a new administration at the VA, and incoming VA leaders either did not understand the work and mission or did not care. Maybe both? From my viewpoint, they seemed less concerned about women veterans than their careers. Truth, compassion, and change took a back seat. They began implementing their own party line: that it happened to men too, we could not say "women," and the CWV no longer had the authority or ability to ensure necessary change or improvement for women. So much for prioritizing women veterans.

My stronger places began crumbling under the weight of this truth.

I almost immediately became concerned about their direction and the director who would come next. Nevertheless, I still believed in McDonough. I believed that he and the people brought on under him would have the same care and concern I had seen. I believed all I had to do was wait for them to find their level. Instead, what happened was that I began seeing the dark truth, which I came to call "The Emperor's Clothes."

I was beginning to see disconnectedness. What I saw seemed more like the Emperor who was convinced he was wearing cloaks of gold—encouraged by the false praise of his minions - but was naked. I saw a man who was either a) disconnected and unconcerned about what was happening under him or b) easily manipulated by those around him. Maybe both? I'm still not sure which, but neither of those make for a good leader. This became obvious when the story and hearings about sexual assault being perpetrated by the

Broken in the Stronger Places: From Resilience to Resourcefulness

deputy assistant secretary for resolution management, diversity and inclusion at the Department of Veterans Affairs came to light in 2024. Along with that came the betrayal survivors feel when a superior knows it is happening and does nothing. Such was McDonough's story. I was gone from the VA by this time, but it struck me deep in my soul nevertheless.

During the new administration's onboarding, people began expressing frustration similar to mine as it became clear that these new appointees did not really care about women and LGBTQIA+ veterans so much as their party line and their own careers. The people in charge of hiring the senior executive service appointees began hiring people with no experience or understanding of veterans and without a basic understanding of how the federal government works—like budgets. And, although there is nothing necessarily wrong with not knowing, they seemed to have zero interest in learning or gaining knowledge and experience related to any veteran population. As these new people came in and began disregarding and overlooking the advice and efforts of those with experience and knowledge, people who had been with the VA for decades began to leave, including many at the junior management level, such as deputy directors.

I was the interim director for four months and was facing exhaustion and burnout. I had no deputy, and we were short-staffed by three. One day, several months into my interim role, I went into the deputy chief of staff's office with my resume and asked to be considered for the position. He said, "You aren't qualified." I looked at his bachelor's degree hanging on the wall, pointed to the section on my resume that showed my master's in social work from Columbia University, along with my decades of experience, and reminded him that I was, in fact, qualified and had been doing a great job for four months. He backtracked, saying he did not mean to say I was not qualified but that they already had some people who had been vetted. He went on to pretend to give me buy-in by interviewing the two final candidates.

Why do I say 'pretend'?" He and the other senior advisor had invited me to write my own questions for the candidates and asked me to share with them, which I did without hesitation, with the understanding that the candidates would not see my questions. During the interview, one candidate rose to the top, answering all the questions exactly how the answers would have sounded if I had given her a script. The two who hired her shared with me that she was their pick. However, almost immediately after she was hired, I began to notice that she did not have the experience needed, and it became clear she was either not capable of or had no intention of doing the things she had agreed to in the interview.

For instance, during the interview, one of my questions was how she felt about pushing back at leadership when necessary (put in the context of the work we did for women veterans). She assured me in the interview that women veterans were her number one priority, she would uphold the CWV mission and mandates, and that she had no problem with pushing back. However, on day two she showed for the first time her unwillingness to push back when she advised she did not submit the budget I had written requesting a necessary additional $300,000 (in government budgets, not a lot of money).

As deputy director, the budget was in my lane. As an experienced deputy director, and as the interim executive director, I wrote the budget with full understanding of the risks and limitations we faced with the budget we had been given. My knowledge of the budget process, the history of our office, and the needs that would best support women veterans informed my budget development. In other words, I knew how much money we needed to request in order to fulfill our congressional mandates and our commitment to women veterans.

Because of COVID, the Veteran Canteen Services (VCS), from whom we received $150,000, disappeared. Leadership at VCS had advised us in February 2021 that because VA canteens had been shut down during COVID, they did not have the profit necessary to continue funding us. They were in the red and had no idea when that might change. It was difficult news that we knew would hurt our outreach program and the work of our advisory committee.

Losing this $150,000 meant that we would have a serious shortfall in paying for outreach, travel, and the convening of the Advisory Committee on Women Veterans. In the request for the $300,000, I included this explanation, as well as pointing out that our increase over the past years was lower than that of the Center for Minority Veterans. I anticipated that the secretary's office would likely not give us that full requested amount, but we had an excellent shot at the replacement of the $150,000 because that's how government budgets work. You ask for a lot more than you want in hopes of getting what you need.

Never having worked for the government and with no understanding of the budget process, this new Director refused to submit my budget. Instead, she removed my request and submitted the original budget we had been given with no changes. I went back to her and explained the potential problems and fallout from her actions. I attempted to convince her that the approach I had taken was not only necessary to our office but encouraged and supported by our budget person in the Office of the Secretary and asked her to resubmit the budget with my increase intact. Her response was that she was unwilling to shake things up with the new administration so soon. The result was that we ended up with only the amount allocated in the original budget we were sent by the Secretary's office, which was entirely insufficient and negatively impacted our ability to conduct in-person outreach and support the advisory committee in conducting hospital visits and in-person meetings. So much for pushing back.

Over the remainder of my time at CWV, I would see the results of how her decision impacted our ability to conduct outreach and provide support to women veterans. The Advisory Committee on Women Veterans was not able to meet in person, in-person congressionally mandated visits to VA hospitals would be out of the question (each visit meant paying travel, per diem and a stipend to each of the twelve members of the Committee), and outreach at national conferences would be limited due to lack of funding. This was one of those disregarding mandates that rubbed me the wrong way. These mandates are not to be interpreted as optional, yet here we were. When other staff members and I tried to explain it to her, she would instruct us to write up the reports in a way that matched PL 101-146. We tried to explain that was not how it worked, but she was unconcerned. She, after all, would not be the person sitting in a chair facing a potentially hostile transition team.

Having been through a presidential transition, I was 100 percent clear about the process. The transition teams speak to the deputy directors, not the directors, who are political appointees. They wanted career people. I had faced the inquisition and understood what would be expected in the next transition: that they would be required to report on what they had done to implement directives and mandates. I also understood it was not going to go well because we were not doing what we were supposed to be doing. It added immense stress to my job, knowing that honesty about our failures would not go well, but neither was lying an option.

In retrospect I came to believe she had been coached to give the answers they knew I wanted to hear during the interview. They wanted her, and they used me to get her. Literally everything she said to me in the interview that she believed or would do was exactly what she *did not do*. Although she is a veteran, she had little understanding of the unique challenges, needs, issues, and experiences of women veterans, and learning or advocating for our needs seemed irrelevant.

During the interview, she talked about the importance of change, of policy implementation and advocacy, of pushing back, of our outreach team and our office growing our initiatives. She spoke of respecting the approximately fifty years of collective experience present on our staff and building on the foundation built by previous directors. But as soon as she took over she began doing the opposite of all of this. She was not a team player, and was a severe micro-manager. Good leaders are never micro-managers. She was entirely uninterested in conducting initiatives, and canceled events that were already planned. Instead, she seemed more concerned about how bright the spotlight was on her.

For the next fourteen months, she and I had differences. She began to exclude me from all meetings and decisions and, toward the end, I discovered that she lied to me about our participation in several areas. While she assured me that she "would ask" or submit a request for me to be involved in committees or task forces, she did not. I learned that she was withholding information from me and staff and not following through with feedback or requests. On its face, this may not seem to be an issue, but it was important because her actions and inactions impacted how we met women veterans in their spaces and advocated for their needs. The lack of outreach and initiatives silenced the voices of women veterans nationwide.

Offices in the government are structured so that the second in command, the deputy directors, have full knowledge of what is going on in their office. It is what I call the "hit by a bus" planning approach. It is a failsafe for the

Broken in the Stronger Places: From Resilience to Resourcefulness

second—the right hand - to know everything so if the director leaves suddenly, the deputy can take over, and the office can continue operating. This played out in real time when they broke the contract of my director and others and sent them on their way, showing that the design worked.

Because my previous director made sure that I was in meetings and had 100 percent awareness of everything that was happening, I was able to step in and take over seamlessly when she left. Under this new director, though, the design was ignored, in spite of warnings I and others gave her. Had she suddenly disappeared, our office would have struggled with catching up because of the fact that no one in the office, even me—the person who was supposed to be the right hand, the failsafe—literally had zero knowledge of what she was doing.

An example of this is her work with a national corporation. She had been meeting with them for about six months and had not brought in any of the CWV staff for planning or input, including me—a reoccurring situation we had discussed repeatedly. We could see meetings on her calendar, so we knew she was meeting with them, but when asked she would give a vague nonanswer. One day, a few weeks before I left, she brought me a talking sheet on the implementation plan for what she had been planning with them.

I scanned it briefly, laid it down, and said, "Without further conversation and a full read of this, I can tell you off the top of my head at least six reasons this will not work. Had you brought in staff, this stuff would have been brought up and it could have been addressed. Now, you either have to start over with the team involved or face failure." She uttered some excuses and walked out. The saddest part of this is that it could have been an excellent partnership, but because her mode of operation was to do everything without her team, it did not have a chance for success.

Why was this her approach? I can only guess it was because, as was her mode of operation, she wanted to be the only person in the know. Her goal was to have her name attached to everything we did, so much so that she excluded myself and the outreach and communication directors from vital meetings. She had no expertise in women veterans or their challenges, issues, experiences, and needs, was not learning, and failed to ask those who did.

In Spring 2022 when she stated that the Deputy Secretary told her VA policy was to not fire medical providers who are sex offenders as long as they retain a state license, I challenged her to do something—to fix it. She insisted there was nothing she could do, to which I responded that there is a legislative mandate, a public law, that defines her role, stating clearly that the director and CWV are to effect policy change, conduct advocacy, and ensure safe, equitable services. This is a policy being enforced without public knowledge, and which she was unwilling to bring to light or change. When I continued to inquire about this policy, she told me it was to protect the VA from being sued. At that point, I reminded her that the VA employed a legion of attorneys who, surely, could find a way around it. Additionally, I suggested that perhaps a lawsuit was what we needed, because it would put medical providers who harm veterans on notice that their days of conducting this behavior were coming to an end. She was uninterested.

I reminded her that women veterans were being harmed by this policy, and it was literally our Congressional mandate to work toward changing laws, policies, and guidelines that harmed or did not serve women veterans. She stuck by her insistence that she could not. To my knowledge, that policy stands today. Who knows how many veterans have been harmed over the years by this policy that protects sex offenders?

From day one she had stopped our initiatives and refused to engage staff in outreach and initiatives, focusing instead on herself and what she believed made her look good. I was watching the Center for Women Veterans change at the hands of someone who did not care about women veterans or our mission, and it pained my soul.

When Hope Is Gone

There's a scene in *The Fifth Element* where Leeloo (the Fifth Element) has been watching the history of the world, and you can see the impact it is having on her as she witnesses reel after reel of wars, bombs, death, and destruction we human beings have meted out against one another over the millennia. [xxxvii] She collapses in on herself and becomes unable to care about doing the job she is supposed to do, devastated by bearing witness to the enormity of

Broken in the Stronger Places: From Resilience to Resourcefulness

the inhumanity of humans. What she sees is humans focused on killing and destroying one another, which leads her to question her mission and whether the world is worth saving.

That has always resonated, but toward the end of my career it became real for me as I collapsed emotionally, mentally, and even physically and became unable to do my work. This collapse was brought about, in part, because of the change in administration and the hopelessness I had begun to feel about change in the VA.

What is the purpose if we cannot make change, when we run out of hope? With every ounce of lost hope, the breaks widened beyond repair.

Throughout my career in the field of domestic violence and sexual assault, and even before that, I was able to use my intellect and fierce determination to make change and approach how I worked—to use my rational, logical self and my sheer tenacity and passion to effect change. This effort brought numerous successes and changes not only on the macro level, but on the micro as well. I understood that it was not affecting the whole of everything, but it was making a difference for those who needed it, and hopefully that would spread. This changemaking is how I was able to continue doing my work over the decades. I was able to continue hearing the stories because my experience and thoughts were guided by the belief that change for one person mattered.

All of this soul and passion had been enough to push me through difficulties and challenges for the sum of my adult life, right up until it was not, but that light was dying, and it was the VA sucking it out of me.

---

xxxv   Center for Women Veterans website, https://www.va.gov/womenvet/cwv/index.asp, viewed 06/20/2024

xxxvi   The Emporer's New Clothes [book]. Anderson, Hans Christian, 1837.

xxxvii   The Fifth Element (1997) [Film]. Luc Besson. Paris, London, Rome, Iceland, Mauritania. Gaumont and Columbia Pictures.

I decided it is better to scream. . . . Silence is the real crime against humanity.

—**Nadezhda Mandelstam**, *Hope Against Hope*

CHAPTER 12

And Just Like That

So, there I was, September 30, 2022, sitting in a meeting with all the same suspects, or leaders as they like to call themselves. It was the VA's Sexual Assault Prevention Committee, which I had finally been invited to attend after almost a year of asking.

My nearly thirty years of experience gave me expertise that would have benefited the Committee and its outcomes, especially given the fact that few of them had experience in the field. It was not my boss who invited me, but a peer who questioned why I was not attending and sent the invitation. She was someone I highly respected who had years of knowledge and experience in the field of violence against women. My boss was thoroughly surprised to see me on the Teams call.

They were talking about the work that was being done—work mandated under the Deborah Sampson Act.[36] It was intended to ensure improved services and care for women veterans. It was the Secretary's committee, because if you have committees and do the stuff and say the words, that means you care, right? You don't have to actually make progressive or real change that will impact their safety, benefits, or change. You just have to say, "Look, we have a committee! Look at these charts, aren't they amazing!"

Broken in the Stronger Places: From Resilience to Resourcefulness

You can carry on, knowing that women are experiencing sexual assault in the offices of your appointees and in your hospitals and clinics and just pretend it does not exist, and as long as no one important knows, your words matter, right? You can cherry pick data and leave out the populations you swore you would prioritize, and if you put them alongside things people want to hear, no one notices. Look how the Emperor's beautiful cloaks of gold shimmer.

Except some of us do notice.

The truth is, few of the people in charge knew anything about sexual assault or prevention. Of the group, the most noticeable was the one person who should have been a subject-matter expert—or at least had a modicum of knowledge: the woman who was the Director of the Office of Assault and Sexual Harassment Prevention. I was somewhat aware of her history with the VA, so when she was appointed to this position, I looked at her VA bio and researched her professional history. In so doing, I found that she knew almost nothing specific to the field of sexual assault and harassment and had no comprehensive history in the field.

The lack of knowledge and experience in the field hindered the effectiveness of their work, which means they ended up with an ineffective process and protocol for the silenced and disempowered victims. I struggled greatly with this reality because I understood that it was not just about our congressional mandate not being fulfilled, but women continuing to be unsafe and underserved. My integrity had begun to feel raw and pained, but by this time, my frustration over what felt like a betrayal of women veterans was approaching "open wound" status.

Regardless of the fact that women veterans continually expressed a lack of personal safety at the VA and complaints about sexual assault and harassment continued to flow into our office, the committee's work seemed to be counter to the best interests of women veterans or, at a minimum, irrelevant to our collective and individual reality.

It was during this meeting that I realized I could not do this any longer. The leaders were all congratulating themselves on the work they had done. Though there was no research or evidence to prove it as a best practice, they had deemed their word salad diagram as "best practice," just as they had with their poorly constructed bystander intervention program that completely left out women as victims of male sexual harassment in the VA. It was an ongoing struggle for me to hear the VA throw about the words "best practice" when in fact what they were doing was not.

Best practices are built from evidence found through data and peer review. Leaving out important findings or changing a recognized best-practice program to fit your needs cancels its best practice standing. VA does both, erroneously applying the phrase even though they just made stuff up to suit them. As a person who has spent decades in the social services field developing and implementing best-practice programs, VA practices were counter to my integrity when it came to program and policy development.

Ironically, while the intent of the Deborah Sampson Act was for the VA to be a safer place for women veterans, they did not really talk about women, instead preferring their white male cisgender default word "veterans," which too often left out those of us who are not default. This is how the VA ends up with policies and programs that do not actually work for everyone. The simplest solution to this language is use inclusive language that states "women veterans, veterans who identify as women, and veteran men." An example of why this is important can be found in discussions and planning for homelessness and suicide. The rates for women are different than they are for men, as are the reasons they become homeless or commit suicide. When we exclude women, this information gets lost, which impacts how program planners and funders approach solutions.

When I brought up women, they kept insisting it happens to all veterans and they could not use the word "woman." And while it is true that it happens to men as well, they refused to acknowledge the fact that, according to their own studies,[xxxviii] it happens that women are the targets of harassment and sexual assault inside VAs with far more frequency than men, and veteran men are statistically most likely perpetrators of this harassment and violence against women. They refused to acknowledge that women are more at risk than men. Par for the course for the VA, they were walking past all their own research relevant to the topic and just doing what they wanted. And still, they called their work best practice. I just could not.

From where I sat, VA leaders were unwilling to accept lessons learned or recommendations made under previous administrations. They all want it to be their great big idea, which is fine, unless you are ignoring millions of dollars' worth of studies and findings.

Despite what I and others had said over the past year, the talking heads in the meeting refused to acknowledge that their bystander intervention program is flawed. Deeply flawed. The designers stood on the shoulders of those who came before them, borrowed from their bodies of work, ignored the best parts, and kept only what they, in their collective incompetence on the subject, wanted. They ignored the recommendations of experts and studies and hobbled together a worthless video that supported their narrative that male veterans cannot be accused of sexual assault or harassment and women do it too.

Since day one of my boss' arrival at CWV fourteen months prior, I had engaged her in numerous conversations about sexual assault and prevention at the VA and the need to involve the Center for Women Veterans and me as the subject-matter expert. In our interactions there was always me explaining facts about sexual assault and harassment, sharing VA and other data, and urging her to get me on that committee.

To be fair, she occasionally allowed that she had no knowledge of sexual assault and harassment or prevention at all except what I gave her. Fortunately, when a request came in for CWV to speak at an internal or external event about the topic, she did ask me to do that part. Usually if there was an email or a topic, she referred to me so that I could answer the questions. This alone is not bad, because not everyone can be or is a subject-matter expert, and she was using me as she should have at these points. However, the problem was her refusal to learn or lead so that she had the necessary tools when working in committees on policy, guidelines, or programs, or to refer me to any of these committees. She relied on me to feed her the details when it was necessary, but when I was not in the room, her lack of knowledge was a detriment.

This was not just the case with this topic, but with women veterans in general. When she spoke about any topic relating to women veterans, it was generally from a position of ignorance, only able to speak to what was on the PowerPoint slide or in her notes. Even when it came to us explaining to her how she needed to report data on the survey we had constructed and disseminated, she refused to listen, which turned into her reporting data incorrectly.

No matter how hard we tried, we could not get her to understand the problem inherent in reporting inaccurate data.

It had taken about a year for CWV to develop a survey that would help not just our office but partners everywhere understand if and why women veterans were or were not using the VA. We had carefully constructed the survey to have wide demographics that VA had few studies on, such as understanding the gaps and needs of LGBTQIA+ veterans. Data could be pulled with multiple specific variables that included age, gender, era, branch, LGBTQIA+ status, and more. It was the first time the VA had engaged in such a study.

Our survey had only one question on MST, which the respondent could opt out of. We had inserted this question so as to sort the survey results by those who reported having MST and those who did not. For instance, that information would help us understand if women who reporting having MST were more or less likely than their counterparts who did not to use benefits and services. Consequently, when reporting the data, the correct approach when showing how veterans with MST differed from those without was to talk about the 'opt out' option and explain that the set was not all survey respondents. Inaccurately reporting data, implying that all members of one group (in this case MST) represented the entire body of respondents, was the equivalent of lying about findings, intentionally or out of ignorance. Either way, not a good look. In spite of repeated coaching on this, she insisted on reporting the MST data as if it was from all respondents and not just those who opted in on the question. Programs developed from erroneous information are less than effective, yet she continued to report inaccurate findings.

As for the Sexual Assault and Prevention Committee, the trend continued insofar as this workgroup: I would give her my input, which was often critical and not in alignment with the suggestions of the workgroup, and then she would tell me she had no authority and had to be careful how she approached whatever the topic was. I had worked with previous directors under her predecessor, and I understood that this was false. She did have the authority assigned to her job, because the office was Congressionally mandated, as were her guidelines and directives. I frequently reminded her that it was our job to push back when it came to women veterans, but she repeatedly failed to do this. Integrity was consistently lost in our work, and my internal struggles, including frustration and concern, with this grew.

During this meeting on September 30, 2022, they were coming to the end of their work. This meeting felt like an opportunity for them to review what they had done and again congratulate themselves on a job well done. Each presenter in the group brought up their own slides to share their amazingness, and then my Director came on. When her slides came up, the first one showed the title "Senior Advisor, Secretary's Workgroup on Sexual Assault and Prevention."

I looked at that slide remembering the repeated requests I had made to her and her ongoing assurances that she had no authority. Her answers: "I'll try, I can't make any promises, I don't have any authority," rang in my ears. I knew exactly what that that title "Senior Advisor" meant, which was that she had authority and was one of the leaders on the Workgroup. The problem was not that she held this title and was engaged, but that she had lied to me and dismissed my requests and recommendations.

Unbeknownst to me, she had been involved but had simply been excluding me and denying that she had involvement. This was how she conducted the business of our office, doing it all herself and hiding her work from the rest of us. She was like a toddler who grabbed everything and said, "mine." It became clear to me when I saw that slide that she had deceived me about her role in the committee and on the workgroup.

As I looked at that slide and realized how much she had kept from me for the past year, as if I was some outsider or stranger, I snapped. As had been the trend with her, she did not want my involvement because she saw spotlights and credit where the rest of us saw effectiveness and improved practices, even though the work is not supposed to be about who gets credit. Whereas my interest and passion was the equity and safety of two million women veterans, hers was the advancement of her career and looking good. Every shred of integrity inside of me that had been violated suddenly tore to pieces.

Heart pounding, breath shallow, I took my mouse in hand, moved my cursor to "Leave Meeting," and clicked. This was just one small incident, but it was on top of everything else that had happened with her over the past year. It was the proverbial straw that broke the camel's back. At that moment all of my stronger places snapped. It feels impossible to explain how everything that had been building steadily for the past fourteen months culminated into this palpable breaking inside of me. I was not sure if I was having a heart attack or an anxiety attack, so I called my friend AnnMarie and explained everything that happened.

She said, "First thing, we need to make sure you are OK. Do I need to come over there? Let's make sure your heart rate is OK and you are breathing properly." She asked me several times if she needed to come to my home and stayed on the phone with me until she believed me when I said I was better.

Then she said, "I want you to pull up Outlook and write this email," and she told me what to write, word for word, which, in summary, was this: I am going on sick leave, my workplace has become a hostile work environment. The CWV has become an unsafe place for me to work, and I will be using my sick leave for time off. I will be working with my therapist and will let you know when and if I will return."

That was the last day I was at work, with a couple of small exceptions that involved staff, since I felt it important to provide them with some support (like completing their performance evaluations), before I left. My decision to leave that day did not happen in a vacuum, because I had been questioning how much longer I could do this. That meeting was just the snapping point.

Not surprisingly, there was no response from her for two days. The HR representative cc'd on the email responded immediately, but nothing from my boss. When she finally responded, she was asking me to take care of four separate tasks, one of which she had taken from me months previous. My response to her was that she could do it herself, and legally she was not allowed to contact me, as I was on an allowed mental health break.

A Ragged Break

This decision to leave was the result of months of stress and anxiety brought about by a combination of my own PTS and the toxic work environment. It was the apex of actions and events of the past fourteen months, but mostly all that had taken place between April and September 2022.

In April, two women who had been sexually assaulted in VA facilities had come to CWV for help, as had one in August who filed a claim with such horrific experiences of rape in the military that not only should she never have been denied by the VA, but she should also have left the military with 100 percent service connection. Instead, she was denied by the VA because of their inept handling of her claim.

This woman veteran who filed the claim had requested a woman examiner, but they connected her with a man. As is the case with many veterans during the claims process, she believed she could not say no to an exam, so she went through with it. Veteran readers, a tip: Yes, you do have the right to say no to an exam and request a different examiner. If you want a woman and find out your examiner is a man, you can ask for a new exam date with a woman provider.

Not only was her examiner a man, but he was also an aggressive man. The two combined brought on a mental health crisis for her that unfolded while she was talking to him, leading to her mentally and emotionally checking out while on the call. The real-life impact of this was that she simply disconnected mentally and answered yes to everything, just so she could end the nightmare that was the exam. This tremendous failure on the part of VBA—a failure that thoroughly traumatized a woman who had brutalized during her military service—ended with her claim being denied.

Her case was in appeal, and when it came to my desk and I took it to the proper authority, explaining everything that had gone wrong in the Veteran Benefits Administration side, I was told there was no way they (VBA appeals) could look at it outside the regular appeals process, and it just had to wait its turn in appeals. It was irrelevant to the people in appeals that VBA had completely and entirely screwed this up egregiously from the beginning, proving incompetence on their part during the compensation and pension (C&P) exam. I made my case and gave them the facts as to the monumental errors of the VBA that had led to the denial, but to no avail. All we were asking for was a new exam, but they refused that allowance. Calling her with this bad news was one of the hardest things I have ever done.

It was just one more failure of the VA, VBA, and the Administration. Historically, I had been successful with cases that needed reexamination, but that was then, and this was now. My internal struggle grew as I came to understand that integrity such as mine had no place in this institution, and my ability to make change was yesterday's news. I was devasted that there was no helping this woman who had been so thoroughly traumatized during the claims process. My stronger parts, now thoroughly weakened, broke.

Between this woman, the two women who had been sexually assaulted at a VA facility, and the statement by VA Deputy Secretary Donald Remy that the VA doctors who committed sexual assaults were able to keep their jobs so long as they maintained their state medical license, something inside of me snapped. They were not concerned about the women who were being assaulted by these predators, nor did they care about the women who will be assaulted in the future by these very same predators. Instead, they were concerned about being sued by the predators. I understood that I could not work in a place that had no concern for the harm they were causing.

By the time September rolled around, my integrity was on fire at the injustice these women faced and the knowledge that there were likely thousands more in the same situations, yet with no recourse. It was further aggravated by the fact that the people in charge of managing these cases had no experience or knowledge in the field, yet they were the ones making the decisions. My mind was bursting with the idea that the VA literally had no intention of protecting their veterans from these experiences.

Never mind the legions of attorneys employed by the VA Central Office in Washington DC and at every VA facility in the United States, their decision was to feed women veterans to sexual predators across the United States because they were afraid of being sued. They chose to protect the offenders and predators instead of their vulnerable population. When my Director delivered this news to me, I was nearly outside myself with disbelief, shock, and anger. The next day as I was getting ready for work, I sat on my bed and sobbed. So, I texted my boss to tell her I could not work that day. When she asked if I was OK, I stated "No, I'll never be OK again."

These things came together like a perfect storm on September 30, and all I could believe was that, in spite of McDonough's assurances that he cared about women veterans, nothing would ever change the fact that he either does not care or he is uninterested. Worse, those appointed under him had no concern for our safety or best interests.

All I could think at the time was that nothing would change. Women will not be safe in VA hospitals or clinics, we have to suffer under the "care" of dangerous doctors, as well as inexperienced appointees who have little concern for the actual welfare of women veterans, even when there is evidence showing we were victimized in the military and/or the VA. For the first time in my career, as my stronger pieces lay broken at my feet, I realized that I was powerless to make change. Hopelessness came to live in the space that used to contain the belief that I could be effective and make change.

The truth is that once you have seen behind the curtain, you cannot unsee those things. Knowing what I knew, I had to make a decision to overlook my integrity and stay or decide that in order to keep my integrity intact in light of the VA's misogynist policies, I had to leave. Given this, I could not find a way to stay.

Later, months after leaving, I was invited to have a conversation with a congresswoman on the House Veterans Affairs Committee. That was when I found out that just as congressional representatives were aware of sexual assault in the military and still take no real action to protect service members, they were aware of sexual assault in the VA facilities and VA policies of protecting perpetrators. My hope that she or anyone else cared enough to make change crashed against the rocks.

I had snapped and walked away because, after forty-plus years of dealing with my own issues and almost thirty years of listening to the stories of thousands of women, I realized I could no longer do the work. My broken places were permanently damaged. Those stronger places that I had so carefully built, repaired, and lacquered were no longer the stronger places. They were broken, to the point of shattering, and I had to leave, for my own soul and sanity.

When two weeks into my mental health leave, after sending the email stating I was taking mental health leave due to the toxic work environment and instructing her not to contact me, she had the audacity to send me an email asking me to manage four different things, one of which was a study on intimate partner violence that I had been the lead on for over a year, I was not in the mood. She had taken over the study management, causing problems and delays. Her decision to take over was not based on her knowing anything at all about the study or the process, but because she wanted to be the only person to manage anything. Once again, her interference had caused efforts to go sideways.

So, my reply was "Do it yourself. You have micromanaged everything. You have taken over everything about my job and staff's, even when you do not know what you are doing. You think you can do it all, you think you can manage actions and events and talk about topics that you have not bothered to learn anything about, so you do it. You take care of it, and do not contact me again."

On October 31, 2022, I had my requested exit interview with the new Deputy Chief of Staff (DCOS) and our human resources representative. There, I delivered a four-page letter expressing my concerns about how the Director was doing business, including concerns that she was mismanaging the budget and failing to abide by our directives and mandates. That meeting fell on deaf ears, with the DCOS expressing platitudes intended to just get me out of her office. She had no interest in facts or addressing problems. She just wanted me gone.

---

xxxviii   VA Women's Health Network. Women Veterans' Experiences with Harassment at VA: What Do We Know and What Has Been Done? https://www.hsrd.research.va.gov/centers/womens_health/Harassment-Research-Snapshot.pdf Viewed 10/21/2024.

I would rather have thirty minutes of wonderful than a lifetime of nothing special.

—**Julia Roberts** *(as Shelby) in Steel Magnolias*

CHAPTER 13

Out of the Fire

My career in the field of violence against women, and sexual assault in particular, ended as abruptly as it began. Just as one day I entered the field and became a warrior for women and girls who were/are victims and survivors of violence, I one day laid down my sword and swore I would hear no more stories—instruction given to me by my therapist. "No more stories, no more advocacy, Liz. For your own mental health, you need to be done."

Although the end I just described was a defining moment, there were a series of personal events that also contributed, leading up to the end. When I look back now, I know that it began with the sudden and unexpected death of my sister Ritha in October 2021. She was for decades the person who had stored all my stories of trauma and pain. As I struggled with her loss, I could feel myself unraveling. What is interesting about this is that the memories of our conversations and the thought of her living with my secrets for so many years had never really been a part of our conversations, or even my psyche, until after she died. Then it pressed down on me like my mother's iron on the wrinkled clothing she used to take in for money.

On top of the memories I held of her was the reality that we never even got to say goodbye because she went into a coma before I got there. My chance to ask her about the things I had asked her to hold on to for me never came.

Broken in the Stronger Places: From Resilience to Resourcefulness

Her loss—the loss of the person who unknowingly and unwittingly was my trauma cushion—had an irreversible impact on my stronger places, and I began even then to feel them coming apart, as if her life-blood had been an ingredient in the glue and lacquer holding them together.

But as I had always done, I pushed down the pain and kept going, albeit not as effectively. I kept moving every day because there were women veterans and staff that needed help. When my staff expressed concern, I assured them I was fine. I'm fine thank you. I'm great. I'm good. I'm fine. The work demanded my attention, and so I threw myself into it, but her loss made me increasingly unable to tolerate the ignorance of my boss and others.

As life tends often to work in circles, so does mine and my story. My mother's story was one of the first I ever heard, and in May 2022 I heard one of my last when I learned a young woman I love with every fiber of my being had been raped, acting as a catalyst for my final breaking point. Her story, as it happened, was one of the last I ever heard.

As I listened to the horrors of what happened to this young woman, no tears came. None ever came, and it was then I realized I was broken inside. The result of my own trauma stuffed away, combined with hearing thousands of stories over the course of nearly thirty years, of sitting and listening and giving my strength so all those women could tell their story—so often for the very first time—to someone who truly listened, resulted in me being broken in my stronger places so much so that I could not shed even one tear for this beautiful young woman, no matter how much my heart was broken for her. When I looked in the mirror, I could almost see the light shining through the cracks and breaks splintering across my body.

In June of 2022, Theresa called and told me my mother had taken a fall. She was OK, but because she had a broken shoulder, she could not return to the assisted living facility until she healed, so Mom was staying at her home. I asked if she was OK and if I needed to come home, but she assured me what the doctors had said. "She's fine. She'll heal." About a week later she called and said they ordered hospice for mom because her condition was worsening.

Even for someone with dementia, her new confusion was astounding, so Mom had been taken off the meds they believed were the cause, but she was not improving. They took a second look at her X-rays and saw that her body was riddled with cancer. They believed it had gone to her brain, and that was what caused the fall and confusion. Days later she was dead. For the second time in eight months someone I loved had died and I had missed my opportunity to come home and say goodbye. I was devastated.

The cracks and breaks deepened.

In August, came the woman veteran whose story crushed my soul, and I knew I had nothing left. The anger boiled out of me as I not only listened to her tell this story of horror, but at the VA, my boss, and the Deputy Secretary for their refusal to help—for their lack of concern and compassion, for showing me that they really did not care about women veterans and that I was wasting my time trying. Any hope I had left escaped my body in one heaving breath.

One month later I would walk away from my career and not look back, completely drained of hope and wondering how on earth I could possibly reassemble my own broken pieces, but never with any amount of regret for the work I did for so long. As a friend pointed out, my resourcefulness was knowing that I needed not only to leave the career I had so carefully and intentionally built, but to get away, alone, and find a way to bring myself back to life. I bought a camper van, put everything I owned in storage, and set out on the road, just me and my Shih Tzu Beyonce, to escape the reality of my life and where my career had brought me.

Finding Hope

As I packed up my home and prepared the van for my escape from the DC area, I know now that I was not in my right mind. The remnants of the nervous breakdown remained with me. All I could think was that I had to leave. I needed to get away, go someplace that was not there, where no one knew me. I needed to get to the sun and try to burn out the cluttered contents of my mind that felt like the junk drawer in the kitchen.

Funny, I remember that, during the first few months of my travels, when people asked where I was from, I would say "I'm escaping from DC." Sometimes people would ask about my work, and I would simply say that I used to work for the VA and saw behind their fucked up curtain, so I walked out one day when I could not take it anymore. A (maybe not?) surprising number of people said some version of: wow, good for you.

My family and some friends expressed relief that I had left my job. Theresa shared that she and other family members had noticed a change in me over the past two years. They could see the stress and how it was wearing on me. She jokingly (?) stated that they were about to draw straws to see who was going to come and drag me away from that hellhole that was my job in DC. And here I thought the "I'm fine, doing great, I'm good" platitudes, delivered with a smile, were fooling people. Turns out, not so much.

When I drove away from Virginia on November 25, 2022, my mind was goal oriented toward being nowhere, but anywhere away from there. Primarily, my focus was on the sun. I recall it being so cold I was desperate to go, yet when I look back at the actual weather for that day, it was only the mid-fifties. The cold had set into my heart and soul in a way that it defined what I felt physically. In my mind, if I could just get warm and be away from there, I would be OK.

I had named my van "Hope" because I had none. For the first time in my life, what I believed was impossible happened: I ran out of hope. I no longer believed that I could hope a miracle into happening, or that it was even worth having hope. A lifetime of ugly, horrible experiences and words that belong not only to me but to the collective woman had moved in, taken over and changed me. The depression was fierce and the anxiety real. For the first time in my life, I bought a weapon to carry with me. I was a different person than I had been two and a half years earlier. Even looking in the mirror, I saw a different, aged, hardened person. Would I, could I, get myself back? Was it too much to ask to think I would be OK?

Driving away, I felt disconnected. My mind and heart were so broken that I noticed reality only through a lens of blurred gray, when I noticed it at all. What I knew was that I had to drive until I could not any more, that I had to take care of my dog, and I had to remember to take the meds the VA had given me for my anxiety and depression. I knew what road I needed to be on only because Google Maps told me what to do. Traffic was traffic and weather was weather. I recall noticing things only through that gray lens, not with excitement, but with a barely discernible recognition of what surrounded

Out of the Fire

me: traffic, weather, cities, Everglades, beach, palm trees. Where am I staying tonight, how much gas do I have, does Beyonce need to get out for a walk?

For weeks, this was it. Driving, stopping, being. When I was in the company of others I put on my smiling face and pretended I was good, but when alone, which was most of the time, I could feel it all there, inside of me. As I started to come out of the fog, my soul began to understand that I was relatively safe so long as I was in the van. Being in the van meant safety from the world and all the bad things it held.

My intuitive dog, purchased as an emotional support dog at the insistence of my VA therapist, earned her keep. She barely left my side and spent many a day and night snuggling me, sharing hugs and kisses when I cried for no apparent reason, assuring me I was not alone and would feel better if I petted her. I rarely talked to people, because I had nothing to say and wanted to offer no conversation or explanation for what I was doing.

I spent a month in Florida, enjoying the warmth and sunshine before moving west along Interstate 10. I had driven down the east coast of Florida to Key West and then journeyed back up to the place where I could head west on Interstate 10. When the cold-spell happened during Christmas, I paid for three nights in a hotel and waited it out. I had spent almost every Christmas alone for years, so holing up in a hotel room with booze and snacks was perfectly acceptable for me. I left my room long enough to journey out to a Cracker Barrel for Christmas dinner, where a very nice couple paid for my dinner. I'm pretty sure they felt sorry for me, but I was touched by their kindness nevertheless.

Other than that dinner, I saw no reason to leave the room unless Beyonce had to go out. She had become used to the routine of van life and she loved a hotel room, so we were both as content as we could be. The only destination was the next one. Unlike many people who live in their vans or RVs, I kept moving, rarely staying more than one night in a place. My need to escape was insistent and ongoing.

The fog began to lift about three weeks into my trip. From more than a panicked, escape-oriented lens, color, space, and time began to return to my life. No longer was I just thinking "tree, beach, sun, traffic." I was becoming present with these things. Looking back, I wonder if I missed anything important during that time.

People who hear about my trip now exclaim how I must have met interesting people and done exciting things, but the (disappointing) answer is "No, no, not really." I was peopled out, and the enhanced trust issues that came with my breaking interfered with most human interactions that could come along, except for women here and there.

While in Florida, I began reading on some of the RV-life Facebook pages about people who were going to Baja, so it was something I decided I needed to do. Healing was happening, and adventure for the sake of adventure was taking the place of the stress and anxiety, so when I met online some folks from my home city of Portland who were looking for someone to cross into Baja with them, I made arrangements. We met up on January 30 and crossed over into Baja. My planned two weeks there turned into a month.

About two weeks into the trip, I had a serious problem with my van. The relay switch on my converter that powered my interior electrical system went out. Since I was in Baja, said old relay switch (it was a 2000 van) was not available to purchase. I had power when plugged in, but nothing otherwise, seriously interfering with my ability to boondock on a beach. Plans foiled… But sometimes life gives you what you need, and for me it was a young man named Irving at a water station in the small, small town of Ciudad Constitucion.

The converter broke while in Loreto, about a week after the trip started. My friends were kind and offered to stay while I worked on getting the van fixed, but we agreed they would go on to our initial destination of La Paz while I tried to decide what was next. My initial instinct was to give up this trip and head north, back to Quartzsite, for the installation of solar power. But first, sunshine and kayaking…

The weather was beautiful, so I drove a bit south from Loreto to Juncalito for kayaking, in order to interrupt my pouting about the situation. There was something about Baja that was beginning to crack my shell more. Maybe it was the unknown, or perhaps the fact that I had a decision to make that had nothing to do with saving someone or changing policy. No one was in a hurry there. It was easy for it to be about me and what I wanted and needed. I like to think, though, that it was also the sun and slow pace.

Out of the Fire

One thing my new friends and I had talked about was whale watching. We had done one trip, but I knew that there was more. So, I finished kayaking and decided that the next day I would drive just a bit further south to Adolfo Lopes Mateo. I could make it there in a few hours, stay the night, and then head north, back to the United States. So, off I went to see the whales, and then to Ciudad Constitucion, where I found a cute oasis of an RV park, and one night turned into two.

After leaving the little oasis on my final morning, I made a stop at the Aqua Purificado (water station) to fill my water tank, and then (in my mind), north. There I met my guy, Irving. He spoke English pretty well, and we struck up a conversation. I gave him a brief rundown, including the broken converter, and explained that I was going to head north to get back to the United States and deal with repairs. Irving, however, had something else in mind.

"You haven't been to La Paz? You must go before leaving. It is beautiful and is only two hours south of here. Who cares about your relay switch, you are on an adventure, yes?" (Irving speaks very good English.) I laughed and told him he reminded me of my son. Although charming, I explained that I still needed to head north.

Throughout my life I have operated on feelings — not always a good thing — but it has mostly worked for me. I believe in trusting your instincts and have encouraged folks to do the same; if it does not feel right, it is not. After leaving the water station I arrived at the intersection with Irving's words in my head and sat there contemplating: turn right and go back to the United States, not having completed my Baja adventure, or turn left, south to La Paz and what was there.

Instincts firing, I turned left.

With that decision, it was almost as if the remainder of the shell that had coated my body like the hard chocolate shell clinging to a Dairy Queen ice cream cone slipped away. For the first time in years, I remembered what freedom felt like, and this was it.

I spent the next two-plus weeks driving around Baja, going down to Cabo San Lucas and then back up, seeing whales, kayaking, hanging out on the beach, engaging in nothingness, and meeting people I still call friend.

Baja was helping me find my smile again, and dealing with things like relay switches and brake repairs were just another problem to be solved, replacing the life crisis that had seeped into my soul in DC.

In February, I returned to the United States and continued my adventure, visiting the Joshua Tree National Forest, wine tasting with a woman veteran friend in California, and ultimately heading further north to visit family. Within months, though, I left Oregon and was back on the road for more adventure.

Sunshine and Gifts

For the next three months, during the heat of the summer, I followed signs, made sudden decisions to turn off onto side roads and byways, and looked for wayside stops of interest. Kayaking, taking in the beauty of remote parks and lakes, and visiting with women veteran friends along the way took up my time, each mile and visit helping me to heal and remember the person I was before the darkness seeped into my soul. I needed to see the mundane things humans create, understanding intuitively that the mundane was exactly what my soul needed, having been the recipient of human-imposed trauma for most of my life. These mundane, quiet adventures included silly things like the Jolly Green Giant statue, largest bottle of ketchup and biggest ball of twine (two of them), which were all on the routes I chose (or detoured to).

Like life, sometimes the adventure turned into "Well, there's four hours I'll never get back," such as the "canyon" in Kansas that Beyonce and I had to drive hell and gone to find because it turned out it was more of a ditch than a canyon. Driving around dirt roads looking for what you expect and finding something else entirely changes your perspective, as long as you understand that balance happens when something unexpected appears. For me, that was a lovely remote Nebraska lake that held wide fields of water lilies and shade for days - a place I may not have found had I not been on that remote road looking for a canyon that is not a canyon (sorry Kansans). I was beginning to remember that life gives us gifts if you are just paying attention, if you are willing to turn off your path and find the remote brewery in the middle of nowhere on your way to the lake. The gifts keep giving even if you are not looking for them but remain open.

The Grief of Life

That summer, I was fortunate to spend time with my friend Lynnie, who was my best friend from high school. It had been years, but everything came together for me to get to Nevada and see her. I stayed for several days, long enough for her and Beyonce to form a mutual love, eliciting a promise that if something happened to me, Auntie Lynnie would be Beyonce's new mom.

Beyonce and I drove away, promising we would see her again. Three months later, on August 27, while Beyonce and I were visiting friends in Kentucky, both she and Beyonce would be taken from my life on the same day. I do not believe in God, but my friend said something that, strangely, made me feel better. She said, "Liz, god knew that your friend needed to have a companion when she crossed over, so she sent Beyonce to take care of her and be with her." Of course, I wanted Beyonce with me, and I wanted my friend Lynn to still be alive, but neither of those things were possible.

As horrible and tragic as that day was, I know in retrospect that the gift the universe gave me was that I had the love and support of the women at Lady Veteran's Connect to get me through those next three days when I could not even get out of bed. Had I been on the road alone, I honestly do not know what I would have done. Those women will always hold a special place in my heart.

Beyonce had been my co-pilot during our long journey. She was the joy that kept me from falling apart completely for so long, the emotional support animal that had worked dozens of hours of overtime on my behalf, and I was unsure what to do without her. Although the plan had been that we would drive north to see friends, as well as sites like Niagara Falls and the changing leaves of New England, I knew I could not finish my trip without her. So, I left Kentucky and drove to Virginia to see my sister Kelley. What was next I did not know, except that I had to get to the DC area for an event. Driving those tear-filled hours to my sister's without my precious friend by my side was incredibly difficult, but I did discover that primal screaming while inside your own vehicle can actually be healing.

A new Jeep Wrangler, purchased in Virginia, replaced the van and the memories it held in and around the smells and items that were constant reminders of my precious Beyonce's absence. Her death had brought my van life to an unexpected end before the year was up, so I turned my view once again to the healing sunshine of Florida to spend the winter. There I found a lovely condo on the Gulf Coast to try to heal and write. Still, every trip in the kayak, every walk along the path of the lagoon near the condo I rented, made me think of her and how much she would have loved that place. I was learning to be without her, but it was not a painless lesson.

I had started writing this book early in January, 2023 and was fairly close to finishing when Beyonce died. Unfortunately, one month after Beyonce's death, life unraveled in the form of extreme family drama. That pain and betrayal wrapped in lies and deceit settled into my body and mind alongside my fresh grief. Whereas my initial intent was to write while in Florida, I found writing to be an impossible task. My superpower that had always been writing had disappeared into the black hole that sucked up the relationships I thought I could always count on.

Although it was still winter, in January I had to leave my condo by the Gulf and follow through with commitments I had made to friends, which included another trip to DC for another event. On the road again, I wondered what was next, and unbidden came the realization that going home was next.

Home.

Going back to Oregon was on my mind. When I moved to the DC area, I knew I would return to Oregon when I retired. It was time. So, I headed west, again through the south, where I was to meet my sister Kelley in Tucson for the annual rock and gem show and then on to Phoenix to visit friends and, eventually, meet my sister Theresa for our planned two-week hiking adventure in Arizona. These trips were a continuation of me tapping into my resourcefulness, knowing what I needed to do in order to heal. These new adventures were different without my van and my dog, but still they gave me much to look forward to, since they all involved connections with people I love. The truth was, though, for the first time since leaving Virginia in November 2022, I felt homeless, so I pointed my Jeep west to come home.

And so, I am, home. It is different than it was when I left in 2011, because that is what happens—things change. I have regular reminders of the ongoing grief I still carry for my sister, my mother, and dog—days those reminders feel fresh as the linen I took out of the dryer today. I move through my hometown with memories and thoughts of things that were and are no longer. I experience daily pain at the loss of one of the most important relationships in my life: a relationship I was convinced would never die but, without conversation, ended abruptly.

Questions regarding decisions, life choices, what I have done and what I could have done better sometimes occupy my mind. My surroundings prompt me to sometimes ask myself if, absent trauma, I could have been a better mother, sister, daughter, friend. I experience regular reminders of relationships lost amid lost hope that others will return, while almost daily contending with healing remaining broken places.

I think of my life, what I gave to achieve my career, and what I forfeited. I am proud and honored that throughout my career I gave so many women my strength and the chance to be heard. There are not many of us, I think, who sit in silence for those who have terrible stories to tell, but for those of you out there, thank you. I see you. Like you, I would not trade a minute of my career for anything else.

In 1997, here in this town standing at the crossroads of What's Next and Why Bother, the questions in front of me were, "Maybe that wasn't the right path for me? Had it all really mattered? Was it worth it? Had I really made a difference?"

Just as I knew then, at the start of my journey, I know now, at the end that the answer to all of this was yes.

To the thousands of women who chose to tell me their stories, it was my honor to listen. Thank you for trusting me to help you fight your fight. I hope that you telling me what you needed me to know helped you, and that you find healing in both your broken and stronger places. To those whose support has been unending, I could not have done it without you.

I wish you all peace.

Recovery is not a cure, and that's a common misunderstanding of the word. When we talk about recovery, we're really talking about rebuilding, regaining. Recovery is a process. It's not an event.

—**Tammie McKelvy**, *licensed professional counselor*

Epilogue

After more than a year since hearing the last story, the dreams stopped. Actually, I am still not sure if they were dreams or auditory hallucinations brought on by my PTS and obsession with work. I would wake up to the sound of a woman screaming and lay in bed for a while, asking myself, *Is this real?*

I would get out of bed and stand by the window, wondering. "Is there a woman out there being assaulted, raped? Should I call the cops? What do I tell them when I call: that I heard the screams, but I don't know if they were real?"

Then I would negotiate with myself: I will stand here for a while and listen and look. If I do not hear or see anything, I will go back to bed. Nothing. Okay, back to bed.

In bed, though, sleep was elusive. I had to stay vigilant, awake, in case it was real and she screamed again. Insomnia, a result of my previous years of choosing work over sleep and these "dreams," became my only long-term bedmate.

Whatever they were, they stopped.

My psychologist at the VA advised that, for my own mental health, I must stay away from working in the field that is my passion. The field that fed my family and my soul for so many decades and brought so much pride, and yet sorrow. I cannot hear another story of sexual or physical violence. I walked out of the play "A Jagged Little Pill" because the words unfolding on that stage landed on me like burning embers that melt the plastic marshmallow package at a campfire. For me, this means avoiding spaces where women veterans gather and share: retreats, meetings, events. There is not enough lacquer or gold to bind together my broken pieces in a way that exposes me to other women's pain ever again. I have learned to stop apologizing for that.

If thirty years ago someone had asked me how I thought it would end, this was not it. I had carried pain, tragedy, death, and anger for so many years that it became me. It turned out I was the stories, and it was all the words from all the stories put together that eventually made up the sharp angles of the invisible golden scars that came to define my broken stronger places.

Moving Toward Next Steps

There's always a "next steps," even when you think you are through, isn't there? In the case of this book, I have distilled a great deal of information throughout these pages, which can leave a person asking, "but what do I do with all of this?" This section will answer that question. In the final pages you will find documents I have put together, mostly for employers and people who work in public-facing spaces, but also useful for people who carry trauma.

For *survivors*, the most common advice I give is to hold on, because there is light at the end of the tunnel. Physics tells us that darkness does not exist on its own: it is merely the absence of light. Furthermore, light is relative. I read an example on this that used the light of the sun as an example. Some of you may know that it takes eight minutes and nineteen seconds for the light from the sun to reach the earth. If the sun suddenly extinguished, it would take that brief amount of time for it to go dark on earth, because the light generated by the sun prior to it going dark would still be out there, traveling toward us, in those moments.

The light is still out there, folks. Even when you think it is hopeless, the light remains. You may sometimes find yourself digging in the kitchen junk drawer for the matches, but once that match is struck, you will have light, even if it is just a spark.

Look for the spark, and if you cannot find it externally, make one using your available resources. In my case, the light in the dark is sometimes friends who listen, sometimes writing, and sometimes traveling as far and as fast as I can away from the source of angst and pain.

Epilogue

You may find that opening up about the topic causes a wide variety of negative emotions or retriggers you, even if your trauma experience happened decades ago. You may experience anger, fear, depression, anxiety, sadness, loathing, and more. That is OK, because this is a natural response. Please do not beat yourself up thinking there is something wrong with you for having these feelings. I will say to you what I have said to thousands of survivors: find support, whether that is a therapist, a support group, other survivors, friends, or families. Use your resources, whatever they are, to take care of yourself.

Getting help is important, not just for yourself, but if you have children, for them as well. I think one of the greatest disservices we did to survivors over the decades was to tell them that if they left, everything would be OK. Added to that is the fact that survivors often do not feel safe in sharing their history because we are the ones who feel shame. We may be in fear of retaliation, even if the assault was a very long time ago, because that is what they threatened us with. We were told no one would believe us, or care. We have watched the news and seen how people have said awful, ugly things about survivors. All of these things mix together in a giant quagmire of emotions and thoughts that keep us silent, ashamed, and fearful. I will tell you this and remind you to repeat it to yourself and other survivors: what happened is not your fault.

I met a woman once who talked about how her ex used to silence her through threats or violence each time she tried to speak without his permission. She said that she had spent years eating her words. Within a few years of leaving him, she began to notice that she was having gastrointestinal problems. Visits to specialists found nothing. She asked me if I thought there was a connection between the abuse and her gastro problems, and my answer was, "Absolutely."

We talked about the emotional, mental, and physical impact those years of abuse left on her, and how she could bring herself back to the health she did not remember having prior to him. I encouraged her to seek help, even if it meant just attending groups or therapeutic classes at her local domestic violence crisis intervention center. A couple of years later I saw her and she shared that she had been in therapy with a woman therapist whose specialty was working with survivors of interpersonal violence, and her stomach problems had disappeared. She was feeling healthier both emotionally and physically.

Broken in the Stronger Places: From Resilience to Resourcefulness

When it comes to the *children exposed to violence*, regardless of their age, I strongly encourage you to get help for them as well. Even if they do not visually witness violence, the auditory exposure and recognition of the aftermath of violence cements itself in their minds. Childhood trauma walks with us into adulthood, folks. Wanting your children to be better is what all parents want, but we cannot wish away trauma. Their trauma can turn into behavioral problems that include violence, substance use, anxiety, depression, and other mental health conditions. After you take the step of making sure they are free from violence, the next step is helping them grapple with the trauma.

Your local domestic violence/sexual assault crisis intervention center can be an amazing resource for you. These organizations are phenomenal, free, and available throughout the country and are staffed by people whose only focus is victims and survivors. They may have groups for children, or possibly on-staff therapists. If they do not, they can make recommendations for where you can take your child. If you do not have insurance or money for therapists, know that their services will likely be free, and they are able to recommend a resource that is free. They will also be able to guide you toward services like Crime Victim Compensation.

For employers, whether you work directly with survivors or not, you are an important resource. Our world is not made for survivors and victims, yet here we all are. The more we all know about interpersonal violence and its dynamics, the better we are as humans, employers, politicians, and more, as this knowledge will improve our compassion and understanding when it comes to human behavior. With some exceptions, asking a person if they are a survivor or victim is not recommended. However, gaining information on the topic will improve your environment and success in helping the people with whom you interact.

If you have never attended a training course on interpersonal violence, I highly recommend. If you are a supervisor, human resources, or owner, consider holding trainings for your staff. Your very best option for this is the local or state domestic violence/sexual assault crisis organization. They can help you achieve a better understanding of interpersonal violence and guide you in appropriate actions and steps on building a safe, healthy environment for staff and clients alike. If your company or organization has an Employee

Epilogue

Assistance Program, work with them to be sure that they have services that support survivors. And by services, I mean appropriate, accessible services by people who have experience in this field.

I used to train veteran service officers in Oregon, and one of the first things I noticed was that sometimes I read notes that said things like "veteran came into the office angry and yelling at me." This sometimes resulted in them refusing to provide help to these veterans or in chastising them, discouraging them from coming into the office. My lesson to these workers was this: unless you did something against or to them, they are not yelling at you. They are yelling at injustice, pain, anger, bad memories, betrayal, and more. They are yelling at all the incredibly awful things that happened to them, and those bad things are the reason they are standing in your office. Do not take it personally, and you will be more successful.

If you have never seen the *iceberg model*, it's a great way to gain understanding of this behavior. Above the water you see behaviors that might include anger, despair, depression, and more. Below the water—what you are unable to see—may be abuse, discrimination, fear, childhood trauma, institutional betrayal, injustice, unemployment, and more. These things below the surface are the reason they are standing in your office yelling. The best thing you can do when this happens is sit, make eye contact with them, listen, and remember that they are not yelling *at* you. They are just yelling, and you happen to be there as the recipient. When they are done, ask "tell me what I need to know to help you."

I worked with a woman once who screamed at me for about ten minutes our first meeting. She was a woman veteran who was houseless, had a trauma history, and was actively dismissed or ignored by everyone at the VA. I made mental notes of what she was saying when she was yelling at me, and when she stopped, I said, "OK, tell me what I need to know to help you. I will be taking notes so I can be sure to get everything right. Is that OK?" She was quiet for a few moments and said, "No one ever offered to listen to me before. They always just get mad because I'm yelling in frustration. They keep telling me that I need therapy, but I hate the VA and I hate therapists." I told her I was OK with her yelling, as long as she wasn't yelling at me.

Broken in the Stronger Places: From Resilience to Resourcefulness

After that I took notes during our long conversation, and she was able to hear me when I said, "We are going to break down your needs into three segments. The first is things I can help you with right away. *Second* is things I can help you with that will take some time and require work and patience. *Third* is things that I cannot help you with. I will not lie to you and tell you these things can be fixed, but I will do is whatever I can to research the problems and connect you with someone who can help."

The upside to this story is that we developed a relationship, and I was able to help her in many ways. When I could not help her I did not make excuses or lie to her. I committed to always telling her the truth. The beginning and end of this story about her is this: listen to people, even when it is hard (like when they are yelling).

Although she had ranted about therapists and how much she hated them, through listening I had heard her say that she did not hate social workers and liked group therapy. After she got to the point where she trusted me, I was able to approach the topic of her connecting to a group at the Veterans Center and talked about a friend there who was a social worker who conducted individual and group sessions. Yes, she was resistant at first, but because what I suggested was something she already stated she liked, that resistance was easily overcome.

Six months later I found out that she had called my friend, and that she had been attending the group sessions weekly for six months. Kindness, compassion, and listening go a very long way.

For *family and friends*, all the above. Your role as a resource can be immeasurable in supporting the survivor, or it can cause the most harm. This is not to suggest that you attempt to "fix" them, but rather that you become educated on the topic so as to become comfortable at being a better support person. It will not always be easy, but it will be worthwhile.

Offer to attend some therapy sessions with them, and then let them and their therapist decide if and when that is helpful. Learn to sit, listen, and be empathetic when they speak. Ask them what they need from you and how you can help, and then ask again and again and again. *Recovery is not an event, but a process.* You can be a positive, helpful part of that process, or you can be someone who, even inadvertently, sets their recovery back or, worse

Epilogue

yet, becomes a saboteur. Know that your intimate relationship will likely be challenged and may not survive, but that might also be part of the process.

Give the survivor space to tell you what they need.

Crisis Resources

Suicide and Crisis Hotline: 988. Confidential support for help with mental health crisis and suicide prevention.

- National Sexual Assault Hotline 1-800-656-4673
- Department of Defense (DOD) SAFE Helpline 1-877-995-5247/Text zip code or installation/base name to 55-247
- National Domestic Violence Hotline 1-800-799-SAFE (7233) / Chat: thehotline.org / Text "START" to 88788
- National Mental Health Hotline 1-866-903-3787
- National Crisis Text Line 74174
- National Runaway Switchboard 1-800-RUNAWAY (786-2929)
- National Human Trafficking Hotline 1-800-373-7888/Text INFO to 233733

Building a safe workplace

You have read the book and (hopefully) learned some useful information about the impact of interpersonal violence and how it affects millions of people, some of whom may well be employed by you. At this point you may be asking yourself "how can I do better?"

Great question!

Whether you are a Top 500 Forbes business that employs thousands of people, or a small community non-profit, ensuring a safe, understanding, and supportive space for your employees will go far in improving employee retention, efficiency, and safety. After all, when a person feels unsafe – especially one who has experienced trauma – it can lead to anxiety, retraumatization, and interruption of care and services. How is this relevant? Because domestic and sexual violence are known to enter workplaces around the world, and because employers have been sued for not having an appropriate response in place when such an event occurs. According to Employers Against Violence[37], these are relevant facts related to domestic violence:

- The annual cost of lost productivity due to domestic violence is estimated at $727.8 million with over 7.9 million paid workdays lost per year.
- 74% of employed battered women were harassed by their partner while at work.

- 78% of abusers use workplace resources at least once to express remorse or anger to, check up on, or threaten the victim.
- The health-related costs of rape, physical assault, stalking, and homicide by intimate partners exceed $5.8 billion each year
- 94% of Corporate Security Directors surveyed rank domestic violence as a high security problem at their company.
- 78% of Human Resources professionals polled by Personnel Journal said that domestic violence is a workplace issue
- The United States Department of Justice estimates that 8% of rapes occur while the victim is working. That number is higher in the military and higher education. Thirty six percent of rape/sexual assault victims lost more than 10 days of work after the assault.

Domestic and sexual violence are always your business, but especially so when they enter your workplace. How do you ensure that your workplace is free from violence or be prepared if an incident occurs? Here are some recommendations.

Workplace Safety

Workplace safety is about doing your best to ensure that employees, clients, and customers are safe from all types of harm. Moving toward a safe space is an important process.

It begins with engaging your workforce. Hire a consultant who is familiar with the topic and this type of organizational planning. Their first step will be the analysis process that helps you identify and address relevant weaknesses and strengths in your organization.

This analysis should involve staff and help you identify key areas for improvement or change. Next, you will be working with the consultant to develop actionable recommendations and strategies that address any issues uncovered. If you are working with a board, this step is vital as you move toward your next step: policy and protocol development.

Bear in mind as you do your work that this process makes for easier development and implementation of your new policies and protocols. Last, do not leave out the evaluation plan. With your consultant, determine what an evaluation will look like. Obviously, in the event of an incident, you will do a debrief so you can determine what needs changed and what worked, but you do not want to wait until something happens to evaluate your plan. Perhaps you will want to do a quarterly drill? Or maybe a simple survey, or use multiple methods. Again, this is something that your consultant, who should be an expert in this work, would help you design.

Furthermore, remember that this is dynamic rather than static. Anyone who has worked in policy understands it is not unusual for policies to have unintended consequences. You can address these unintended consequences, as well as lessons learned, as they arise, by conducting regular assessments. Never be afraid of adjusting when someone involved with your organization shares that there is a problem, or something is not working

These are some of the components you should address as part of training and development:

- Actions to take if violence is perpetrated by an employee against another employee in your workplace.
- Actions to take when violence that comes into the workplace involve an employee's partner, spouse, ex, or other family member.
- Processes and guidelines to support an employee who is a victim or survivor of interpersonal violence
- Strong, legal processes, protocols, and policies that guide you if a perpetrator of interpersonal violence is your employer.
- A plan for what to do in the event violence or a threat of violence occurs. Appropriate responses, codes, safe rooms, and more can help prevent lethal outcomes.
- Policies and protocols that cover proper procedures if a client/customer, and/or a person(s) in your employ reports harassment, assault, or other. This includes having a plan that addresses a scenario where the person doing the harm is in a supervisory or executive position.

Employee Assistance Program (EAP)

- If you have an EAP, discuss with them whether their resources are trained in providing care and services to people with experiences of interpersonal and/or workplace violence.
- Whether you have an EAP or not, a great partner is your local domestic violence shelter and crisis intervention center. They are the most qualified to provide services, care, and support to victims and survivors and their children. Along that line, also include resources that focus those who are immigrants, people of color, and LGBTQIA+.
- Make sure signs that give information about available help are posted in the bathrooms as well as public areas.

Environment:

This may seem like the least important item on the list, but your environment speaks volumes to everyone coming into your space. Your consultant should be including this in your analysis.

- If you have artwork, do a walkthrough in all your spaces and look at your art. Assess if it is single-gender or single race artwork or photos only. If the answer is yes, add art that is inclusive, or simply hang landscape or other types of art.
- While you are doing this walkthrough, determine if there are images or symbols that are offensive to women, LGBTQIA+, people of color, or other marginalized groups, or images or symbols that make people feel unsafe. For instance, is someone displaying a sign or image that is sexual, sexist, racist, or anti-LGBTQ+? If you have staff displaying political signs, clothing, or caps, consider how divisive this could be. Have anything that could be contrary to a safe space removed and develop a protocol or policy about such displays.
- Again, sit in different offices and ask yourself if they are designed in a way that a person feels (or is) safe. Are offices laid out in a way that

could impart an unsafe feeling for anyone occupying the office where they may feel trapped in a volatile or other situation?
- If you have a lounge-type space dedicated to clients or staff, pay attention to who is using that space, their language, and how it adds or detracts from your environment. Frequently drop by that space to learn if it is the safe, relaxing space you intended or if it feels more like a bar atmosphere. While you may mean to harbor an environment that is inclusive and friendly, it is important to regularly determine if it feels like a safe or unsafe space.

Developing a workplace safety plan takes thoughtful planning, knowledge, and effort. This document is simply a high-level overview to provide some ideas on what to consider and how to get started. As mentioned earlier, my advice is to hire a consultant who has knowledge and experience on this topic – one who is aware that workplace safety is not just about accidents but who also understands the need to address violence.

Domestic violence and sexual assault are an insidious part of our society that affect millions, and it is everyone's business. Make it yours for your business.

Building a trauma and survivor informed organization

A few years ago, I taught a university class where we talked briefly about trauma-informed care. The big question was "Yes, but what does it mean and how does it translate?" I learned from some of my students that although they were in a social work environment, there was no class or instruction on trauma-informed care. While they were hearing the phrase repeatedly, they had no real understanding of its principles. To help those who are unfamiliar with the principles behind trauma-informed care, I am providing this document as a *starting point* designed to give you a high-level overview of trauma-informed care.

Although conversations of new concepts and processes often come with the concern that it will cost the organization money, that is not the case with establishing trauma-informed care practices: they are about behavior and practice, not purchasing equipment or hiring special staff. They will help improve your organization and the care and services you offer to the people who entrust themselves to you.

As an example of how trauma-informed care can be implemented without cost, a simple action is merely changing your approach: letting the client/patient know what you are doing before you do it, especially if it involves crossing their physical and emotional boundaries. A simple statement like "I have to touch you here, is that okay? I must ask you some difficult questions, is that okay?" Using this approach, you give the survivors a warning of what is to come and honor their boundaries, as well as giving them agency over what is happening to them.

The following principles come from the Trauma-Informed Care Implementation Resource Center by the Center for Health Care Strategies. They were adopted from the Substance Abuse and Mental Health Services Administration's "Guiding Principles of Trauma-Informed Care." While their focus is on health care settings, understand that trauma-informed care guidelines and principles can cross professions and be as useful in non-healthcare settings, such as mental health clinics and social services organizations. All can benefit from an understanding of trauma-informed care.

In order to maintain the intent and context of the developers, I have printed them here as they are listed on the website.[38]

- Safety - Throughout organization, patients and staff feel physically and psychologically safe.
- Trustworthiness + Transparency = Decisions are made with transparency, and with the goal of building and maintaining trust.
- Peer Support - Individuals with shared experiences are integrated into the organization and viewed as integral to service delivery.
- Collaboration - Power differences — between staff and clients and among organizational staff — are leveled to support shared decision-making.
- Empowerment -Patient and staff strengths are recognized, built on, and validated — this includes a belief in resilience and the ability to heal from trauma.
- Humility + Responsiveness - Biases and stereotypes (e.g., based on race, ethnicity, sexual orientation, age, geography) and historical trauma are recognized and addressed.

Two key components of trauma-informed care that are too often overlooked are cultural humility and anti-racism. As part of the process of understanding

Building a trauma and survivor informed organization

trauma, considering race and culture and how those meet the very real existence of historical trauma is vital to how we do our work.

Again, relying on the work of the Center for Health Care Strategies, following are some definitions and recommendations for including these two approaches in your trauma-informed toolbox. As with the previous list, bear in mind that this is a starting point. Like trauma itself, it is a process, not an event. This simply begins your work.

- Cultural humility – "a respectful approach toward individuals of other cultures that continuously pushes one to challenge cultural biases."[39] As explained by Allison Briscoe-Smith, PhD, it is important to recognize that trauma-informed care and cultural humility are synonymous concepts. As Dr. Briscoe-Smith informs us, one cannot separate trauma-informed care without also acknowledging and understanding the underlying cause of the trauma in the person they are treating.

Looking through the cultural humility lens requires an examination of practices and whether or how you are supporting individuals and communities that are different than your own. For example, for people whose first language is not English, communicating in English, even if they know the language, can be difficult, especially when in crisis. This is the time to work with them where they are, not where you want them to be, which includes how you are open to communication.

Be mindful. If you notice they are struggling with conveying thoughts and stress seems to be increasing, bring in an interpreter. Although you may not or cannot hire someone who speaks different languages, there are several language lines available for use. These lines are staffed 24/7/365 and offer interpreters in numerous languages. They will cost you money, but the amount of stress and anxiety they save for clients, patients, and employees makes it worthwhile. Language is just one example. Cultural humility involves growing your own knowledge about other cultures and learning to adjust your interactions in such a way that you understand how their experiences, fears, and historical traumas may look different than your expectations. More importantly, it improves how you design programs, treatment plans, and whether they are relevant, appropriate, and successful for everyone.

- Anti-Racism – As pointed out on the Center for Health Care Strategies page, "Racism is trauma and should be treated as such in any comprehensive trauma-informed care framework."[40] If when you read this you think some version of "We treat everyone the same; we don't see color," I would submit that you definitely need to delve into under-standing and practicing anti-racism.

The path toward anti-racism is to recognize that we live in a world where racism exists, acknowledge our part in it, and recognize that it is a foundation for trauma. To do better, learn how to become an ally. Learn to understand and acknowledge how racism affects communities of color. Accept the fact that people of color have spent lifetimes figuring out how to move through a world that tells them they are "the other," disrespects, is dangerous for, and even hates them. They live with the trauma experiences and stories of their lives and the lives of those that came before them.

When you are feeling discomfort with all of this, that is good. Know that you are on the right path and keep going.

As part of these cultural and anti-racism practices, an examination of your workforce and practices should also be conducted. Following are some recommendations on approaches that support inclusive hiring and business practice. However, I suggest that for a true examination of your organization practices in this area, you hire a consultant who specializes.

Hiring practices:

Of course, your job and service announcements say you do not discriminate and state that everyone should apply, but if you put all your staff in one room, would it look like an inclusive group, or do they all look alike? If it is the latter, ask what are you doing to intentionally hire a diverse staff and how you can do better? Examples or how to embrace inclusivity:

Building a trauma and survivor informed organization

Do your applications and other written documents use male pronouns? If the answer is yes, rewrite them all to either say "they" or in a way that there is no need for pronouns.

Are you recruiting to specific groups or areas? Do you try to have one or more people on staff who are bilingual? Alternatively, do you have access to a language line?

If recruiting from (or to) colleges and universities, do you reach out to schools that have a diverse population?

Have you done an internal audit of your employees and clientele to get an honest picture of the population you serve or hire? In other words, if your clientele includes people of color, immigrants, or women, does your staff reflect that population? I met a veteran service officer once who only ever wrote claims for straight, white cisgender males. He insisted that it was because those were the only veterans who came into his office. Further examination showed that women, LGBTQ+, and veterans of color did not come to see him because they did not feel safe. In other words: it was not them, it was him. Don't be like him.

When hiring, is your interview panel made up of more than one group? In other words, are they all white, all men, all young, all old? If your hiring or interview panel all looks the same, the message received by interviewees may be that their difference makes them unwelcome.

When you are staffing tables at events, do you have women, people of color and other marginalized groups at the table, or is it men only? Do you have materials that are welcoming to everyone?

Veterans:

Examine your hiring practices and if/how you support veterans and ensure inclusivity. As I mentioned in the book, "veteran" is white, male default. How do you support all veterans, including women, LGBTQIA+, people of color, and immigrants? Here are some considerations:

Ensure that any reference to veterans is not centered on the male language and pronouns.

If you ask men if they served, do you also ask woman?

Broken in the Stronger Places: From Resilience to Resourcefulness

Any veteran-related displays should be inclusive of race and gender. Don't be afraid of the LGBTQIA+ flags and displays.

Learn the unique challenges, needs, and experiences of women veterans, veterans of color, and LGBTQIA+ veterans.

This completes this section on trauma-informed care. If you made it this far, thank you for persevering through some difficult information. It is not easy to hear the hard stuff that tells us we might need to change how we are doing our work, but it is important.

As the saying goes, "you got this." Just keep moving forward, one step at a time, and please, take care of you as you do this hard work.

Resourcefulness: Tools that get us through

So, what is resourcefulness? It's what helps us find solutions to the problems in front of us, lean in to our support systems, and adapt to challenges in front of us in a way that we can regain a sense of control and agency.

As I mentioned in the book, my resourcefulness is what got me through the worst years. Most importantly, it got me through the time period after I had my breakdown at the VA, when my PTSD and anxiety spiked and I felt lost and untethered. At the time I did not think about it. I just knew that I *had* to get in my van and keep driving until I was done. It took over a year, and I did not necessarily know in that moment that I was healing, but looking back, that trip embodied my resourcefulness and was my healing.

What are some examples of resourcefulness?

- Engaging in self-care activities, whether that's yoga every morning or a one-year road trip.
- Accessing available tools to manage in the moment. Examples of these tools are online support groups and apps.
- Identifying those things that trigger us so that when they come into our path, we are prepared and better able to manage them.

Broken in the Stronger Places: From Resilience to Resourcefulness

- Self-advocacy. Sometimes, especially as survivors of interpersonal violence, we may struggle with advocating for ourselves, navigating health and behavioral health systems, finding therapy that works for us, or setting good boundaries. An example of how you might do this: if you suspect that your visit to the doctor might be difficult (maybe they are not good at listening to you?), write down what it is you want to say so that you have that in your hand and mind. While there, do not hesitate to look at your note and read that to the doctor. Reading it may make you feel less nervous.
- Work on your resilience building via the tools you have or have been given. This helps you find solutions to challenges and trigger events and helps you rebound more easily during difficult times.
- Learn relaxation techniques like breathing, yoga, and mediation. Maybe it's escaping to go fish somewhere, or sitting in a dark theater eating popcorn with a lot of butter. Find your happy place and use it.
- Creative problem-solving. Know what works for you, especially when you feel overwhelmed. Perhaps it's sitting alone and thinking about it, maybe it's driving with loud music in the background, or even just sitting and writing out a list that includes pros and cons.
- Embrace your support systems. Sometimes you just need someone you can talk to, whether it's your mom, your best friend, someone you met at an event and found a connection with, or lunch at the community center. No matter who or what, know who your battle buddies are and connect when necessary.

These tools are not set in stone: there is no right or wrong. Think about what works for you, and then do that. If you want to learn more about resourcefulness and recovery, you can find more information online or talk to your therapist about tools you can add to your toolbox.

Resilience Tools

As covered in the book, resilience is a skill or dynamic process. We are not born with it, but we can and do develop it – some differently than others. Briefly, it is what helps us positively adapt in the face of trauma or adversity.

Resourcefulness: Tools that get us through

This document provides resilience tools taken from Mental Health America (MHA)[41] that can be helpful for those who have experienced trauma, recently or in the past. Credit goes to MHA for the following resilience tools, found on their website, but more can be found elsewhere.

Connect with others – many of us have experienced the truth in this statement: it is possible to be surrounded by people and still feel alone. Tips for connecting:

- Connect with others at places you already go to
- Use shared experience as a topic of conversation
- Give compliments
- Make time to be social
- Not all connections have to be done in person
- Accept invitations
- Pay attention to what other people are interested in
- Organize activities
- Stay positive – Negativity in our lives can affect our moods, actions, and health. Practice gratitude. Gratitude meditation has become very popular for a reason. It's a great way to start the day and clear your head of negativity. Avoid negative thinking, which can decrease performance and effectiveness in your life and work. Worse, negative self-talk can become thoughts we believe.

What are some MHA tips for staying positive?

1. Write about a positive future or, if you aren't a writer, use your imagination to imagine positive outcomes
2. Search for the silver lining. Sound silly? Maybe, but according to MHA, it can show great strength.
3. Get physically active. When depression and anxiety set in, getting off the couch and doing something can be incredibly difficult, but engaging in activity is not just good for your heart, your blood pressure, your weight, your immune system, your energy, and more, it can help improve your mood, you. It reduces stress, anger, and tension and

decreases anxiety and depression. Depending on the type of exercise you are doing, set a goal for 3 – 5 days a week at a minimum of 20 minutes per day.
4. Help others. Helping others through acts of volunteerism or otherwise (this includes donating money) has been shown to improve happiness, reduce stress, and improve how you feel about yourself. It can serve as a reminder that you are lucky in your life, that you are needed in this world, and add a sense of purpose. Get out there and do good for yourself and others.
5. Get enough sleep. Too many Americans, and especially those of us with PTS, have poor sleep habits due to overworking, stress, and more. MHA offers these tips for improving sleep:
    - To sleep longer—and better—consider these suggestions:
    - Set a regular bedtime
    - Limit caffeine
    - De-stress yourself
    - Get out in the sun
    - Exercise
    - Don't eat right before bed
    - Nap smart
    - Say no to nicotine
    - Go easy on the drinks
    - Limit distractions
    - Make your bed a sleep haven
6. Create joy and satisfaction. As the old saying goes, "laughter is the best medicine." A decrease in pain is just one of the benefits of laughter. Heart, lungs, anxiety, and muscles can all be improved through laughter. While it is certainly not a substitute for taking care of your health in all the important ways, it does lend itself to better health. Recommendations from MHA include:
    - Reading funny books or listening to jokes, comedy, podcasts, and more. Laughing at yourself or the situation can help you get through tough times.

Resourcefulness: Tools that get us through

- Go have some fun. Have you forgotten or dropped the things that used to give you pleasure? Try picking them up again.
- Find your flow. We all have those moments, whether it is a hobby, writing, or engaging in challenging activities. What gets you into the zone and how long has it been since you were there?

7. Eat well. What are your eating habits like? Have you given up cooking, or have you just never experimented with it? Now is a great time to get back into it. Life is busy and sometimes people get stuck in the routine of relying on fast food, but the fat, carbs, and sugar is a storm of nastiness that negatively impacts not only your body but your mental health. There is a popular myth that eating fast food is cheaper, which is why so many people use it as an excuse. Try this challenge to get you started: plan a menu for a week and then shop and cook for that week. If it works for you, do it again the next week. If you end up skipping a night, that is okay, no one will take away your birthday. You can always start up the next day. To get you started, here's a fantastic Better Homes and Gardens website that offers 32 meals for under $3 a serving.[42] See you in the kitchen!

8. Take care of your spirit. Nope, not talking about religion or any particular higher being, although it can be those things. MHA says this, "being spiritual means observing rituals, studying texts, and attending religious services, well, religiously. For others, it's not at all about traditional structures or notions of God." It is connecting to whatever you consider meaningful or holy. It can mean going to church, or a hike in the forest, or a trip to the beach. Regardless of how you get your spirituality fix, it can improve your mood and decrease anxiety and depression.

9. Deal better with hard times. Fact: you have coping skills, or you would not have gotten this far. If you have favorite coping skills, keep doing that. If you ae struggling with identifying or relying on them, here are some that you might be able to use:
   - Write about it. Journaling is a wonderful exercise. Alternatively, a great way to get something off your chest is to write that

letter to someone but then do not send it. Just writing it out is a great way to get it out of your system.
- Tackle your problems. Make a list of the problems, and then think of solutions and write those down. Do not get bogged down in looking for perfect solutions, because that may end up in a spiral. Instead, choose a solution that works – the best option.
- Determine your options for getting to the other side. Weighing the pros and cons helps.
- How do you eat an elephant? One piece at a time. Don't try to solve all the problems all at once. Make a reasonable plan, and then work the plan.
- Shift your thinking. If you get stuck in the negatives or "I cant's" or "it's impossible" spiral, jump out. How realistic are your worries? Or you making it more than it is? Focus on the good in your life. And, as much as it may not be something you want to do, think of it as an opportunity to learn. What is the positive that has come out of this?
- Get support. Call on friends, family members, your therapist, whomever. Call a crisis or help line and talk it out. Never be afraid to ask for help. There's always someone out there who has your back.

10. Get professional help if you need it. Sadly, there is a terrible stigma in our world that burdens those seeking mental health care, but think of it this way: if you have a heart problem, you go to the doctor, and maybe you take meds. You don't not go because you are embarrassed. There's a list of resources at the front of the book, and a more comprehensive list on my website. You deserve to be healthy. Make the call.

There's an app for that!

The National Center for PTSD and VA have spent years collaborating on the development of apps for PTSD, military sexual trauma, recovery, health, and more. These apps are free and available for anyone, even those who are not veterans. I have used a number of them and know others who have. This is a short list of apps relevant to people who have experienced trauma. More are available on the website, as well as some for loved ones and providers. Take a look and see if there is something here for you:

**None of these apps are a replacement for therapy with a trained mental health professional

PTSD Coach - App users can track and manage their symptoms, learn more about PTSD and available treatments, and find additional support and help.

https://mobile.va.gov/app/ptsd-coach

Beyond MST - Beyond MST is a free, secure, trauma-sensitive mobile app that was created specifically to support the health and well-being of survivors of sexual assault or harassment during military service. Find coping tools and free resources to work through challenges associated with Military Sexual Trauma (MST).

https://mobile.va.gov/app/beyond-mst

Mindfulness Coach - Learn how to practice mindfulness to reduce stress and improve emotional balance.

https://mobile.va.gov/app/mindfulness-coach

MHA for Veterans - Allows you to take a variety of mental health assessments from the comfort and convenience of home. You can complete assessments assigned by your provider and receive scores and feedback in real time on a smartphone, tablet, or computer.

https:// mobile.va.gov/app/mha-veterans

Stay Quit Coach – designed to help anyone who would like to quit or reduce use of cigarettes, electronic nicotine delivery systems, cigars and chewing tobacco.

https://mobile.va.gov/app/stay-quit-coach

VetChange – for veterans and service members who are concerned about their drinking and how it relates to post-traumatic stress, and for all people who are interested in developing healthier drinking behaviors.

https://mobile.va.gov/app/vetchange

Caring for Women Veterans – Whether you are a VA or non-VA care team member, the Caring4WomenVeterans App has useful information to help you serve the unique physical and mental health needs of women Veterans.

https://mobile.va.gov/app/caring-4-women-veterans

Safety Plan - Create a custom step-by-step action plan to keep yourself sfe when experiencing thoughts about suicide or self-harm.

https://mobile.va.gov/app/safety-plan

There's an app for that!

Pain Coach – Pain Coach is an interactive app that was created for anyone who experiences chronic pain or has any pain that disrupts their life. The app uses cutting edge, evidence-informed strategies to help people manage chronic pain.

https://mobile.va.gov/app/pain-coach

Insomnia Coach - The Insomnia Coach app was created for everyone, including Veterans and Service members, to help manage insomnia. The app is based on Cognitive Behavioral Therapy for Insomnia (CBT-I).

https://mobile.va.gov/app/insomnia-coach

Acknowledgments

Writing a book is neither a direct line from start to finish nor an easy task. Beginning in October 2023, a very difficult unraveling of family support led to my work on this book nearly coming to an end. Fortunately, while some siblings resolved themselves to anger, two of my sisters, Theresa and Kelley, threw their unwavering support behind me and have been with me for the hardest part of the journey. They recognized that our mother's story was so intertwined with my own that it needed to be told. Thank you for your kindness along this journey and for trusting me.

In my life, I learned to trust those who have skill sets beyond or different from my own. Carly Newberg, author, consultant, and yoga teacher extraordinaire, I hope you understand how much your support and advice along this path meant to me. You were invaluable not just in the writing and publishing but also emotionally as well. I am sure you learned more than you wanted about me, and thanks will never be enough.

A task such as this cannot be successful without people you trust to give you their advice and opinions. My crew was Katrina Hoff, Dr. Qwynn Galloway-Salazar, Dr. Carolina Gonzales-Prats, Dr. Clarice Bailey, Theresa Johnson, and Kelley Finch—friends and family members who volunteered as readers. Your work, honesty, and expertise got me around the final bend. Michelle Dallocchio, Lioness, friend, extraordinary artist, and author: your

Broken in the Stronger Places: From Resilience to Resourcefulness

willingness to share your words of wisdom, support, and encouragement across the ocean mattered so much.

Millions of people today live with post-traumatic stress and its lifelong symptoms. Sometimes, as veterans, we are fortunate to have access to VA psychologists who give us a path to healing. I will always be grateful to the psychologists who helped me and whose caring manners will always matter a great deal to me.

My friends AnnMarie Halterman and Tiffany Wheeler, thank you. Thank you for holding me up when my pieces were lying on the ground in shards. Thank you for sharing your home and wrapping me in your family's arms.

When my best friend, my precious Shih Tzu Beyonce, died, I am not entirely sure what things would have looked like for me had I been alone. Fortunately, I was with a phenomenal, caring, compassionate group of women at Lady Veterans Connect in Kentucky. Your gentle kindness and concern were important as I struggled to move forward without my companion.

There is a talented singer named Jess Glynn, who wrote a song called "Take Me Home." This song, on repeat, got me through so many difficult days and nights that weighed on me while my soul lay shattered and broken all those months before and after I left my job. You, my women veteran friends and supporters, constantly reminded me that there was always someone safe who had me when I was the most in need. Ms. Glynn's words assure us that "space and time will make it better" and bring healing, and it was you, my veteran sisters, who held me tight throughout the process. You knew my faith was broken, and I will be eternally grateful that you knew when to take the wheel.[xxxix]

When I escaped from DC after leaving my job, I traveled in a camper van. It was my great good fortune to have friends, new and old, who gave me a driveway while I traveled, looking for hope in a hopeless world. Thank you not only for the friendship but also for the meals, drinks, joyful conversations, and the reminder that all is not lost, even when it seems so.

Often, the path to healing begins with validation that something happened and acknowledgment of what is wrong. That path was laid for me by my dear friend Gus Bedwell, the world's finest Veteran Service Officer, who was bold enough and caring enough to bring up my military sexual trauma and encouraged me to apply for those service-connected benefits. You have

Acknowledgments

been a constant blessing. I still owe you a cup of coffee for being right about my hearing loss, by the way.

Sometimes, we need a friend to just say something so simple, like, "You need to finish that book," in order to get us back on track. Clarice Bailey, thank you for being that person and so much more.

Friends keep us going, especially in our dark and difficult times. My friends who have supported me throughout this project, encouraging me to keep writing—each and every one of you—I appreciate you all. Barbara Howe, thank you for being my sounding board, sharing your home, and blessing me with your friendship.

This book would not exist without all the women over the decades who trusted me enough to tell me their stories. You gave me a life and career that satisfied my soul every day. I hope you have found health, peace, love, and healing.

I would not be here or who I am today without my mother, who never believed she was good enough, all while raising seven children on her own and teaching us valuable lessons. She had, since childhood, faced fierce opponents, whether they were fears of what came for her in the dark, divorce, a judgmental community, poverty, or the daunting task of raising seven children on her own. Always, she found a way. It is not something she was told she could or could not do, but something she did because she had to. My mother was the queen of lacquering and covering broken places with shiny metal as a distraction. I wish she were here today and dementia-free so I could talk to her about this and thank her for being the best mother she could be. I miss you every day, Mom.

And finally, my sister Ritha. Every single day, I wish she were here. I wish I could ask how she knew what she needed to do for me, how she held my secrets and me close over the years without me even acknowledging what she was doing. I wish she could read this book and that I could thank her. Everyone should have such a sister and friend. I will never stop missing you.

---

xxxix   Glynn, Jess. Track 4. Take Me Home. I Cry When I Laugh. Atlantic Records, 2015, https://youtu.be/P0N0h_EOS-c?si=aoNBXm01ciBVOJZP.

About the Author

Elizabeth Estabrooks served as the deputy director at the Department of Veterans Affairs (VA) Center for Women Veterans (CWV) in Washington, DC, where she operated as the subject-matter expert on women veteran issues, concerns, and needs both within and outside the VA, speaking vehemently in favor of changes that improved safety and equity for women veterans. She was the lead on organizational and strategic planning, led development and implementation of new initiatives to support and enhance CWV's mission and vision, and worked with researchers to lead the production of two congressionally mandated studies:

1) Study on Unemployment Rate of Post-9/11 Women Veterans, and

2) The Prevalence of Intimate Partner Violence in the Veteran Population.

She was also the VA lead on the development of a first-ever VA woman veterans' survey to identify and understand low rates of VA benefits and health-care usage by women.

Prior to assuming her role as deputy director, Elizabeth served as the Oregon woman veterans coordinator with the Oregon Department of Veterans Affairs, where she brought decades of knowledge and experience gained from her career working on relevant issues that included domestic violence, (military) sexual assault, peer support services, community safety, gender- and culturally responsive services, and adult learning. In 2017, Elizabeth co-founded the I Am Not Invisible campaign and photo project for women veterans: a project that, due to her efforts, was adopted as a permanent program by the VA Center for Women Veterans in 2018.

Previously, she worked as an independent consultant advising clients that included the Office of Juvenile Justice and Delinquency Prevention; Oregon Department of Human Services; Oregon Department of Public Safety Standards and Training; Battered Women's Justice Project; Mental Health Partnerships of Pennsylvania; and the Edmonton Police Department in Edmonton, Alberta, Canada.

Her earliest foray into the field of violence against women was first as a board member and then as executive director of MayDay, Inc., Baker County's domestic and sexual violence crisis intervention center, from 1993–1997. While there, she obtained funding to open the first-ever shelter in the community.

Elizabeth is a peacetime Cold War veteran of the United States Army, serving at Harvey Barracks in Kitzingen, Germany. She holds a bachelor of science degree in gender studies and political science from Eastern Oregon University, where she graduated summa cum laude and a master of science in social work from Columbia University in New York. She was appointed to the VA Secretary's Task Force on Inclusion, Diversity, Equity, and Access in 2021 and the VA National Domestic Violence Task Force in 2012 and was a 2013 Fisher-Cummings Washington, DC, Fellow.

She now travels and focuses on writing a blog and three books, speaking and engaging as a freelance changemaker, and consulting as a subject-matter expert on women veterans.

Contacting the author:

Elizabeth A. Estabrooks
Phone: (541)350-6525
elizabeth@awomansvoicepress.com
Website: https://www.awomansvoicepress.com

Glossary

Criterion A Stressor, Diagnostic and Statistical Manual of Mental Disorders (DSM-5): Events that involve actual or threatened death, serious injury, or threat to the physical integrity of oneself or others

Domestic Violence (See Intimate Partner Violence)

Intimate Partner Violence (Domestic Violence): Defined by the Department of Justice as: "…a pattern of abusive behavior in any relationship that is used by one partner to gain or maintain power and control over another intimate partner. Domestic violence can be physical, sexual, emotional, economic, psychological, or technological actions or threats of actions or other patterns of coercive behavior that influence another person within an intimate partner relationship. This includes any behaviors that intimidate, manipulate, humiliate, isolate, frighten, terrorize, coerce, threaten, blame, hurt, injure, or wound someone."

LGBTQIA+: An acronym that stands for lesbian, gay, bisexual, transgender, queer or questioning, intersex, and asexual. The "+" represents other identities that are not included in the acronym

Broken in the Stronger Places: From Resilience to Resourcefulness

Lautenberg Amendment: Passed September 30, 1996, it prohibits those convicted of domestic violence misdemeanors from owning or posing firearms of any kind. The Amendment applies to both civilians that include law enforcement, as well as military members. It also applies to those who sell firearms to individuals convicted of a domestic violence misdemeanor.

Military Sexual Assault: Sexual harassment, assault, and/or rape that occurs against someone while they are serving on active duty in the U.S. military.

Military Sexual Trauma: Psychological trauma that results from sexual assault, battery, or harassment that occurred while serving on active duty or training orders. The program applies to all active-duty service members, National Guard, Reservists, and military veterans, regardless of gender, era of service, discharge status, or if the crime was reported." Unfortunately, this code also uses the above written VA definition of sexual harassment.

Post-Traumatic Stress (Disorder): Post Traumatic Stress is a mental health condition that is a mental, physical, and/or emotional stemming from a stressful, traumatic event that put someone in danger of serious injury, harm, or death.

Rape: "The penetration, no matter how slight, of the vagina or anus with any body part or object, or oral penetration by a sex organ of another person, without the consent of the victim." The U.S. Department of Justice now definition has expanded to include: any gender of victim and perpetrator, not just women being raped by men. It also recognizes that rape with an object can be as traumatic as penile/vaginal rape. This definition also includes instances in which the victim is unable to give consent because of temporary or permanent mental or physical incapacity. Furthermore, because many rapes are facilitated by drugs or alcohol, the new definition recognizes that a victim can be incapacitated and thus unable to consent because of ingestion of drugs or alcohol. (National Sexual Violence Resource Center, Let's Talk Definitions of Terms, January, 2025.)

Glossary

Sexual Assault: According to the Office on Violence Against Women, the term "sexual assault" means any nonconsensual sexual act proscribed by Federal, tribal, or State law, including when the victim lacks capacity to consent. State laws vary in the definitions used for sexual assault. (National Sexual Violence Resource Center, Let's Talk Definitions of Terms, January, 2025.)

Some forms of sexual assault include:

- Penetration of the victim's body, also known as rape.
- Attempted rape.
- Forcing a victim to perform sexual acts, such as oral sex or penetration of the perpetrator's body.
- Fondling or unwanted sexual touching.

Sexual Harassment:

VA: Sexual harassment: means unsolicited verbal or physical contact of a sexual nature which is threatening in character.

Equal Employment Opportunity Commission: Harassment can include "sexual harassment" or unwelcome sexual advances, requests for sexual favors, and other verbal or physical harassment of a sexual nature.

Harassment does not have to be of a sexual nature, however, and can include offensive remarks about a person's sex. For example, it is illegal to harass a woman by making offensive comments about women in general.

Both victim and the harasser can be either a woman or a man, and the victim and harasser can be the same sex.

Sexual Misconduct: Terminology typically related to institutions of higher education but also applied to the acts committed in the general population, as well as the U.S. military. One definition is that sexual misconduct is a broad term encompassing any unwelcome behavior of a sexual nature that is committed without consent or by force, intimidation, coercion, or manipulation. Sexual misconduct can be committed by a person of any gender, and it can occur between people of the same or different gender. (National Sexual Violence Resource Center, Let's Talk Definitions of Terms, January, 2025.)

Sexual Violence: defined as a sexual act that is committed or attempted by another person without freely given consent of the victim or against someone who is unable to consent or refuse. It includes forced or alcohol/ drug facilitated penetration of a victim; forced or alcohol/drug facilitated incidents in which the victim was made to penetrate a perpetrator or someone else; non-physically pressured unwanted penetration; intentional sexual touching; or non-contact acts of a sexual nature. Sexual violence can also occur when a perpetrator forces or coerces a victim to engage in sexual acts with a third party. Sexual violence involves a lack of freely given consent as well as situations in which the victim is unable to consent or refuse. (National Sexual Violence Resource Center, Let's Talk Definitions of Terms, January, 2025.)

Sexual Abuse: When a person knowingly causes another person to engage in a sex act by threatening or placing the other person in fear, or if someone engages in a sexual act with a person who is incapable of appraising the nature of the act or unable to give consent. (National Sexual Violence Resource Center, Let's Talk Definitions of Terms, January, 2025.)

Trauma-informed Care: A shift from "what's wrong with you" to "what happened to you." It acknowledges that using such practices potentially improves patient engagement, treatment adherence, and health outcomes, as well as provider and staff wellness. As adopted from Substance Abuse and Mental Health Services Administration (SAMSHA)

- Realize the widespread impact of trauma and understand paths for recovery.
- Recognize the signs and symptoms of trauma in patients, families, and staff.
- Integrate knowledge about trauma into policies, procedures, and practices; and
- Actively avoid re-traumatization.

Glossary

VA Service-Connected Disability: An injury or illness that was caused by or worsened during active military service. Disabilities can be physical or mental health conditions, such as Lou Gehrig's Disease or post-traumatic stress disorder (PTSD). Veterans with service-connected disabilities may be eligible for tax-free monthly payments from the VA. The amount of compensation is based on a disability rating percentage assigned by the Department of Veterans Affairs, which ranges from 0% to 100%.

Service-Connected Disability Claim: In order for a veteran to obtain service-connected disability, they must file a claim (similar to a social security disability claim) for these benefits. There are five main methods to establish service connection: direct service connection, service connection through aggravation, presumptive service connection (e.g. toxic water or chemical exposure), secondary service connection, and service connection for injuries caused by VA health care. The claim process involves application, evidence of service connection, and exams.

Vicarious Trauma: Am occupational challenge for people working and volunteering in the fields of victim services, law enforcement, emergency medical services, fire services, and other allied professions, due to their continuous exposure to victims of trauma and violence. This work-related trauma exposure can occur from such experiences as listening to individual clients recount their victimization; looking at videos of exploited children; reviewing case files; hearing about or responding to the aftermath of violence and other traumatic events day after day; and responding to mass violence incidents that have resulted in numerous injuries and deaths. (Office for Victims of Crime, What is Vicarious Trauma?)

---

xl   U.S. Department of Justice Office on Violence Against Women. https://www.justice.gov/ovw/domestic-violence. Viewed 09/16/2024

References

1   Vicarious trauma is an occupational challenge for people working and volunteering in the fields of victim services, law enforcement, emergency medical services, fire services, and other allied professions, due to their continuous exposure to victims of trauma and violence. https://ovc.ojp.gov/program/vtt/what-is-vicarious-trauma.

2   A Woman's Voice Press, www.awomansvoicepress.com.

3   ProPublica. What Mental Health Care Protections Exist in Your State? https://www.propublica.org/article/mental-health-wiltn-states. Viewed 12/20/2024

4   Recommended for practitioners in health care, social services, and the mental health field, a trauma-informed approach is one that uses a "what happened to you" instead of "what's wrong with you" methodology to understand how a person's past experiences may be impacting their current health or other status. One of the most important characteristics of this approach is that it recognizes and seeks to avoid retraumatization.

5   This is no longer the case. Toward the end of the twentieth century, rules were changed throughout the military to allow single parents to join, with family plans and more in place.

6   Relaxin' Jackson is the nickname given to Ft. Jackson.

7   "Quality" is the word used in the report, so it is the word I have chosen to retain here.

8   Struck V Secretary of Defense, 460 F.2d 1372 (9th Cir. 1971). A lawsuit brought by Air Force Captain Susan Struck who fought the military regulation that forced women to discharge or receive an abortion in order to remain in the service. Heard and resolved in the Ninth Circuit Court of Appeals

9   Peralta, E. 2013. Panetta Is Lifting Ban On Women In Combat Roles. National Public Radio. https://www.npr.org/sections/thetwo-way/2013/01/23/170093351/panetta-is-lifting-ban-on-women-in-combat-roles. Viewed 10/20/2024.

10   Advanced individualized training, or AIT, is the post-basic training that all service

Broken in the Stronger Places: From Resilience to Resourcefulness

members attend in order to have the skills and training to perform their job. The time varies according to the type of occupation chosen.

11   A semi-permanent base that troops use when they are away from a major installation or fort. It is a way to keep troops ready for combat and to marshal them.

12   Stand-downs (SD) are typically one- to three-day events providing supplies and services to homeless Veterans, such as food, shelter, clothing, health screenings and VA Social Security benefits counseling. Veterans can also receive referrals to other assistance such as health care, housing solutions, employment, substance use treatment and mental health counseling. They are collaborative events, coordinated between local VA Medical Centers, the Department of Labor (DOL), other government agencies and community-based homeless service providers.

13   Although there is no evidence of sexual assault before 1950, it is acknowledged that rape has been prevalent in our society for as long as stories have been told on the subject. Based on this long-running culture of rape in our society, it is very likely that women in the military since the American Revolution have experienced sexual harassment, assault and rape during their service. However, there is little to no mention of sexual assault in the military prior to the implementation of Article 120 of the Uniform Code of Military Justice.

14   The Feres Doctrine stems from a 1950 Supreme Court decision that precludes service members from being able to sue the military for any wrongful injury or death that may occur "incident to service." It includes sexual assault and harassment. https://www.protectourdefenders.com/feres-doctrine-and-lawsuits-against-the-us-military-explained/

15   Secretary of Defense at the time of book publication.

16   While this has remained true throughout military history, Secretary Austin helped pass a new military code, effective January 1, 2025, that makes sexual harassment an offense. However, it will be up to leaders to enforce this as an action. Time will tell the effectiveness.

17   The duchess slant: upper body at attention and facing forward with knees bent and legs pressed together, knees angled slightly to one side and back, ankles crossed. I failed the interview in that instant.

18   Changed to Ft. Gregg-Adams in 2023 in honor of Lt. Gen. Arthur J. Gregg, a three-star general who served for thirty-six years, and Lt. Col. Charity Adams, the first Black officer in the Women's Army Auxiliary Corps in World War II.

19   A corrugated galvanized steel structure used as our office building.

20   AKA, deuce and a half.

21   A hierarchical structure that outlines how authority is ranked and how people report to each other in an organization.

22   A senior noncommissioned officer (NCO) in a US Army company, battery, or troop. They are responsible for providing guidance, discipline, and support to the soldiers in their unit.

23   German currency prior to the euro.

24   Struck V Secretary of Defense, 460 F.2d 1372 (9th Cir. 1971). A lawsuit brought by

References

Air Force Captain Susan Struck who fought the military regulation that forced women to discharge or receive an abortion in order to remain in the service. Heard and resolved in the Ninth Circuit Court of Appeals

25 The senior noncommissioned officer (NCO) of a company-sized unit. They are responsible for the leadership and professional development of their soldiers, including grooming enlisted soldiers for promotions.

26 An "alert" was an event that occurred when we were notified in the middle of the night to report to the company area, collect our weapons and gas masks, and report to our duty stations. These were often simply practice drills, but on occasion something would happen in the world that would be a catalyst for the military to call troops out on alert. The taking of the Iranian hostages was just such a time.

27 A government television and radio broadcast service provided by the US military to those stationed or assigned overseas.

28 Finding Nemo [Film], Stanton, 2003. 01:00:22

29 The MOS determines your specific job or role within the military. They are defined as codes. For instance, my MOS was 76D/P, which was a Supply Specialist.

30 2002, Achieving Better Health Outcomes: The Oregon Benchmark Experience Howard M. Leichter and Jeffrey Tryens. www.milbank.org/wp-content/uploads/2016/06/ACHIEVING-BETTER-HEALTH-OUTCOMES-The-Oregon-Benchmark-Experience.pdf.

31 Notwithstanding the provisions of subsection (1) of this section, when a peace officer responds to an incident of domestic disturbance and has probable cause to believe that an assault has occurred between family or household members, as defined in ORS 107.705 (Definitions for ORS 107.700 to 107.735), or to believe that one such person has placed the other in fear of imminent serious physical injury, the officer shall arrest and take into custody the alleged assailant or potential assailant.

32 Every veteran who enters a VA medical facility is to be screened for MST. The questionnaire has changed over the years, currently reduced to two questions: "a) Did you receive uninvited and unwanted sexual attention, such as touching, cornering, pressure for sexual favors, or verbal remarks?" b) Did someone ever use force or threat of force to have sexual contact with you against your will?" In the early-/mid-2000s, however, there were four (or five?) questions that asked essentially the same questions as today's two.

33 A veteran service officer is an individual who is trained and accredited in assisting veterans and family members with obtaining benefits, most notably service-connected benefits from the Department of Veterans Affairs. They may be employed by state, county, or tribal governments, or they may be volunteers with a national veteran organization (Veterans of Foreign Wars, Disabled American Veterans, Vietnam Veterans of America, American Legion, etc.).

34 With the passage of HB3479 and SB946, the Oregon Women Veterans Coordinator and Oregon LGBTQ Coordinator became permanent positions at the ODVA. These Coordinators were required to focus on outreach and assistance to only the population they served. Since 2015, Oregon has added Coordinators for tribal veterans; student veterans, and justice-involved veterans. ODVA culture and efforts have shifted to one that reflects more

Broken in the Stronger Places: From Resilience to Resourcefulness

inclusivity, diversity, and equitability for all veterans.

35   The law that established the VA Center for Women Veterans in 1994. https://www.congress.gov/103/statute/STATUTE-108/STATUTE-108-Pg4645.pdf

36   H.R.3224 — 116th Congress (2019-2020). This bill implements or expands various programs related to health care and benefits for women veterans at the Department of Veterans Affairs (VA).

37   Employers Against Violence, https://www.eadvma.org/facts-and-statistics.html. Viewed 10/24/2024

38   Trauma-Informed Care Implementation Resource Center by the Center for Health Care Strategies. https://www.traumainformedcare.chcs.org/what-is-trauma-informed-care/

39   Center for Health Care Strategies. Cultural Humility: A Key Element of Trauma-Informed Care https://www.chcs.org/cultural-humility-key-element-trauma-informed-care/

40   Center for Health Care Strategies. Incorporating Racial Equity into Trauma-Informed Carehttps://www.chcs.org/resource/incorporating-racial-equity-into-trauma-informed-care/

41   Mental Health America. Ten Tools for Resiliency. https://mhanational.org/ten-tools

42   https://www.bhg.com/recipes/healthy/dinner/cheap-heart-healthy-dinner-ideas/

www.ingramcontent.com/pod-product-compliance
Lightning Source LLC
Chambersburg PA
CBHW052028030426
42337CB00027B/4909